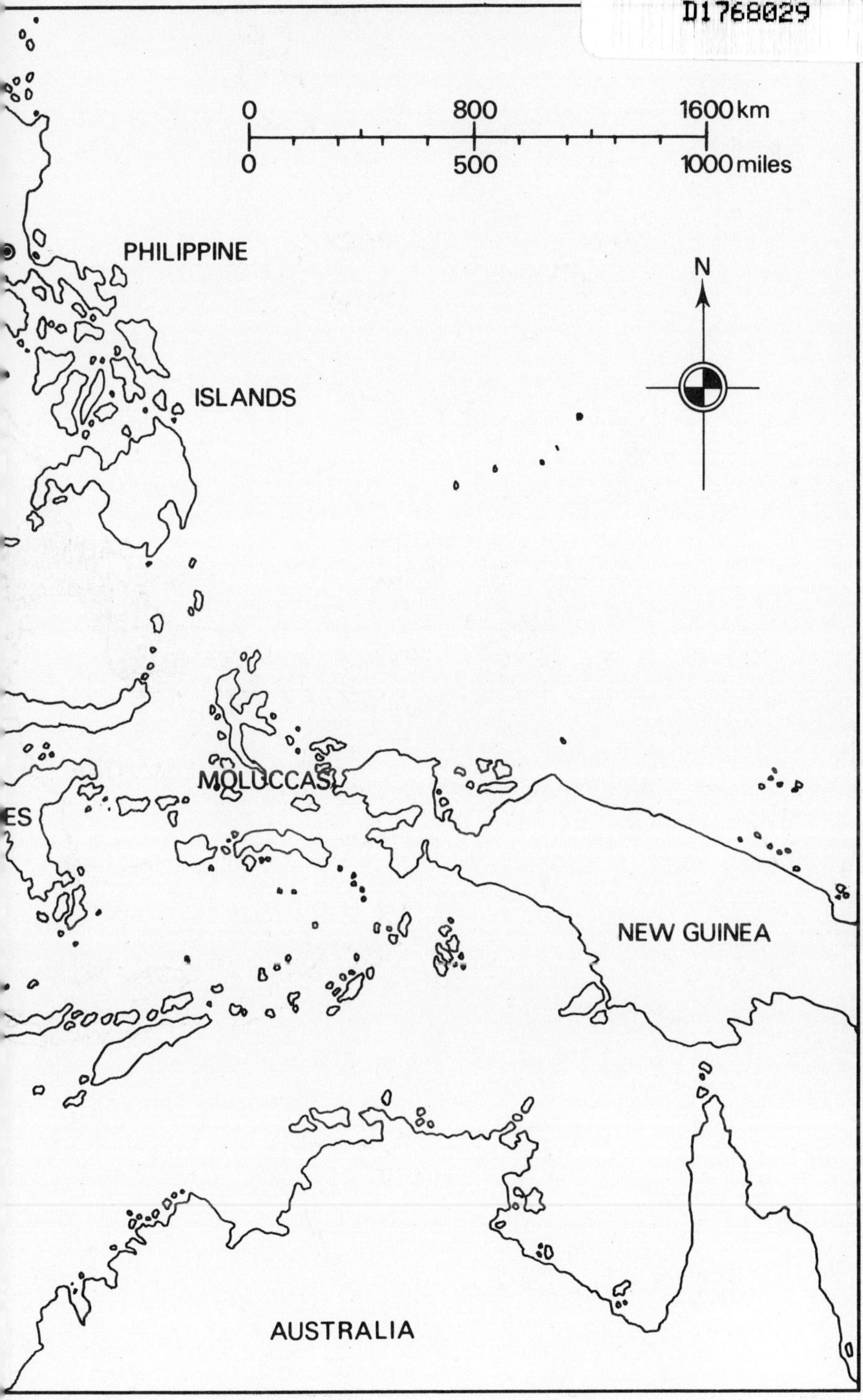
0
800
1600 km
0
500
1000 miles
N
PHILIPPINE
ISLANDS
MOLUCCAS
ES
NEW GUINEA
AUSTRALIA

Tun Razak:
His Life and Times

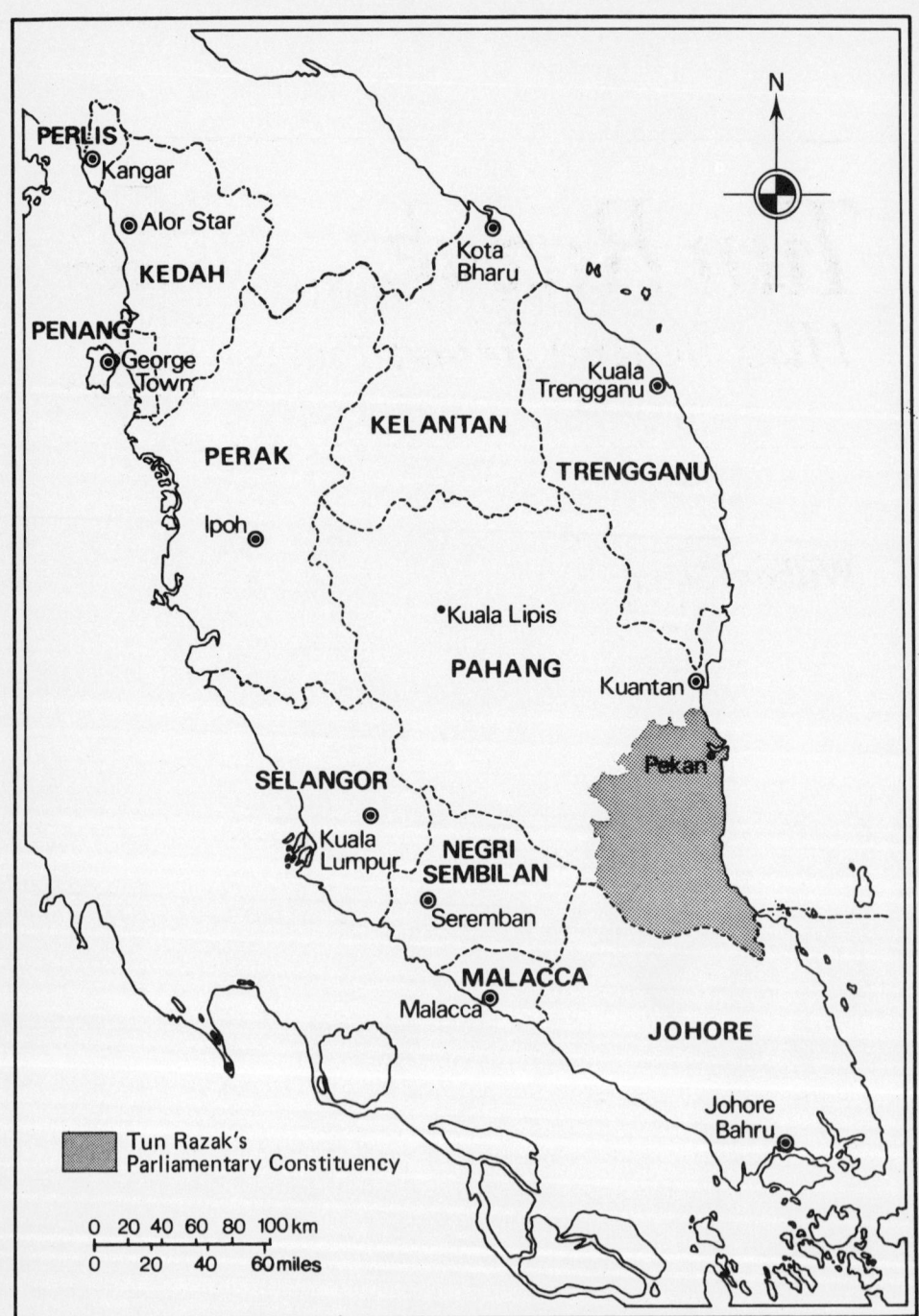

Peninsular Malaysia

Tun Razak
His Life and Times

Longman

William Shaw

LONGMAN GROUP LTD
London and New York

LONGMAN MALAYSIA SDN. BERHAD
Wisma Damansara, Jalan Semantan, Kuala Lumpur
25, First Lokyang Road, Singapore 22

Associated companies, branches and
representatives throughout the world

© Longman Malaysia Sdn. Bhd.

All rights reserved. No part of publication may be reproduced, stored in a retrieval system, or transmitted in any form or by any means, electronic, mechanical, photocopying, recording, or otherwise, without the prior permission of the copyright owner.

First published 1976
ISBN 0 582 72414 7
ISBN 0 582 72415 5

Text set in 11/12 Baskerville
Printed by Chong Moh & Company.

Preface

The greater part of this biography was written before the sudden and untimely death of Tun Razak; and the author, who was in Malaysia at the time, had been hoping to have one final interview with the late Prime Minister on the latter's return from medical treatment in London. But it was not to be.

It should be said, therefore, that this account of Tun Razak's life and achievements makes no attempt to be a final assessment of his contribution to Malaysian history. It does however set out to record, within the context of Malaysian history, the very important part that Tun Razak played in his country's affairs over a period of twenty-five years from 1951 to 1976. It does not attempt an account of his personal or private life; essentially it is a political biography which places the life of the late Tun Razak within the context of his times — the modern history of Malaysia and Southeast Asia.

The author and his publishers would like to place on record their appreciation of the unfailing kindness and courtesy of the late Tun Haji Abdul Razak bin Datuk Hussein on the occasions when, as an extremely overworked Prime Minister, he agreed to be interviewed.

Acknowledgements

The publishers are very grateful to the following for permission to use illustrations:

the late Tun Haji Abdul Razak bin Datuk Hussein for numbers 1, 3, 4, 5, 6, 7, 8, 9, 11, 12; the Department of Information, Malaysia, for numbers 10, 13, 14, 18, 19, 21, 22, 23, 24, 25, 26, 27, 28, 29, 30, 31; the Press Association Ltd. for numbers 15 and 17; N.J. Ryan for number 2; Fox Photos Ltd. for number 20; and the Editor of the *Far Eastern Economic Review* for the cover photograph.

Contents

Part One; Political Apprenticeship
1. Bugis Ancestry — 1
2. School Days — 12
3. War — 26
4. Japanese Occupation — 43
5. Post-War Problems — 55
6. Student in London — 69

Part Two: The Road to Power — 81
7. UMNO and the Alliance — 83
8. Minister of Education — 95
9. Independence — 105
10. The 1959 Elections — 117
11. National and Rural Development — 127
12. The Haj — 138
13. Malaysia — 148
14. The 1964 Elections — 160
15. Singapore Leaves Malaysia — 173

Part Three: Dictator and Democrat — 187
16. Prelude to Tragedy — 189
17. Black Tuesday — May 13th 1969 — 202
18. From Director of Operations to Prime Minister — 212
19. Re-Alignment in Foreign Policy — 222
20. Restructuring the Economy — 232

Epilogue — 246
References — 250
Bibliography — 258
Index — 262

List of Photographs

Plate 1	The Malay School at Langgar The Malay College, Kuala Kangsar
Plate 2	Malay College prefects and pupils
Plate 3	Students in London in 1948
Plate 4	Malayan Students Association dinner Opening of Malaya Hall in London in 1949
Plate 5	Called to the Bar in London and Kuala Lumpur
Plate 6	Wedding in Johore
Plate 7	The UMNO General Assembly 1951 The Razak Education Committee 1955
Plate 8	The Commonwealth Prime Ministers Conferences in London 1962 and in Singapore 1972.
Plate 9	With President Sukarno in 1959.
Plate 10	Land Development and Operations Rooms
Plate 11	With Prime Minister Harold Wilson in 1964; and with President Lyndon Johnson in 1966.
Plate 12	Chancellor of the National University The first Razak Cabinet
Plate 13	The 1974 General Election The 1975 UMNO General Assembly
Plate 14	With Chairman Mao Tse-tung in 1974 With President Suharto in 1975
Plate 15	Relaxation at golf and hockey
Plate 16	Tun Abdul Razak and his family.

Part One
Political Apprenticeship

Chapter One
Bugis Ancestry

On May 13th, 1969, directly following a bitterly fought general election, the sovereign state of Malaysia came close to civil war. On that day, less than six years after its formation, the multi-racial Federation was brought to the very brink of disaster. This was due to a combination of causes: among them, racial chauvinism, religious fanaticism, economic inequalities and the fears of an indigenous people faced, through an accident of history over which they had no control, with an immigrant population little less in number than themselves[1].

In Kuala Lumpur, the Federal Capital, Malaysian Malays fought against Malaysians of Chinese and Indian origin; shops and houses were looted and burned and men, women and children killed or mutilated. The police temporarily lost control of the situation and troops, armoured cars and helicopters were needed to prevent mob violence from spreading. The existing system of government had proved inadequate to withstand inherited, long-fermenting, internal pressures and quickly had to be replaced by something more effective. Parliament and the State Legislatures were suspended and the country placed under a National Operations Council which, through the newly proclaimed Emergency Regulations, was granted almost dictatorial powers. Malaysia then needed a strong and ruthless man to head this Council and make it work; one who would play no favourites and bow to no pressure groups. It found that man in the Deputy Prime Minister and Minister of Defence in the outgoing government, Tun Haji Abdul Razak.

At the time, however, this appointment caused considerable consternation among many in the non-Malay communities, for Abdul Razak, due to the energy with which he had championed the cause of the Malay peasant when Minister of National and Rural Development, was considered by them to be not only a racialist, but one particularly biased against the Chinese. He was, claimed rumour-mongers, a religious fanatic who would discontinue, even reverse, the liberal and humanitarian policies so courageously pursued by the Prime Minister, Tunku Abdul Rahman. The foreign correspondents of the international press were equally unenthusiastic, for in addition to being generally hostile to the interim government's handling of the riots, for the suppression of which he, as caretaker Minister for Home Affairs, was ultimately responsible, they were less than impressed with the personal qualities that they chose to attribute to the man himself.

Unfortunately for Abdul Razak he possessed neither his leader's charisma nor his flare for public relations. He seldom smiled in public and his lack of cordiality, limp handshake and the flat, unemotional delivery of his speeches were all unimpressive and made him appear, at least on casual acquaintance, too stolid and withdrawn in comparison with the extrovert and ebullient, Cambridge-educated, prince who had led the country for the past twelve years.

In 1951 Abdul Razak had modestly, and some felt unwisely, declined to accept the leadership of his own political party, the United Malays National Organisation, (UMNO); and in consequence had forfeited the opportunity of leading his country's fight for freedom from colonial rule and the chance eventually to become its first Prime Minister. For half a generation after Independence he had apparently been content to play second fiddle to the Tunku and remain in the background, efficient as an administrator, but uninspiring to Asians accustomed to more flamboyant and articulate leadership. He was, it seemed, the all-time 'Number Two', the loyal assistant, the dependable back-up man. 'When the Tunku goes,' wrote one foreign correspondent, qualified as an expert by a recent three-day visit to the country, 'Razak must surely follow.'

But the doubts of the lamenting Jeremiahs proved to be unfounded, because the man who looked and sometimes acted like an accountant took a firm grip on the country and rapidly brought the extremists, whether they were Malay, Chinese or Indian, to heel. There was soon no doubt who was master of the situation; and peace and security returned. The fears of discrimination against the non-Malays proved to be groundless also, for although Abdul Razak was a zealous and devoted Muslim, dedicated to the economic advancement of his own race, he came out strongly for tolerance and moderation both in religious and in mundane matters. Because he used the great powers that his office conferred upon him wisely and honestly, he eventually won the acceptance and respect of the great majority of his fellow countrymen, regardless of their racial origins. But most important of all, when the time was right he voluntarily gave up his near dictatorial powers and, taking over the Premiership from his friend and mentor Tunku Abdul Rahman, led the country back to democracy, albeit with a few necessary restrictions built into the Constitution to guard against any recurrence of the May 13th tragedy.

So successful were Abdul Razak's policies of nation building that by 1972 the leader of a predominantly non-Malay opposition party, formerly unreservedly critical and suspicious of his government's actions, could publicly say of him: 'Tun Razak's moderation and sense of justice impressed us and we felt that we could take a chance ... by joining (him in) a coalition government. We have no regrets. We believe we have done the right thing.'[2]

*****   *****   *****

When, in the aftermath of the Second World War, Malay nationalists began to agitate for independence for the whole Peninsula, they were confronted by a major problem not of their own making. Due to the past immigration policies of their colonial masters, their own people — though indigenous to the area — were in grave danger, should Singapore be included in the proposed new independent State, of becoming a minority in their own country. Not just a simple minority, but an economically depressed one as well. That the British at last recognised some of the dangers inherent in this situation, which had been caused mainly by their avarice, became plain in 1948 when they formed the Federation of Malaya; for by excluding Singapore, with its relatively large Chinese population, from the new state, they at least attempted in some way to safeguard the political, if not the economic position of the people to whom, sooner or later, they would inevitably have to hand over power.

In 1959, two years after Malaya had finally become a sovereign state, Singapore attained internal self-government; and it became obvious that despite British reluctance to give up their premier naval and military base in the Far East, full independence for that island, either alone or through federation with another state, could not be long delayed. For the Malays then, political, financial and military necessity required that this transition of Singapore from colonialism to full independence should be achieved through incorporation into the Malayan Federation, if only to prevent this strategically situated territory from falling into the hands of the Communists. This meant that once again the Malays were faced with the problem of retaining their racial identity and political hegemony; and eventually their leaders evolved a plan of desperation, involving a calculated risk, whereby the danger of them being swamped by the Chinese could perhaps be resolved by the formation of a new, enlarged Federation that would include not just Singapore, but also the British Crown Colonies of North Borneo and Sarawak and the independent, though British 'protected', Malay Sultanate of Brunei.

These leaders were, of course, well aware that only a minority of the inhabitants of the first two of these Borneo territories were akin to the Malays by race, or even Muslim in religion; but they hoped that the greater part of them, the non-Chinese element, would at least share an interest in cooperating with other indigenous communities in presenting a united political front against any combination of immigrant organisations aspiring to gain control of the government of this new nation. The British were pleased at the prospect of being able to shed further remnants of their by now politically embarrassing and economically unrewarding empire while securing their stability after independence. They agreed with the proposals provided that the position of the native Borneans was adequately safeguarded. Thus, through pressure of circumstances imposed by earlier generations, Malaysia was born prematurely in 1963 with the seeds of fundamental racial and economic tensions already present in its body. A sickness that has plagued its internal political life ever since. A genetic fault the origins of which go far back into history.

HISTORICAL BACKGROUND

In prehistoric times, so experts tell us, the Malay Peninsula formed a land bridge over which waves of migrant people moved south from the mainland of Asia into the Indonesian Archipelago, the Philippine Islands and Australasia. The last such series of migrations, which occurred at various times between 2500 and 1500 B.C., were made by those Austronesian people, or Proto-Malays, who were then inhabiting an area of south-west China that later became the Provinces of Szechuan and Yunnan. They found the dense jungles and fever-ridden swamps of the Malay Peninsula unsuitable for large-scale settlement and most moved on; but those who elected to stay first drove the aboriginal inhabitants, themselves the descendants of earlier waves of immigrants, into the inhospitable interior, then went on eventually to set up numerous small palisaded towns and villages at strategic sites around the coastline or along the banks of the principal navigable rivers. Over the centuries these independent colonies developed into a conglomeration of small sovereign Malay states which proved too weak, however, to resist the encroachments of a succession of Asian imperialistic powers, so that at various times they fell under the suzerainty, usually tenuous, of empires based upon Sumatra, Java or Siam. Not until the fifteenth century of the present era did the indigenous people succeed in gaining control of their own destiny when, for a few glorious decades, the whole Peninsula formed part of a great Malay empire.

The centre of this empire was the fortified city of Malacca, a port at the 'meeting of the monsoons', from which a well-positioned Malay fleet was able to control and tax shipping passing through the narrow straits between Sumatra and the mainland. Gradually, all the embryonic states of the Peninsula became tributaries of the Malacca kings, who also sent out punitive expeditions that subjugated large areas of Western Sumatra and so secured the hinterland on both sides of the strategic straits on which their prosperity depended. Trade and

culture flourished in the capital, for the conversion to Islam, first of
the Malay aristocracy and later of the bulk of the ordinary people,
enabled the town to develop into an important international centre of
Muslim thought and learning; while traders from all over Asia and the
Middle East came to Malacca to exchange their merchandise or even
to take up residence there, so that the port evolved into one of the
richest markets in the Orient.

During the second half of the fifteenth century, however, the
Portuguese, then one of the foremost maritime nations in Europe,
began their predatory advance down the west coast of Africa. By the
turn of the sixteenth century they had entered the Indian Ocean
where, spurred on by the double incentive of trade and religious
missionary zeal, they inaugurated the era of European colonialism in
the Far East. After the necessary fortified trading posts, which also
served them as naval bases, had been established around the coast of
India, they turned covetous eyes upon Malacca; and in 1511 a
seaborne expedition was able, due to a superiority in weapons and
military discipline, to seize the Malay capital. The fall of Malacca
began a new fragmentation of the Peninsula that was not to be
reversed until after the end of the Second World War.

During the period of their ascendancy, the Portuguese fortified
and defended Malacca so effectively that they defeated all attempts by
the Malays to recapture it; and, although it eventually passed by the
fortunes of war first to Holland and then to Britain, it remained a
European stronghold until independence was attained in 1957. The
fugitive Malacca royal family finally established itself in the south of
the Peninsula, where the former Ruler invested himself with the newly
created title of Sultan of Johore; but the days of glory had passed and
the once proud empire went into gradual decline. In time Siam
reimposed her suzerainty over the northern part of the Peninsula; and
the Sumatran States, and even the territories in west-central Malaya,
broke away, until little more than the Riau Archipelago, Singapore,
Johore and Pahang remained.

By the provisions of the Anglo-Dutch Treaty of 1824, Britain was
left as the sole European colonial power in the Malay Peninsula; although until well into the 1870's her rule was confined to the three
Straits Settlements of Singapore, Penang and Malacca. Intervention in
the central Malay states began from 1874, however, and gradually
British officials, ultimately responsible to the Governor of the Straits
Settlements, took over each individual Principality's administration.
In theory at least each of these states remained independent, being
bound to Britain only by Treaty, so that it was designated a protectorate
rather than a Colony.

On July 1st, 1895, the four central Malay States of Pahang,
Selangor, Perak and Negri Sembilan formed a Federation with an

integrated civil service; and from the beginning of January, 1896, their Rulers, relinquishing much of their sovereignty, accepted a British Resident-General, whose advice and policies they agreed to follow in everything, except for matters pertaining to Malay customs and the Islamic religion. Subordinate to this Resident-General were four senior British officials, styled Residents, responsible for the administration of the individual participating states. The northern Principalities of Kedah, Kelantan, Trengganu and Perlis remained under Siamese suzerainty until 1909 when, by Treaty, they were transferred to the British sphere of influence. Johore did not accept a British Adviser until 1914, although European administrative officers, under contract to the Malay Ruler, were employed much earlier. These latter five states, despite a certain amount of British pressure, remained outside of the Federation until after the end of the Second World War.

FOREIGN LABOUR

Although Chinese and Indians had been resident in the Peninsula for some hundreds of years, their numbers were of minor importance until the third decade of the nineteenth century. Before that, the majority of immigrants entering the Malay States had been Indonesians whose language, culture and religion was close enough to that of the indigenous people to permit them to integrate without difficulty. With the establishment of Singapore as a permanent British base and the opening up of Johore, Perak and Selangor by the Malays for foreign commercial exploitation, however, large numbers of Chinese and Indians were brought in wherever local labour was scarce or unwilling to undertake the work. The Malay peasant generally displayed little interest in changing his traditional way of life and means of livelihood, effectively resisting even the efforts of his own feudal aristocracy to turn him into a hired mine worker or estate labourer. Malay landlords, especially those who had entered into joint ventures with Chinese merchants in order to obtain adequate finance, therefore found it expedient to recruit Chinese coolies for this work. Thus many foreign communities, nurtured through capitalist exploitation, grew up side by side with indigenous ones which, though hostile to this invasion, were yet impotent to resist it. This hostility grew, for these aliens, although they soon came to consider themselves to be permanent residents, made little or no attempt to adopt the customs of the country or to integrate with its people, but instead formed insular communities retaining their own religion, culture and language or dialect. Many of these Chinese communities, especially those directly associated with branches of the obiquitous Hung League, or Triad Secret Society, eventually became so powerful that they were able to defy constituted authority and even, on occasions, wage war in support of those Malay princes, or lesser territorial Chieftains, whose policies suited them best.

Dangerous as this situation was when the individual Malay States were autonomous and almost completely undeveloped, it became far worse when sudden economic progress, in which unfortunately very few of the indigenous people shared, followed in the wake of the establishment of British 'protection'. Work was then plentiful, for there were railways and roads to be built and huge areas of ground to be cleared and planted, and for this vast numbers of Tamil labourers were recruited and brought in from India and Ceylon. At the same time many thousands of Chinese, fleeing from their homeland because of oppression and near famine, learning of the boom in Malaya made their way there in the expectation of finding work as general labourers, artisans or itinerant hawkers. Some proved so successful, diligent and skilful in their various occupations that they were able to accumulate sufficient capital to set themselves up as small shopkeepers, merchants or even entrepreneurs. Regardless of their status, however, few wished permanently to leave the country of their adoption; and as soon as they achieved sufficient economic and social security began to remit passage money home so that the younger members of their families, or girls of marriageable age who had been selected for them by their parents or by marriage-brokers, could join them. Thus family life began for them and large numbers of Chinese and Indian children were born and raised who, though educated in the traditions of their parents' homeland, were themselves to know no other home than Malaya.

Immigrant foreign workers and their dependants continued to enter the Peninsula unchecked until early in the 1930's, when the effects of the worldwide trade recession forced the various responsible authorities in both the Malay States and the Straits Settlements to halt the flow so that unemployment, which had already reached a dangerous level, should not escalate into civil disturbance. But these restrictions came too late to benefit the Malays, who were already being conditioned by certain nationalist writers to fear a 'yellow peril'[3] that in time would make them strangers in their own land.

*****   *****   *****

From the fall of Malacca until 1699 the twin states of Johore and Pahang were ruled by a dynasty of Malay princes who were themselves blood descendants of the deposed royal family; but in that year Mahmud, the Sultan of Johore, was assassinated by one of his own nobles and the Malacca line came to an end. Mahmud, a paranoid sexual pervert who was subject to hallucinations and fits of uncontrollable rage had, according to popular legend[4], had the abdomen of a lady-in-waiting at the Court cut open in order to confirm his suspicions that she had stolen and eaten a slice of jackfruit from the royal table. The lady died and her husband, a warrior Chief, plotted revenge against the murderer. With the connivance of various high officers of state, including the powerful Chief Minister (*Bendahara*) who had his own reasons for wishing Mahmud dead, he disposed of the royal bodyguard and then, knowing that as it was Friday, the Muslim holy day, Mahmud would make the obligatory attendance at the midday service, lay in wait for his king on the route between the palace and the mosque.

Eventually the royal murderer appeared riding, as Malay aristocrats were at that time wont to do, upon the back of one of his servants. No one interfered as the distraught husband plunged a short stabbing spear repeatedly into the back of his demented sovereign. Mahmud left no heir; and so by Malay custom the throne passed to that same Chief Minister who had secretly condoned the assassination. From that time a member of the Johore royal family, entitled the *Dato Bendahara,* was appointed as Viceroy to rule the dependency of Pahang on behalf of his Sultan.

THE BUGIS

In those early days, the Johore Rulers depended for their power mainly upon the fighting qualities of a force of Bugis mercenary warriors, recruited from the Indonesian island of Celebes, who were famous for their reckless courage in hand-to-hand combat and notorious for 'running amuck' whenever frustrated. When, in times of peace, these mercenaries were denied the loot that was to them the most attractive part of military service they could prove to be not only an embarrassment to the Johore Ruler, who found them far easier to hire than to fire, but also a real threat to the security of the state.

They were hated too by the Malay aristocracy, for whole communities of them had settled permanently within the Johore dominions, where they all too frequently fought with the local magnates over the possession of land and villages. When, therefore, Johore was attacked in 1718 by the forces of a Sumatran prince, many of the Sultan's followers supported the invader in the hope of ending Bugis political and military power. This defection enabled the Sumatran to usurp the kingdom; although he held it for only four years. In 1722 he was overthrown by the Bugis, who thereafter placed a son of the first *Bendahara* Sultan upon the throne. So powerful were the Bugis from that time, that they succeeded in installing one of their own Chiefs as Under-King, and it was he, in fact, who was the real ruler of the Sultanate.

This fortunate circumstance, from the point of view of the Bugis, led to greatly increased emmigration from the Celebes into the Johore empire; and one of these immigrants, said to have been a deposed prince of Macassar[5], was an ancestor of Malaysia's second Prime Minister. This warrior prince settled in Pahang close to the royal capital of Pekan, married a local lady, and later became so domesticated that he is credited with having personally improved and reorganised the Principality's silk weaving industry. He seems also to have been a good and just administrator, for when he died his grave became a *keramat,* or shrine at which the ordinary people prayed for help and guidance.[6]

The great grand-daughter of this Bugis prince married a Malay nobleman who brought into the family the major title of *Orang Kaya Indera Shahbandar.* This noble, who was more usually simply called the *Dato Shahbandar,* or Lord of the Ports, was charged with the administration of a large feudal territory in South Pahang which was held in trust for the Sultan of Johore. In fact he and three other feudal magnates of equal rank, supported by a larger number of secondary and minor Chiefs, really ran the country, though by virtue of authority delegated to them by the Viceroy.

These four major nobles exercised a power over life and property within their own fiefs that was limited only when the Viceroy could command a sufficient personal following among the other land-owners to restrain them. They were the royal tax collectors; traditionally indispensible at the installation of a new Viceroy or Ruler; and in time of war were required to support their overlord with armed retainers and a feudal levy of their peasantry. In later, more settled times, when the country was administered by a British-type civil service, however, the *Dato Shahbandar* became more nearly the equivalent of an hereditary Earl Marshal, or the noble responsible for palace ceremonial.

Until 1853 the Pahang Viceroy governed on behalf of Johore, but in that year Bendahara Ali declared himself an independent Ruler, although the polite fiction of the Sultan's personal suzerainty over the State was maintained for another eleven years. Ali's successor continued to use the title of *Bendahara* until 1882[7] when he assumed the rank of Sultan, a title that was officially recognised by his principal Territorial Chiefs two years later. By virtue of an Agreement dated October 8th, 1887, Pahang became a British Protectorate; and in the following year accepted a British Resident as its chief administrator.

Four years later, on April 5th, 1892, a dissident Malay Chief known as the *Panglima Muda* of Jempul raided the area around Pekan, the royal capital, and murdered two European employees of the Pahang Exploration Company[8] while they were supervising the cutting of timber in the jungle. This rebel, whose uprising against the Sultan was in fact directed mainly against the British, who at that time were rapidly stripping the feudal Chiefs of their powers and turning them into little more than pensioners of the colonial administration, then began his retreat back towards his own territory.

The only force available to stop him was that commanded by Ali, the seventh *Dato Shahbandar,* who was therefore instructed by the European officer administering the area to arrest the rebels. But Ali, although loyal to his Ruler, was personally in sympathy with resistance to the British and so failed to oppose the retreat. The colonial authorities had the last word, however, for when Ali died the title that should have descended to Abdul Razak's paternal grandfather, Awang Muhammad Taib, passed out of the family for a generation. This, it seems, was not so much due to Ali's tentative support of the rebels, as to palace intrigue over the royal succession in which Awang had unwittingly become involved; for even when the title was restored to the family in 1930, this same claimant was passed over once again and Abdul Razak's father, Hussein, ennobled in his place.

In the last two decades of the nineteenth century the dispossessed Territorial Chiefs of the 'protected' Malay States were often given courtesy positions as 'advisers' to the British civil servants controlling those same districts which they had formerly ruled[9]. Their lack of education for and experience in European-style administration made them largely ineffective, however, and so it was considered advisable to provide a central training establishment specifically designed to fit the more promising sons of Malay princely and aristocratic families to fill certain medium grade jobs in the civil service. The very top positions in this service were, as one might expect in a colonial administration, filled by expatriate Europeans; but the necessity of finding suitable local officers of subordinate and junior grade had to some extent been solved by founding a number of secondary and grammar schools in which English was the medium of instruction. To these, in 1905, was added the Malay College, situated at Kuala Kangsar in the State of Perak. This was run on the lines of an English Public School of that period, but with a curriculum specifically designed to turn out both a privileged elite of government-orientated administrative officers and a supply of potential Sultans better qualified than their predecessors to lead their states in the way that the British authorities wanted them led.

Included among one of the early batches of Malay aristocratic youths selected for this experiment was Abdul Razak's father who, after having completed his secondary education at the College, stayed on to undertake a specialist course as an Administrative Probationer. At the beginning of 1916, when he was still only eighteen, he received his first official appointment as a subordinate Malay Officer. Four years later he married a charming but unsophisticated young Malay girl named Fatimah, after a daughter of the Prophet Muhammad, from Pulau Keladi, a village near Pekan; and settled her in his family's country house, which was only a mile or so away on the opposite side of the Pahang River. Eventually, to his joy, Hussein learned that his wife was pregnant.

Two months before her baby was due to be born, Fatimah crossed the river to her home village and there formally engaged the services of the local midwife by presenting her with the traditional gifts. At that period magic and belief in the supernatural still played an important part in the everyday lives of many Malays, especially those living in the rural areas; and so the midwife, who was also a noted clairvoyant, was asked to cast the child's horoscope and by means of divination give guidance concerning the manner in which the mother should conduct herself during the period of waiting. For a small fee she also prepared a charm to ensure that the birth would be easy and without danger. Then, satisfied that she had done all in her power to provide her child with an auspicious start in life, the proud mother returned home.

Chapter Two
School Days

When her time was near, Fatimah decided to move back across the river so as to be with her parents in her home village of Pulau Keladi, for her husband was at that time living at the other end of the State, in Raub, where he was employed in the District Office, the regional centre for local administration. The house in which her child was to be born on March 11th, 1922, not as a Malayan or Malaysian citizen, for no such nationality then existed, but as a subject of His Royal Highness the Sultan of Pahang and a British Protected Person, was a typically Malay plank-walled village structure roofed with nipah-palm fronds, that stood close to the river in an unfenced compound that was shaded by coconut palms and banana trees. Because of the floods that occurred when the river overflowed its banks each year during the rainy season, this house was raised some four feet above the ground on wooden piles; providing beneath the building a cool retreat from the tropical sun, a sheltered storage space, and living quarters for the usual mixed bag of scrawny free-range poultry that besides forming an invaluable source of food, also kept the area free of poisonous centipedes and other pests.

A flight of wooden steps led up to a deep, open verandah that was traditionally the principal reception room in which male guests were entertained; the women being happy to remain modestly out of sight in the kitchen. From this verandah a curtained doorway gave access to the body of the house, which consisted of a single large room that served both as sleeping quarters and as a workshop. Here Western-style furniture was kept to a minimum, the only concessions to the family's modern upper-class status being provided by a large double-bed draped with a hand-woven coverlet and a glass-fronted cabinet in which the best imported china was displayed like trophies. In the place of honour stood a hand-operated wooden loom, for Pulau Keladi was the centre of a silk-weaving industry that had thrived in Pahang from time immemorial.

As the time of birth drew near, the midwife busied herself with selecting the most propitious place in the central room for the child to make its first public appearance. This was ascertained by dropping the charmed blade of a *parang,* the Malay multi-purpose jungle machete, down through different parts of the raised, slatted floor, until eventually it remained standing upright in the earth below. This indicated the auspicious spot above which the delivery couch was to be placed. After suitable magical incantations had been muttered, prickly leaves were placed beneath the house to ward off the dreaded birth vampires, while a net was hung suspended above the bed to entrap any other kind of evil spirit that might try to harm the baby when at its most defenceless.

Finally, a large tray was filled with husked rice and covered with a small mat surmounted by seven silk sarongs, which were in turn covered by another mat upon which it was intended that the precious infant should lay. Thus Hussein's firstborn came into the world, just after noon, protected from evil and misfortune by ancient ceremonies made beautiful by the motherly love that inspired them. He was bathed and fumigated in the smoke of incense and then handed to his father, who formally adopted him by whispering a Muslim religious formula into his son's ear. The child was then placed upon the pile of seven sarongs and laid on the bed beside his mother. Each day one of these sarongs was removed until, on the seventh, all were gone. On that day the boy received his name, Abdul Razak, meaning Servant of God the Provider, derived, as are the names of so many Muslims, from one of the ninety-nine glorious attributes of Allah the Exalted.

When the naming ceremony had been completed, the child was placed for the first time in his swinging cot; a hammock-like structure that was suspended on long cords from the rafters. Each day thereafter he was taken out and bathed in water in which an iron nail and a tough candlenut had, after a formal ritual, been immersed, in order that, through contact with their magic properties, his body might grow hard and strong.

Soon after his child was born, Hussein had the good fortune to be posted to the District Office in Pekan and so was able to live with his family in Pulau Keladi, travelling the six miles to and from the office by boat. This ideal existence lasted for less than two years, however, and then he was promoted to Assistant District Officer and transferred to Temerloh. This promotion, though otherwise welcome to an ambitious young man, came at an inopportune time, for his wife was about to give birth to another child. Before leaving for his new position he therefore arranged for Abdul Razak to be taken to the other side of the river to live in the village of Jambu Langgar with his paternal grandparents. There, despite his family's affluence relative to the near subsistence level living standards of the majority of their neighbours, the household among whom the young Razak was raised lived a simple life. Although their home, the family's principal residence in the State, was by far the largest and most imposing house in the district, it had neither electricity nor modern sanitation; the river serving as their common bathroom.

JAMBU LANGGAR

The majority of the people in Jambu Langgar depended for their livelihood on rice-planting, fishing and weaving; growing the greater part of their own food and raising a little surplus for sale in order to be able to afford a few minor imported luxuries. Many of the village women, including those in Abdul Razak's own family, wove silk sarongs as a means of supplementing the incomes of their menfolk. These garments were made on locally manufacturered wooden hand-looms little more advanced in design that those that had been introduced into Pahang in the 1720's by Abdul Razak's Bugis ancestor. It usually took a woman about a week to set up her loom for a three to five garment run and then another to complete the first sarong, for which she could expect to receive seven or eight Malayan dollars[1] from the purchasing agent in Pekan; a useful sum of money for a villager in those days, when a man could eat a simple meal in a coffeeshop for about five cents.

Everyone in the village had to work and Abdul Razak, though only a small child, was no exception. His job was to tend his grandfather's buffaloes, riding upon the back of the leader when he took them to and from the rice-fields. These monstrous beasts, which seem so docile when handled by small Malay children, have an unexplained hatred of Europeans and to the delight of countless villagers throughout the Peninsula have trampled the dignity of many a pompous expatriate official who has had to scuttle to safety to avoid their unwelcome attentions.

In 1925 Hussein took a second wife, for under Islamic law a Muslim may, subject to certain restrictions imposed by the Prophet of Islam, be married to up to four women at any one time. But his son was probably too young at that time to suffer any serious traumatic effects from the partial desertion of his mother, with whom anyway he was not living; but it may be significant that there was never any indication that he himself ever even contemplated marrying anyone other than his first wife. There was no bitterness in the family, for the situation was of course a usual and generally accepted one, and Abdul Razak throughout life remained on good terms with his many half brothers and sisters.

Despite the lack of man-made amenities for entertainment in the village, life held its fair share of simple pleasures for the small boy. He fished and swam and stole fruit from nearby orchards, although there was plenty on his own family land; and every so often there was the excitement of a trip across the river to visit his mother and little sister, or a shopping expedition to Pekan. The royal capital was then a very small town of mainly attap-roofed wooden buildings, many of which lined the river bank with their front verandahs, supported on stilts, projecting out over the water. This was because the river was still the main highway and market place, for there were few properly constructed roads in Pahang in those days and the majority of people travelled, and transported their goods, by rowing-boat or raft.

When he was six years old Abdul Razak began to attend the village school. This was situated about a mile away from where he lived and he reached it by walking barefoot along a dirt path. He did this not because his parents could not afford to buy him shoes, although like some contemporary Western politicians he later sometimes engaged in the harmless fantasy of imagining that this was the case, but because that was the way that the majority of the other village children went about, and he needed to conform. This school, which was for boys only, was housed in a single long plank-and-attap shed, raised well above the ground because of the annual floods. There he studied through standards one to four, starting at eight in the morning and finishing five hours later. Instruction, which was rather elementary, was given on six mornings a week with only Friday, the Muslim holy day, free of lessons. This kind of schooling was not really designed to produce future Prime Ministers for sovereign states, but was rather intended, as the Colonial Government had made quite clear, to 'make the son of the fisherman or peasant a more intelligent fisherman or peasant than his father had been, and a man whose education will enable him to understand how his own lot in life fits in with the scheme of life around him'[2].

In the early years of the British Protectorate the education of boys in Malay villages in Pahang was provided by the Surau, that is prayer-house, or by Quranic schools which were run by private teachers for personal profit. There, from about the age of five, the child learned to read the Holy Quran in Arabic, studied the practices of the Islamic religion, and was taught to read and write in the Malay-Arabic script. The successful completion of these studies was a great event in any Muslim boy's life and a cause for a communal celebration paid for, of course, by his parents. For a very long time, this was all the education that most rural Malays considered it necessary that their children should receive.

By the turn of the twentieth century, however, the government of the Federated Malay States had opened a few state financed colleges in which the medium of instruction was English and a much larger number of elementary schools where the pupils were taught in Malay. The latter had often evolved from existing Quranic schools, the staffs of which had merely been transferred on to the government payroll. These schools offered a morning session of general education which did not include religious instruction; although the same teachers were permitted to remedy this in the afternoons by providing private tuition for those children whose parents were willing to pay for the privilege.[3]

Abdul Razak was one of those who took both types of education; and the fact that half of his early schooling was in Islamic subjects gives some indication of the important part that religion played, and indeed still does play, in the lives of the rural Malays; for to the Muslim, Islam and the Holy Quran provide a comprehensive guide to every aspect of human behaviour, guiding him 'from his birth to his death and from the grave to the other world'[4].

ROYAL ACCESSION

On March 3rd, 1930, Abdul Razak's father inherited the title of *Orang Kaya Indera Shahbandar;* a position that automatically qualified him for a seat on the State Council of Pahang and entitled him to be styled as *Dato,* in this case roughly equivalent to Lord, Hussein. Abdul Razak was, on this occasion, considered too young to attend when his father was formally placed in this post; but two years later, when a new Sultan of Pahang ascended the throne he was, as a close relative of one of the State's four major territorial Chiefs and a likely successor to the title, given a place of honour at the ceremony. His father had an important role to play in the latter part of this installation. Indeed the *Dato Shahbandar* was directly responsible for organising all male participation in palace ceremonial, while his first wife, Fatimah, had a similar responsibility for the women's side.

As this great occasion approached public attention throughout the state centred on the sleepy little town of Pekan; for each day crowds of Malays, colourful in their best clothing, arrived from the outlying districts to wander along the long double row of gaily decorated Chinese shops that formed the new commercial centre. At night the entire town was lit up until long after midnight, when at last the gongs and other musical instruments that had provided the accompaniment for the traditional Malay dancing were silent. Many visitors had arrived from other states and those among them who were unable to find accommodation in the town were lodged in private houseboats on the river. On the day preceding the ceremony Sir Cecil Clementi, the Governor of the Straits Settlements and High Commissioner of the Federated Malay States, resplendent in white uniform, sword and official plumed helmet, arrived with a large party from Singapore on board the government steamer *Sea Belle* and was met at the Customs Jetty by the Sultan-to-be, Dato Shahbandar Hussein and all of the other major Chiefs of Pahang.

At 8.45 am on Sunday June 23rd., a single shot was fired from a gun in the compound of the police barracks to let everyone know that one of the principal preliminary ceremonies was about to begin. Abdul Razak and his family, who had crossed the river at dawn, joined a

School Days

large crowd of loyal subjects who had assembled to watch the bathing, or purification ceremony. This took place at the *Sri Terentang* Palace, an old but dignified wooden building situated about a mile inland from the river. In the grounds of this palace stood the Ruler's bathing pavilion, an ornate seven-tiered roofed structure built upon a huge raised dais.[5] Around this imposing edifice swarmed a great crowd of Pahang Malays and foreign visitors, all eagerly awaiting the arrival of the royal party.

The Prince's procession approached through the ranks of a guard of honour made up from the state's minor Chieftains, administrative officers in the government service and religious dignitaries, each in traditional Malay dress and armed with a *keris,* a short stabbing sword of a design peculiar to the East Indian Archipelago. First came one of the principal Officers of State, the *Tunku Panglima Besar,* dressed all in red; and behind him a courtier bearing the broad-bladed spear that has been a major symbol of royalty in Pahang from the time, many centuries before, when Hinduism was the state religion. These were followed by two further gentlemen spear-bearers, directly preceding the Sultan-to-be who walked under a royal umbrella made from yellow silk. His highness was escorted by a bodyguard of twenty spearmen, all dressed alike in yellow coats and black sarongs over white trousers. The Royal Consort, walking under a separate coloured umbrella, followed her husband. She was accompanied by her mother, who was wife to the Sultan of Perak, and by a princess of the House of Johore; and was escorted by thirty ladies-in-waiting and an all-male bodyguard. This procession proceeded slowly toward the bathing pavilion walking beneath a white awning and along a path that had been covered with white cloth. Upon entering the pavilion the guards, umbrella-carriers and spear-bearers lined the lower tiers, while the royal escorts and ladies-in-waiting accompanied the Prince and his Consort to the roofed platform situated at the top of the structure.

The ceremony that followed, which though it was of ancient Indian origin had been modified so as to be acceptable to the Islamic religion, was conducted mainly by women. After the prince and his princess had seated themselves on the thrones provided they were blessed by being sprinkled with rice that had been stained yellow with tumeric, first by the Sultan of Perak, the prince's father-in-law, then by the youngest surviving brother of the late Ruler of Pahang and finally by one of the State's principal religious officers, the Chief *Kathi*. Then, to the accompaniment of prayers led by the *Kathi,* the women attendants ritually bathed the prince and his consort with holy water taken from nine different streams within the State and contained in nine separate silver vessels. When this purification ceremony was finished, the procession was re-formed and to the regular discharge of a 17-gun salute the royal couple returned to their palace, the *Istana Pantai*, to await the official installation.

Later that same morning the prince and his consort, after inspecting a guard of honour mounted by seventy-two officers and men of the Malay Company of the Pahang Volunteer Infantry and the Battalion's drum and fife band, proceeded to the great audience hall of the palace in a procession similar in composition to that of the purification ceremony. Inside the hall the prince and princess sat upon two Chinese blackwood thrones, ornamented with gold, that were set upon a dais. Slightly below the level of these thrones and to the right of the prince sat Sir Cecil Clementi; while the Sultan of Perak occupied the corresponding position on the left of the princess. Immediately behind the Sultan-to-be stood the principal spear-bearer, flanked on one side by Dato Hussein and on the other by the Prince's European A.D.C.; the one in traditional Malay costume and the other in the full dress uniform of the Federated Malay States Police. Behind these two equerries were massed the colourful spearmen of the guard; while in front of the throne two officials of the Royal Household stood guard with drawn swords. In the body of the hall, drawn up in lines to the right and to the left, were the invited guests, Abdul Razak and his mother among them.

The actual ceremony of installation began when Dato Hussein, as *Orang Kaya Indera Shahbandar,* came forward bearing a document which announced the accession to the throne of Pahang of Prince Abu Bakar as Sultan. This he handed to the *Tunku Arif Bendahara,* second brother of the new Ruler, who made the Proclamation in Malay. A further document was then handed to the Prince who read from it the Oath of Office and then signed it. After this signature had been witnessed by Sir Cecil Clementi and the Resident of Pahang, and only after that, the Sultan was considered to have been officially installed.

Normally there were only four Europeans stationed in Pekan — and none of course in Jambu Langgar — and so this was the first time, seeing these two high officials of an alien power sitting there in their service uniforms and plumed helmets, that the young Razak had realised that his sovereign could rule only after foreign administrators had signified their assent. Though still a child, it made a deep and lasting impression upon him. As he was to say forty years later, he felt even then that the Malays were just acting out a charade for the amusement of the colonial officials in whose hands all power, advancement and patronage lay.

The new Sultan was next accorded the homage of his feudal aristocracy. First to approach the throne was the *Tunku Arif Temenggong,* the Sultan's youngest brother, who paid homage on behalf of the members of the Royal Family and of the four major territorial Chiefs.

He knelt four times in front of the dais, each time advancing a little closer to the throne and on each occasion proclaiming in Malay the nobility's allegiance to their Ruler. At the conclusion of this, as a special mark of deference, he knelt directly before his prince and pressed his forehead against the Sultan's hand. He was followed by three other homage-bearers, representing three lower grades of the aristocracy and gentry, who followed a similar procedure except that they did not kneel on the dias or touch the Ruler's hand. The ceremony ended with a second salute of 17 guns fired from the police station compound.

The final seal of British approval was placed upon the new Sultan the next morning, in the same audience hall, when he was invested with the insignia of a Companion of the Most Distinguished Order of Saint Michael and Saint George. On this occasion His Highness was accompanied by the Crown Prince of Perak and the *Tunku Besar* of Pahang, both of whom were already Companions of the same Order. The Royal Warrants were read out first in English by the Sultan's private secretary and then in Malay by Dato Hussein, after which the Ruler was invested by Sir Cecil Clementi acting on behalf of the King-Emperor, George the Fifth.

THE MALAY COLLEGE

Toward the end of 1933 Abdul Razak was selected by the Resident of Pahang to attend the Malay College at Kuala Kangsar, his father's *alma mater,* with the intention that he too should be trained for a career in the civil service; for even if he eventually succeeded to his father's title of *Orang Kaya Indera Shahbandar* he would still, under the laws of Pahang, be able to continue his career as long as his appointments were confined to his home state. At this point, however, he had to face the fact that as he had absolutely no knowledge of the English language, which was the medium of instruction at the Malay College, he would have to master this difficult subject before he could even begin seriously to participate in the ordinary lessons. Fortunately provision had already been made for other boys who had found themselves in similar circumstances, so that special instruction was available as part of the first year curriculum.

At last the great day arrived and Abdul Razak said goodbye to his friends and relations in the village and set out on what, for a boy who had never previously been outside of his own State, was a considerable adventure. Accompanied by his father and both paternal grandparents, he travelled by car first to Kuala Lumpur, the capital of the Federal Malay States, and then, after a welcome night's rest, on to the royal capital of Perak.

The quiet and rather introverted young Razak was duly registered at the College as a boarder on January 26th, 1934, and, although everything was so very dissimilar to the quiet village life that he had been used to, soon settled into the school routine. On ordinary schooldays reveille was at 6 am, with the first lesson starting an hour later. There was a break at 8.30 for a European-style breakfast of bread and butter, eggs and tea; and then form work again from 9.15 until the lunch break at 1 pm. In the afternoons every boy, whatever his own inclinations, was forced to take a short siesta so that the headmaster could work without undue noise; although those who had been careless or lazy in form usually found themselves in the detention class writing lines instead of sleeping or reading.

From the time of Abdul Razak's arrival until 1938 the school was under the headmastership of a strict disciplinarian named Bazell, who insisted on the boys being correctly dressed at all times and in comporting themselves like young gentlemen, as the British at that time understood the term. As one left-wing nationalist[6] and former pupil put it when interviewed in the 1970's, 'we were taught to drink tea and soup like upper-class Englishmen, that is without making a noise'. This public school image did nothing at all to increase the popularity of the Malay College boys in the town, where they were generally regarded as arrogant snobs aping the manners of Europeans. This antipathy was particularly noticeable at the school's sporting events, when spectators from the town invariably cheered for the visiting team. Despite this aristocratic image, however, everybody, regardless of his background or family wealth, was supposed to receive the same amount of pocket-money — one Malayan dollar a week. In a creditable attempt to ensure that this was so, the headmaster kept a large bag of fifty cent coins in his study and every Friday personally handed his allowance to the individual pupil.

His previous lack of instruction in the language notwithstanding, Abdul Razak managed to score seventy-one out of a hundred in English subjects in the examinations held at the end of his first year at the College. The headmaster's report said of him: 'he has been given double promotion this year and is now in Standard III. He has ability and is a consistent worker.'

It was during this year that Abdul Razak was first introduced to one of the favourite sports of the College boys, water tobogganing. The most popular site for this was a place overlooking the river some seven or eight miles outside the town. Armed with picnic baskets the boys would go off *en masse* to where, in a secluded spot far from the main road, a jungle stream poured over a huge rock to cascade down a long precipitous slope into a deep natural pool below. Here the intrepid tobogganist, equipped with an areca palm frond to sit upon whilst sliding, took off from a strategically positioned ledge and, with legs thrust out in front of him and hands frantically clutching the front end of his seat to help him maintain balance, rushed with exhilarating speed down the eighty or ninety foot slide to the comparative safety of pool below; counting the battering his body took on the way down a small price to pay for the approval and acculamation of his peers. It was a contest played as an early form of 'chicken'; born out of the necessity felt by every adolescent boy to establish his own identity, separate from the one his doting family had wished upon him, by finding acceptance within the social hierarchy of his own generation.

Sustained by such interludes from work, Abdul Razak continued to get good reports throughout his school career, he passed the Junior Cambridge Examination in July 1937 and obtained his School Certificate a year later. His report for 1937 described him as a very promising boy with both ability and character. To this his form master had added acidly, 'but he must learn to write legibly'. In the same report too, under mathematics, appeared the criticism: 'has ability but rushes to conclusions (often wrong) too quickly ... he would be very good if he could cultivate accuracy. His methods are invariably correct, but his results are often wrong. He is a very quick worker and could afford to go slower. Often he can't read his own figures, so should try to be more tidy'.

This 1937 report was accompanied by a letter from the Pahang State Secretariat that must have given Dato Hussein considerable pleasure, for it read: 'I am directed to refer to the report of the Headmaster, Malay College, Kuala Kangsar, on your son Abdul Razak, and to say that your son is continuing to earn good reports at the College and to show promise for his future success in life. I am to add that on the recommendation of the Headmaster, the Resident has pleasure in remitting the school fees in full for the next year.'

FISHING INTERLUDE

In this same year, while he was back home on holiday, the 15-year-old Abdul Razak attended a fish drive on the Pahang River that was one of the highlights of the celebrations arranged for the Ruler of Pahang's birthday. Two days before the drive was due to begin, Abdul Razak was permitted to accompany and help the workers who were sent ahead to construct the barricade of stakes, closely interlaced with strips of split bamboo, that was to act as a trap. This was set up at the junction which the tributary that was actually to be fished made with the main river.

On the appointed day a considerable fleet of small river craft assembled off Pekan and then, led by the Sultan in his royal barge, made their way up the river to the scheduled starting place. That night the whole party was put to work pounding tuba roots [7] and mixing the resultant extract, containing the stupefying drug that would bring the fish to the surface, with water to form a milky white fluid. They worked in family groups by the light of flares and, while pounding away, amused themselves by making up topical Malay pantuns, or poetic verses in four line stanzas, each section in turn trying to surpass the efforts of those who had gone before them and so win the applause of their co-workers.

At dawn the milky liquid was poured into the river where it spread rapidly, clouding the water; and after about ten minutes the first fish began to appear on the surface, floating helplessly. The smaller ones were netted and the larger ones gaffed with either trident-like or single-barbed spears. Although many of the bigger fish seemed to be little affected by the drug, they nevertheless fled before the advancing white cloud that menaced them, until they were finally trapped against the barricade at the junction of the river. There, though they fought desperately to escape, but were eventually speared and brought ashore. The drive then ended with a great communal feast in which many hundreds of fish, impaled on sharpened sticks, were grilled over open fires and then eaten on the spot with white rice, chillies, and the little spicey tidbits, intended to titivate the palate, that Malays delight in savouring.

EMBRYO PHILOSOPHER

Although he had been quite happy to work alongside the other village children in the rice fields of Jambu Langgar, Abdul Razak had always possessed a driving ambition to lead; a full measure of what the nineteenth century philosopher Nietzsche, declared to be the dominant motive behind all human endeavour, the will to power — a fundamental agressive instinct that drives men on toward ever higher goals. In the limited world of the Malay College this meant that in addition to distinguishing himself academically, he must also strive to become an outstanding sportsman and seek positions of power or distinction in the school societies. By 1938 he was not only Captain of his House, but had been appointed Head Boy of the entire student body. He was, too, a versatile sportsman who had already gained his school colours for hockey, tennis and squash, and house colours for cricket. He was particularly proud of being vice-captain of the school soccer XI; and with reason, for the College magazine for 1939 reported that at centre-half he was 'the backbone of the College defence. Very difficult to pass. Heads well and has a good left foot kick, but is ineffective with his right foot.' Which was rather surprising as he was right-handed.

School Days 23

Late in 1939, not long after the Second World War had broken out in Europe, Abdul Razak's first contribution to English literature, an essay entitled 'Progress is a Myth', was published in the Malay College magazine. In it he wrote:

That wise man of all ages, Solomon, said: 'There is no new thing upon the earth, and all novelty is but oblivion'. Men today are proud, and in some ways boastful of the things which they have improved and discovered. They think that all the scientific discoveries and mathematical theories which are part of their everyday life were not dreamed of by the ancient Greeks and Romans. They think that the Egyptians were able to erect such colossal pyramids simply by infinite labour and not because of the advancement of their civilization or the cleverness of their engineers.

Certainly the average man today would be bewildered and puzzled to hear that all the mathematical arts which are within the reach of the human brain today were known to the Egyptians; and that in building the huge pyramids these arts were used .....

Although modern people pride themselves on their beautiful buildings and magnificent skyscrapers, the architecture of the Greeks and Romans was much finer than that of today. Paradoxically, it can be said that the civilization of the ancient Greeks and Romans was much higher than that of the present day. No artist today can imitate the Greek art and no architect can produce the same fine architecture as that of the Romans .....

The progress of man, if there is any such thing, must be very slow. Every human being has to start, as it were, from zero. Every child who is born into the world knows nothing about anything which its predecessors have discovered and learnt. It has, through its brief existence, to learn everything that has already been known and also it has to try to improve on that knowledge. If only a man could start from where his forefathers had left off, the progress of man might be tremendous.

What is still worse is the fact that a civilization may be destroyed by a world catastrophe. The great civilizations of the Greeks and Romans are completely separate from the present civilization. Endless wars brought their civilizations to complete destruction, so that the people who came after them had to start afresh. There are some of the remains of the literature, arts and architecture of the Greeks and Romans which modern civilization has as its mother and nurse. It is perhaps therefore too pessimistic to say that our present civilization will soon be destroyed by a world catastrophe, of which the seeds have just been sown. The modern scientific discoveries seem to result only in world disaster. Aeroplanes seem to bring no other result to the world than that of killing its inhabitants and destroying its beautiful towns and buildings. The machine-guns, the submarines and the big guns destroy men. The radio is used for spreading propaganda. It therefore appears that progress is merely a road to catastrophe.

Now Great Britain and Germany are at war, which may in all likelihood involve and cause disaster to the whole world. If such a catastrophe cannot be avoided, men have not yet progressed at all. A war with daggers, shields and spears is no more barbarous than one with aeroplanes, submarines and machine-guns. Both wars mean the killing of men; and the killing of men is an act of savagery and barbarity.

Men have doubtless made great progress in some directions for modern ships are obviously better and faster than the sailing ships and rowing boats of the ancients. The radio and the telephone are modern wonders which the Greeks and Romans never dreamt of having. Furthermore, although modern people may not be wiser than the Greeks and Romans, education today is spread among a larger number of the community, and the delight of reading and writing is within the reach of almost everyone. Thus men should be more educated, and they should be able to be masters of themselves.

The whole trouble in the world today is caused by the conflict between man and himself. Every man should be master of himself before there can be everlasting peace in the world. There should be world unity, in which the rule of force has been banished and replaced by that of law. The League of Nations was an attempt to federate the world, but unfortunately it was a failure.

The present war between Great Britain and Germany is a conflict of principles. The result of the war will show whether the rule of force or the rule of law will exist on earth. Britain is trying to stop Germany from dominating the world by force. She is fighting for the peace of the world, and it is the hope of the world that Germany will be totally crushed so that there will be a lasting peace .....

Although by modern standards the opinions expressed about the objectives of the war may seem surprisingly pro-British in a highly intelligent indigenous youth living under colonial rule, it should be remembered that not only had Abdul Razak been for several formative years subject to the influence of patriotically inclined British school masters, but that the conservative brand of Malay nationalism to which the majority of his people then subscribed, was directed not against the expatriate establishment, but against the immigrant races living in the Peninsula, particularly the Chinese. This growing antipathy between the various races was demonstrated during a debate staged by the Malay College Literary, Dramatic and Debating Society, of which Abdul Razak was in 1939 the Vice-President, when the motion 'that in the opinion of this House padi-planting should be open to all Asiatics'[8] was crushingly defeated by 72 votes to 4; the four supporters including the proposer and seconder who, of course, had no option. It was said at the time that because feeling ran so high, even among the junior boys, the standard of debate was higher than had ever been achieved before. Abdul Razak, although he remained neutral and merely invigilated this particular discussion, was already showing signs of emerging as a formidable debater; and in fact went on to become the President of his College Union. His contemporaries remember him, even at that time, however, as being more than usually serious and reserved for a boy of his age; and as seldom smiling, for even when he cracked a joke it was normally with a straight face.

STUDENT PROBATIONER

In the middle of 1939 Abdul Razak was appointed a Student-Probationer in the Malay Administrative Service, his application having been supported by the following report from the Principal of the Malay College:

> Che Abdul Razak is seventeen years of age. He is Head Boy of the School, and is a boy of strong character. He is a good leader and is absolutely reliable. He has done well both in school and on the playing fields, having played for the College at both football and hockey; winning colours in both games. He is captain of tennis, captain of his House, and a sergeant in the College Cadet Corps. I have no hesitation in recommending him for a Probationership in the Malay Administrative Service, since he is quite definitely, in my opinion, the type of young man required.

The Student-Probationers, the majority of whom were recruited from other secondary or high schools, received a year's training course at the Malay College, following a special syllabus that included English, mathematics, history, geography and, as specialist subjects, elementary law and surveying. They were also encouraged to take part in all of the extra-curricular College activities and sports. Abdul Razak received uniformly good marks during this period, but as usual was in trouble with the mathematics master, who recorded that 'he is forgetful and rushes headlong into errors. Will nearly always fall into a trap set in any question. He is intelligent and should do well when he learns to take more care.'

On May 31st, 1940, Abdul Razak left the Malay College with a scholarship that entitled him to take a three-year course in economics, law and history at Raffles College. This was a centre for higher education that had been set up in Singapore in 1928 to offer diploma, but not degree courses, in a wide range of subjects. It was, until after the end of the Second World War, the nearest to a University available within the Malay Peninsula.

Chapter Three
War

Raffles College turned out to be a hybrid creation, run partly on the lines of a British Public School of the period and partly on those of a University and so Abdul Razak, as a freshman, found himself subject to the usual ragging which was, however, much milder and more gentlemanly than it is at the University of Malaya today. For the first month of their stay the freshmen had to fetch and carry for the seniors and call them 'sir'. They were not permitted to wear normal neckties but instead were given pieces of unsewn calico to knot around their necks. If any freshman was discovered wearing a proper tie, this was snipped off just below the knot with a pair of scissors. The staid and unsmiling Abdul Razak attracted more than his fair share of the ragging and was forced to do countless press-ups, was 'dunked' in the bathroom, and once, for a particularly heinous but now forgotten crime, forced to push a mothball across the floor of the bathroom with the tip of his nose. But he took it all in good part and managed to preserve the quiet dignity that despite his youth had already become so important to him.

All of the Malay Administrative Service students were accommodated in the same block, in dormitories that had each been divided into a number of private cubicles; but as the partitions of these stopped some two feet short of the ceiling to allow for better ventilation in the tropical heat, it was easy for anyone to climb into the rooms when the doors were locked. Sometimes when the occupants were out, seniors took the opportunity to raid their cubicles and throw bedding and clothing all over the place. Such raids were called 'earthquakes'. The ragging month ended with a dance and general social evening at which the 'freshies' had to provide the entertainment by giving a concert to celebrate their acceptance into normal College society. From that time onward, everywhere the new students went outside the dormitory area they had to appear dressed formally in long-sleeved shirts, ties and white jackets.

As soon as he began to attend classes, Abdul Razak realised that the boys who had been educated at the Malay College were generally well below the standard of those students who had come from less privileged schools like the Victoria and Raffles Institutions. This, it seemed to him, was due mainly to the aristocratic exclusiveness of the intake at Kuala Kangsar; for the majority of the sons or nephews of

Sultans and princes were financially independent and so had no compelling need to work hard in order to ensure success in future careers. Because of this, those who had ambition met such weak opposition in rising to the top of their classes that they became over-confident of their own abilities and so failed properly to exert themselves. This was a situation which in later years, when he became Minister of Education, Abdul Razak was able to rectify; and so effective was the democratization of the intake that when his fourth son failed the qualifying entrance examination for the Malay College, he was refused a place.

BURGEONING NATIONALISM

Multi-racial Raffles College was a great change from the very Malay atmosphere of Abdul Razak's previous school at Kuala Kangsar and for the first time he, who had become used to an underlying mildly anti-Chinese feeling among a Malay majority, found himself on the receiving end of similar sentiments in an environment that was predominantly Chinese. Normally, of course, all of the racial communities represented at the College got on fairly well together, but he soon found that there was a feeling among certain of the Chinese and Indians that the colonial authorities, especially those of the Malay States, were too biased in favour of the Malays in, among other things, the award of scholarships. So the Malays, who in fact formed only a small percentage of the student population of the College, felt that they had to close ranks and stick together. Their extra-curricula activities tended, therefore, to centre around the Muslim Society, a social club in which those College students whose religion was Islam mixed with their counterparts from the King Edward VII College of Medicine, with whom they organised dances and picnics.

It was whilst he was in this Society that Abdul Razak, who served on the committee and later as its secretary, first really became interested, if only marginally, in what then passed as Malay nationalism and politics. This came about because his fellow members, who were unable to air their frustrations during staff-supervised College debates that were deliberately confined to non-controversial or academic subjects, took to turning their picnics, and those discussion groups held in their residential quarters, into clandestine protest meetings. At these the muslim students, Abdul Razak among them, often expressed themselves with the generous fervour and uninhibited radicalism of youth in condemnation of the ultra-conservative policies of the colonial government. They especially resented that their efforts should be rewarded only with a diploma instead of a degree; the lack of scholarships to overseas Universities; that Asians, and particularly

Malays, in the government service, doctors for example, should not be accorded opportunities and pay equal to those of expatriate Europeans; and that the Malay Administrative Service Probationers were, on graduation, given only inferior positions in the governing of their own Malay States.

Although, of course, he had no way of knowing it at the time, Abdul Razak was already meeting some of the men who would later be his political colleagues or adversaries, or the leaders of his country's civil service after independence. One such, who became a firm friend after they had met at various gatherings of the Muslim Society during 1941, was a first year student named Ghazali Shafie, a Malay youth from his home state of Pahang, with whom he was to have a long association in wartime anti-Japanese activities, in the civil service and in politics. This was indeed an example of the attraction of opposites, for 'Gaz' as he was affectionately known to all, was and is a brash and ebullient personality, the absolute antithesis of the stolid, unemotional Abdul Razak.

Another who was to have a considerable effect on his future political life, but who at that time he knew only by sight and reputation, was Sardon Haji Jubir; later to become an influential Malay politician, particularly associated with his party's youth movement, and a cabinet minister. Sardon, who had recently returned to Singapore from the United Kingdom after having qualified as a barrister, was the main guest speaker at the last pre-Japanese-invasion meeting of the Raffles College Muslim Society, when he called upon those Malays with education and social position to help raise the economic standard of the oppressed majority of their race. He was not at that time looked upon as a nationalist spokesman, but rather was respected by Malays as one of the comparatively few members of their race to have graduated overseas.

Many of the students who returned from the United Kingdom, especially those from Oxford or Cambridge, were feted as nationalists merely because they brought back with them editions of the Left Book Club and controversial works like Emerson's *Malaysia* which, though not officially banned, were not readily available in Malaya. The real hard-core nationalists were, in fact, former students of the Sultan Idris Teachers' Training College and the members of the Kesatuan Melaya Muda (K.M.M.) or Union of Malay Youth; but the Raffles College students, because of their background and upbringing, were more readily influenced by the Oxbridge graduates with their fine British accents, briar pipes and non-conformist beer drinking.

Before the end of the Japanese Occupation there was really no such thing as Malayan nationalism, mainly because no Malayan nation existed to rally the peoples' loyalty and affection. While the French, Dutch and even the Americans were faced in their Southeast

Asian colonial territories with strong and disciplined political movements aimed at driving them out, the British in Malaya were, thanks largely to the multi-racial nature of the society which they had themselves created, and the fragmentation of the Peninsula which pre-dated their occupation, left in comparative peace. There was, of course, occasional economic unrest within certain sections of the non-Malay population, although this was mild in comparison with that experienced in many other countries at the time; but such nationalism as existed, with the exception of that of the Communists and a few numerically insignificant groups of extremists, was aimed mainly at targets other than the colonial administration. The Chinese and Indians were interested chiefly in the problems of their own countries of origin, still referred to by the majority of them as their homelands, while even the Malays often looked outside the Peninsula to the Pan-Islamic movement for their inspiration.

The earliest Malay revolts against the British administration, the Perak War of 1875 to 1876 and the Pahang Disturbances of 1892 to 1894 for example, were not, in fact, popular movements of the common people resisting an aggressor, but rather risings of feudal Chiefs against the suppression of their right to levy taxes and their replacement as arbitrary administrators and petty rulers by professional civil servants. The ordinary people had no concept of a Malayan nation, for no such entity existed, their loyalty being to the particular State in which they resided and to its individual Ruler. In the first two decades of the twentieth century, however, two more broadly-based systems of nationalism began to emerge due mainly to the efforts of two totally dissimilar groupings of the rising generation of Malay intellectuals. The first was supported and advocated by traditionalists who had received their education in the Muslim colleges and universities of the Middle East and had as its ultimate aim the inclusion of a theocratic Malay State within a Pan-Islamic Empire; while the second, a more mundane and far less aristocratic movement, was greatly influenced by nationalist sentiments imported from the Dutch East Indies, and was therefore orientated more in the direction of a Greater Indonesian Commonwealth.

The first of these movements suffered a reverse from which it never recovered when, on October 29th, 1923, the Sultan of Turkey, who was also the *Khalifah* or Vicegerent of Islam, was deposed by his own National Assembly. In order to lessen the anger that this aroused in other Muslim countries, the new Republic temporarily retained the ex-Sultan's eldest son as *Khalifah*; but on March 3rd, 1924, President Mustapha Kemal, well aware of the danger of being overthrown as long as such a rallying point remained available to unite opposition within the country, and to gain support for it abroad, abolished the holy office absolutely.

The second and longer lasting movement received a great boost when in 1922 the government of the Federated Malay States opened the Sultan Idris Teachers' Training College at Tanjong Malim, in Perak, in order to produce for its state-supported Malay schools an adequate supply of properly qualified teachers. Unfortunately there were at that time no other secondary or high schools using Malay as the medium of instruction and no suitable textbooks in that language printed in the Peninsula; and so the students at the Training College imported most of their reading matter from the Dutch East Indies. This soon exposed them to the influence of Indonesian nationalism and especially of its extreme left wing after a number of revolutionary Indonesian leaders had sought refuge in Malaya following the abortive 1926 Communist-led uprising against the Dutch.

In 1937 a number of the former students of this establishment joined with some of the Indonesian political refugees to form a left-wing, anti-colonialist party called the *Kesatuan Melayu Muda*. For several years thereafter the K.M.M., which had established loose ties with the Chinese dominated Malayan Communist Party,[1] ran a newspaper in Singapore which attacked not only British colonialism, but also the privileges enjoyed by the Malay Sultans and their feudal aristocracies. As war in the Pacific area became inevitable, the leaders of this revolutionary Malay party made an accommodation with the Japanese whereby they agreed to assist their invasion forces with information about British troop movements and military installations and to provide them, wherever necessary, with guides to lead them through the jungle. This plan became known to the internal security forces, however, and as soon as war broke out the majority of the party's leaders were arrested and detained in Changi jail; where they remained until released by the Japanese in February 1942.

There was however a third and at this time the most important of the Malay nationalist movements. Conservative in outlook, it was concerned with improving the lot of the Malays generally, but prepared to do it with the cooperation of the British as long as the colonial government supported the indigenous people and stated openly that one day, ever if that day was so far off as to be out of sight, the country would be handed back to them and to them alone. For as long as this proviso was accepted, there was little opposition to the British staying. The great outcry against colonialism came only in the post-war period, when the British, obsessed with what they considered to be the fifth column activities of the K.M.M. and its allies, and feeling an obligation to the Chinese community which had resisted the Japanese during their military occupation of Malaya, reversed their former policies. This about face was marked by an attempt to reduce the hereditary Rulers of the various States to mere colonial puppets and also to deprive the Malays of their birthright by offering citizenship to all those immigrants who had either been born in Malaya, or who considered it to be their permanent home.

Theoretically all British colonies and dependent territories were supposed to be progressing, under the tutelage of their colonial masters, toward self-government; and in the case of Malaya this had gone forward in the leisurely and dignified manner so beloved of the *ancien regime*. The major communities were all represented in the Legislative and Federal Councils and the Malays, and in some cases the other races, in the State Councils; but all of these bodies had built-in official majorities, that were able whenever necessary to safeguard the *status quo*. In the Straits Settlements the first Malay Legislative Councillor was appointed in 1924 and this success encouraged the more influential of his compatriots in the Crown Colony to form the political organisation necessary to back him. This society, the Singapore Malay Union, was inaugurated in May 1926.[2]

For the next eleven years this organisation confined its activities to Singapore Island, but in 1937 a branch was opened in Malacca. A year later a similar, but undependent, society was set up in the Malay state of Pahang, with a member of the royal family as President and Abdul Razak's father, Dato Hussein, as Vice-President. Other states followed this example, and in August 1939 a conference of seven of these Malay Unions was held in Kuala Lumpur[3] to discuss cooperation and the possibility of joint action. This was an event which quickly led to the formation of similar societies in all of the remaining Malay States so that when, toward the end of 1940, a second conference was held in Singapore, the Peninsula Malays had, for the very first time, an embryo political movement organised, if loosely, on a national basis.

The more radical elements associated with the K.M.M. and its allies were not impressed with, or interested in joining, this conservative move towards national unity, however, for they were committed to being satisfied with nothing less than independence through federation with Indonesia. While this attitude was largely inspired by those of Indonesian extraction among the leadership, it was also acceptable to the bulk of the rank and file Peninsula Malays, on the principle that it was better to be assimilated into a society allied in race and religion than be swamped by alien Chinese. This attitude hardened still further after the publication of official estimates for 1941 which showed that if the Straits Settlements and the Malay States were taken together, the Malays formed only 41 per cent of the total population, while roughly 43 per cent were Chinese and nearly 14 per cent had their origins in the Indian sub-continent.[4]

In earlier days those Chinese who had entered the Peninsula to work as labourers had shown little inclination to become involved in politics, although on occasions their mutual protection societies, organised on a tribal or clan basis, such as the various lodges of the

Hung League or Triad Society, had led them into Malay dynastic struggles, armed opposition to the establishment, and attempts at territorial domination by force. With the extension of British 'protection' and subsequent rule by central governments disposing of considerable military power, the Societies were forced underground, became fragmented, and soon degenerated into numerous small criminal organisations. The bulk of the Chinese then became disenchanted with politics until 1911, when a revolution in mainland China overthrew the monarchy and inaugurated a Republic. This revolution, which caused the disappearance of the traditional ruling class, led to an unprecedented desire for knowledge among the more ambitious peasants and workers who, for the first time, saw a chance to escape from their perennial situation of grinding poverty. Not surprisingly, this movement spread overseas to the many China-orientated communities living in Southeast Asia; and Dr Sun Yat Sen's revolutionary government, realising that it had been presented with an outstanding opportunity to increase its influence by means of propaganda, willingly despatched school teachers, who were also nationalist agents, to man the new private schools that patriotic merchants were building.

By the mid-1920's, however, the *Kuomintang,* or Chinese Nationalist Party, had been extensively infiltrated by Communists who, in the Malay Peninsula as in other territories, worked to take over the school propaganda networks and to use them for their own ends. In Malaya this took the form of conditioning the pupils to believe that once the British had been driven out, the future of the Peninsula lay in colonisation by China. Before long, however, two factors appeared to weaken, although not to break, the Communist hold on the Chinese private schools: the first, an upsurge of nationalist hatred toward communism in Malaya following a series of bloody purges carried out by Chiang Kai Shek in China, which smashed the extreme left wing of the Kuomintang; and the second, the introduction into these schools of undercover police agents working for the British colonial governments. The Communists, driven from the shelter of an organisation that enjoyed the support of the great majority of Malayan Chinese, formed their own clandestine political party and went underground.

During the early 1930's the combined effects of the Sino-Japanese war and the world-wide economic recession had led larger than usual numbers of Chinese to seek a better life in Malaya. Eventually, this influx into a country already badly hit by the depression aggravated the existing problem of unemployment to such an extent that in 1933 it became necessary to pass an Aliens Ordinance in order to restrict the number of male immigrants. For a time, however, female immigrants, unless they were known prostitutes [5], were permitted to enter freely in order to correct the serious imbalance within the community between men and women. So effective did this measure prove to be, in fact, that it changed the whole social structure of Chinese life within Malaya; leading to greater domesticity and with it, inevitably, increased demands for political representation and equality of rights with the indigenous peoples.[6]

In 1937 the Japanese invaded China once again; and in the following year the Chinese communities of the Peninsula set up a Pan-Malayan organisation, called the Anti-Enemy Backing-up Society, in order to enforce a boycott that they had imposed upon the sale or import of Japanese goods. Soon, however, the leadership of this patriotic movement was usurped by the Communists who, while pretending to pursue its original objectives, made of it a weapon to attack the British through the medium of strikes and demonstrations.[7] This civil unrest reached its peak when, following the military catastrophe of the fall of France, the hard-pressed British capitulated to Japanese threats and closed the Burma Road supply route into China. It did not cease until June 22nd, 1941, when Germany attacked Russia and the immediate alliance between that latter country and Great Britain made of the Malayan Communist Party an uneasy collaborator with the colonial authorities.

Although there had been Indian settlers in the Peninsula for more than a thousand years before the outbreak of the Pacific War, their presence, until quite recent times, had posed no great problems for the Malays who, until their conversion to Islam, had themselves followed Saivite Hinduism, so that inter-marriage was not only possible but usual. With the establishment of British settlements at Penang, Malacca and Singapore, however, many more Indians entered the country, though only the Muslim element among them showed much inclination to integrate with the indigenous people. This situation was exacerbated when following British intervention in the Malay States, large numbers of Indians and Ceylon Tamils were recruited to work there. They brought with them their own religion, culture, and social systems, and an incipient nationalism that was concerned solely with their homeland.

Although it was known to the internal security services that professional agitators from the Indian nationalist movement had, from about 1910, settled in Singapore for the purpose of harassing the colonial authorities,[8] little was heard of them by the general public of the Straits Settlements until the second year of the first world-war. Then, on February 15th 1915, men of the 5th Light Infantry Regiment of the Indian Army mutinied in Singapore. They were joined by disaffected elements of the only other regular battalion in the Peninsula at the time, the Malay States Guides, a regiment that, despite its name, was totally Indian in composition; and the revolt was put down only after marines and armed sailors had been landed from a number of Japanese and other Allied warships that were on patrol in the area.

In the period between the two world-wars Indian nationalist agents continued to use Singapore as their main base in Southeast Asia, although they gradually spread their activities into the Malay States and Thailand. For most of this period the majority of Indians in Malaya remained apathetic about politics; but the situation changed dramatically in May 1937 when Pandit Nehru made an officially approved visit to the Peninsula, and in a series of inflammatory speeches called upon all Indians, no matter where they lived and worked, to fight for the independence, not of Malaya, but of India. This set the stage for Indian political thinking in the Peninsula for the next eight years; for although there was a certain amount of politically motivated industrial unrest during the remainder of the pre-war colonial period, the real interests of these nationalists lay solely in driving the British out of India.

Such then were the forces of potential conflict and disruption that lay, apparently dormant, beneath the deceptively placid surface of life in colonial Singapore; forces the existence of which were slowly revealed to Abdul Razak through mixing with an ever-increasing circle of acquaintances and listening patiently, and as objectively as he was able, to their views on topics about which they obviously felt very strongly. Gradually he began to see the interactions of life in the Peninsula in a new perspective and to realise that many of the preconceived ideas which, in his formative years, he had adopted from others, needed to be re-examined and in some cases modified.

Another facet of his new environment that had considerable bearing upon Abdul Razak's growing political awareness and dissatisfaction with existing conditions stemmed from contact, for the first time, with large numbers of Europeans of varying types and backgrounds. Whereas previously he had had dealings mainly with the masters at the Malay College and senior government officials in the service of the Federated Malay States, most of whom were sympathetic to Malay culture and traditions and sufficiently well educated to display tact and courtesy, he now came up against a kind of colour bar and the careless insults of an ill-mannered lower-middle class who had all too often been promoted above their capabilities.

The European community of Singapore at that time fell into three general categories: government servants, the Services, and those engaged in some form of commerce; each section with its own fiercely preserved social hierarchy and tabus. The majority wore their white skins like the insignia of an hereditary aristocracy and banished humility from both their vocabularies and their thoughts. Those at the top could afford to be more tolerant and liberal, but those holding minor positions felt that they had to struggle continually to assert their supposed superiority. The worst offenders were their wives and daughters who had often brought with them from Britain all the petty snobberies and Victorian prejudices of their suburban or provincial origins. A man who in Britain had been a clerk was in Singapore styled, by courtesy, an 'accountant'; every commercial assistant was a 'manager'; and every policeman an officer. A wife who had formerly darned her husband's socks suddenly had servants to cook and clean for her, to look after her children and to drive her to visit her equally over-leisured friends.

The colour bar was mild in comparison with that operating in many other colonial territories, but it existed. The treatment of Eurasians, who were accepted as equals neither by Europeans nor Asians, was as cruel as it was stupid and unwarranted; and even Abdul Razak, who by such people's own tenets was their superior in social position and in many cases education, was often treated as though he were a second class citizen in his own homeland. None of this helped to win many friends for the British in the coming struggle with the Japanese, although it did influence the local people in their subsequent actions.

PRELUDE TO WAR

Although the war was still far away, the fighting in Russia and the Middle East dominated the radio news bulletins and newspaper reports; and so people's thoughts, despite official assurances, turned to the possibility of an extension of hostilities to the Far East. In September 1940 the Japanese had occupied French bases in northern Indo-China and in July the following year had taken control of the south as well. This brought them within air striking distance of the whole of the Malay Peninsula.

Morale remained high, however, for the British had an awesome reputation for power that had not been seriously challenged in the Far East since the days of the Indian Mutiny; and with the trappings of military might well displayed about the island, few civilians in Singapore could have had any idea just how illusory that power was. It took the Japanese army, navy and airforce just seventy days, once it decided to move, to shatter it for ever.

The British laid the foundations of their own defeat at the beginning of the twentieth century when, feeling themselves menaced by an expansion of the German navy, they withdrew their own capital ships from the Far East to Europe and left Japan free to fill the vacuum. From 1919, after the Germans had scuttled their surrendered fleet at Scapa Flow, Japan became the third greatest naval power in the world; able to dispose of a far larger force than ever Britain would dare to withdraw for long from European waters and the Mediterranean. Successive British governments were, of course, not unaware of the danger that this fleet posed to Australasia and India and compromised by voting funds for the construction of a modern fortified naval base, to be sited at Singapore, at which, in times of emergency, a defending naval task force could be concentrated. By the time war broke out in Europe in 1939 the defences of the base were still far from complete, however, and military estimates at the time suggested that it was incapable of withstanding more than a minor raid from the sea [9].

Ill-armed and over-extended in fighting Germany and Italy in Europe and the Middle East, Britain had little thought to spare for the defences of Singapore which, in December 1941 when the Japanese attacked, were still grossly inadequate. The peoples of Malaya and Singapore, however, shared Winston Churchill's ignorance of just how naked the island really was.

*****   *****   *****

On Monday, December 1st, the people of Singapore were shocked to learn through the radio and their newspapers that the Governor, Sir Shenton Thomas, had declared a State of Emergency and authorised the mobilization of all of the Colony's reserve and volunteer military, air and naval forces. It was emphasized in official quarters, however, that this was merely a normal precaution and did not mean that there had been any further deterioration of the situation in the Far East. None of this made much of an impression on the students at Raffles Colleges, who were fully occupied with last minute preparations for the examinations that had to be faced before they could return home for the Christmas holidays.

The next day the Malay States too called up their reserve units; but the really big news was provided by the arrival at the Singapore Naval Base of the battleship *Prince of Wales,* flagship of the newly constituted Far Eastern Fleet, accompanied by the powerful battle-cruiser *Repulse* and four destroyers, a reinforcement that was greeted with much official and press jubilation. Their presence was also made known to the outside world through a radio broadcast which did not, of course, reveal that the new aircraft-carrier *Indomitable,* which it had been intended should provide air cover for these vulnerable capital ships, had recently gone around in the West Indies and could not quickly be replaced. [10]

In the town centre the department stores and other shops were all gaily decorated for Christmas and in Little's Cafe and the Tanglin Club European ladies took their 'elevenses' and spoke disparagingly of the Japanese. The streets were crowded with servicemen and every day there were air-raid drills and the reassuring sound of anti-aircraft gunfire. On Friday, December 5th, the Raffles College Literary and Dramatic Society presented Oscar Wilde's 'The Importance of Being Ernest' to a distinguished gathering in the great hall, all profits going to swell the War Fund [11]; while for those with less cultured tastes there was Ginger Rogers on the screen at the Alhambra, with competing attractions offered elsewhere by Tyrone Power, Spencer Tracy and Ann Sothern.

On December 7th the Sunday newspapers reported that at about eleven-thirty the previous morning a Royal Air Force reconnaissance plane had sighted a Japanese convoy of troop-transports, escorted by warships, south of Indo-China and sailing westward. They went on to state that all Service formations in the Peninsula had been brought to a state of first degree readiness and that temporary restrictions on travel north of Kuala Lumpur had been imposed on the railway system of the Federated Malay States. The public was also urged not to travel unnecessarily elsewhere, as the trains were needed for the movement of troops and supplies; while those people who were already away from home were advised to return immediately.

Abdul Razak, like many other second and third year students, was a member of the Auxiliary Medical Service of the Passive Defence Organisation and was attached as a section leader to the first aid post and ambulance station that had been set up in the College grounds. By that time a fairly competent organisation for dealing with the casualties, structural damage and disruption of essential services to be expected during attacks from the air had been set up in Singapore under the name of the A.R.P., or Air Raid Precautions, Services. The majority of its members were Asian volunteers.

Despite the long experience of the British of aerial bombardment in Europe, no properly constructed air raid shelters had been built for public use; although some rather primitive refugee camps had been sited in open areas well ourside of the town in case mass evacuation should become necessary. There was also no general blackout in operation, for it had been decided long before that it was pointless to try to enforce one in advance of an attack; as in a tropical climate there was bound to be violent opposition to any attempt to block up windows and so stifle the inhabitants. Instead, a plan had been formulated whereby all electricity would automatically be cut off at the mains whenever a warning was received at night that enemy aircraft were approaching.[12]

Such a warning was received at about three-thirty in the morning of Monday December 8th, when a radar station on the east coast of Johore reported that a formation of unidentified aircraft was heading for Singapore. Immediately, all anti-aircraft batteries and fighter stations were prepared for action and the regular police and fire services alerted. It was then discovered that as the colonial government's campaign of self-deception had been 'business as usual', the civilian A.R.P. services had remained unmobilized. This meant that as they, not the military, were responsible for blacking out the town, the Japanese raiding force, later stated to have consisted of a mere seventeen naval bombers operating from an airfield in southern Indo-China,[13] found the street lighting still on and some of the government buildings illuminated as part of the Christmas celebrations. Not that this really mattered, for the raid took place in brilliant moonlight.

At first the students at the College ignored the air-raid sirens, for the many practice alerts in the past had made them blasé. They were soon brought from their beds, however, when the usual anti-aircraft gunfire was punctuated by the thud and shock of exploding bombs; and crowded out on to the roofs and balconies of the hostels where, oblivious to the danger in their excitement, they were thrilled by the spectacle of bombers circling overhead, occasionally caught in the converging beams of the searchlights. The gunfire was ineffective, for none of the raiders was destroyed, but fortunately the bombing was fairly light and soon over. Although night fighters were armed and ready to take off, they were not sent up, as it was feared that they would merely confuse the defence controllers who, for some reason not specified, had not been sufficiently trained in the coordination of fighters, searchlights and guns at night[14]. To most civilians this air-raid was the first terrifying intimation that the Pacific War had begun.

The 'all-clear' sounded at about 4.30 am and a few minutes later all the street lamps and municipal fairy-lights went out; for by then the passive defence workers had voluntarily mobilized themselves. They went into action with unexpected but welcome efficiency putting out fires and rescuing the injured from damaged buildings. Within a few hours public transport was working to schedule and shops and offices operating as though aerial bombardment was an everyday occurrence. The attack, which had been concentrated mainly against the airfields of Seletar and Tengah had done little damage to those military installations, but some bombs had fallen in residential areas where, in the absence of shelters, they had caused many casualties.

Abdul Razak and his friends, who had still not been officially called up, missed breakfast in order to go into the town and view the damage. They had, of course, seen newsreel films of air-raids in China and in Europe, but being actually involved in one was a frightening new experience. In Battery Road they saw the effect that a direct hit had had on a, fortunately unoccupied, office block; while in nearby Raffles Place, one of the island's most popular shopping centres, a whole row of shops and offices, including Robinson's new departmental store which had only recently been moved to that site, had been blasted and gutted. This damage, though slight by the standards of war-torn Europe, came as a shock to the Malayan students, for many of the fires were still smouldering and some charred and mutilated corpses were being removed from the shattered buildings.

From the newspapers [15] which they obtained on their way back to the College, Abdul Razak and his companions learned that,

> Japan declared war on Great Britain and the United States as from dawn today. Before the declaration Japanese air attacks were carried out on Singapore Island and Honolulu and elsewhere. Japanese troops attempted to land in North Malaya near Kota Bahru. They were repulsed with small arms fire and aircraft attacks. Some troops landed and were reported today infiltrating toward Kota Bahru.

Later in the day General Percival, Commander-in-Chief of the Imperial Land Forces in the Peninsula, issued the following optimistic statement: [16]

> .....We are ready. We have had plenty of warning and our preparations have been made and tested .... We are confident. Our defences are strong and our weapons efficient .... We see before us Japan drained for years by the exhausting claims of her wanton assault on China .... Confidence, resolution, enterprise and devotion to the cause will inspire every one of us in the fighting services, while from the civilian population, Malay, Chinese or Indian, we expect that patience, endourance and serenity which is the great virtue of the East and which will go far to assist the fighting men to gain a final and complete victory.

A further military communique was issued later that same day. This, while admitting that the airfields in Kelantan had been under aerial attack, ended with the cheerful, if misleading, news that all the Japanese warships and troop-transports were sailing away from the Malayan coast and that those troops who had landed from them were pinned down on the beaches under heavy fire. All therefore seemed to be going well; especially when, just after nightfall, the *Prince of Wales, Repulse* and an escort of destroyers left Singapore to give battle, for the prestige of the Royal Navy was still very high. That night Abdul Razak and his friends went to bed in a fever of speculative excitement; and were woken early the next morning by the sound of renewed anti-aircraft gunfire. The circling planes were merely on reconnaissance, however, and no bombs were dropped. The all-clear sounded some fifteen minutes later.

During the afternoon of Wednesday, December 10th, the students were informed by the Principal, Professor Dyer, that by order of the government their examinations had been cancelled and that the College was to be turned into an auxiliary military hospital. All the first and second year students were advised to return home as speedily as possible, while those in the third year were to be conscripted into the passive defence forces. Stunned by the sudden interruption of his academic career, although at the time he could not believe that it would be more than very temporary, Abdul Razak began to pack his belongings.

That evening he heard the radio broadcast by Mr Duff Cooper in which the Resident Cabinet Minister in Singapore and Chairman of the newly formed War Council announced the shattering news that both the *Prince of Wales* and the *Repulse* had been sunk by Japanese aircraft. The sheer unexpectedness and extent of this humiliating defeat, after all the bombast and fustian of official pronouncements over the past few weeks, had an even more serious effect on Asian morale than on Europeans, and marked the beginning of the end of British military prestige in the Far East.

Early the next morning Abdul Razak and the other first and second year students were sent away from the College and forced to seek accommodation wherever they could, for the buildings were needed without delay, they were told, to house the many hundreds of survivors from the sunken capital ships who had been brought to Singapore by the destroyers that had rescued them. The majority of those who came from the north of Malaya experienced some difficulty in returning home immediately, as many of the passenger trains were still being used to move troops and military equipment to the border with Siam, and so had to stay with friends in Singapore until they could organise some other form of transportation.

The war news fed to the people of Singapore was deliberately vague and misleadingly optimistic, but in spite of this it soon became obvious to everyone that things were going badly for General Percival's forces. On the evening of Saturday the 13th December, less than a week after the invasion had begun, Radio Malaya's Singapore station announced that the evacuation of European women and children from Penang would take place immediately and appealed to the people to take these refugees into their homes. The evacuees arrived in Singapore by train on the morning of December 15th and all the women with children were taken directly to the docks, where they boarded a ship bound for the Netherlands East Indies.[17] The following day the Governor said, in an address to the Legislative Council[18], that, '... in any withdrawal ... there will be no distinction of race. No European civilian male or female will be ordered by the civil government to withdraw. We stand by the people of this country, with whom we live and work, in this ordeal.'

When, however, it became generally known that all of the remaining European civilians and military forces had that day abandoned Penang; and that no arrangements whatsoever had been made to evacuate those among the Asian population who wished to leave, there was widespread anger and disgust. This was deliberately fanned by the already active fifth column, which made great play with this total lack of concern for the safety and well-being of the people whom the British were supposedly 'protecting'. Whether the British authorities did in fact callously abandon defenceless Asians to their fate is not now really of much consequence; but what is important is that a future Prime Minister of an independent Malaysia thought then, and continued to think, that they did so.

All of this made Abdul Razak extremely anxious to get home, for any Japanese force thrusting south through Kelantan must eventually reach his home state of Pahang. He managed to squeeze on to a slow, blacked-out train that took him to Kuala Lumpur and from there went on by road to Bentong, where his father was serving as the District Officer. By the time that he reached his father's house he was a very angry and disillusioned young man, for while in the capital of the Federated Malay States he had learned that two battalions of the 8th Brigade, the main British-Indian military force defending the East Coast, had already been evacuated from Kelantan and were preparing defensive positions in central Pahang. This meant that only a rearguard, composed partly of Malay troops, had remained behind to destroy the railway bridges and other installations before themselves retreating. It also meant that Pahang, his State, was next on the list to be fought over by two alien and imperialistic powers, with the likelihood that the predominantly Malay population, unarmed, helpless and with no real stake in the bloody squabble other than self-preservation, would have to bear the brunt of the material destruction and loss of life.

To make matters worse, on December 26th he heard of a Christmas broadcast that had been made the previous day by the Governor of the Straits Settlements, who was also High Commissioner for the Federated Malay States, in which, referring to the offer by a number of leading Chinese of their community's help in resisting the common enemy, he had said:[19]

> You can realise the immense contribution which the Chinese can, and will, render to the war effort by mobilizing themselves in this way, by helping to preserve the peace, by preventing panic, by assisting in the distribution of food, by producing labour, by joining the defence forces and in a multitude of other ways. I have had similar assurances of unstinted cooperation from leaders of the Indian community, and I have, of course, accepted them with equal gratitude.

'Although the Malays had two battalions of regular troops and a large number of volunteers actively serving with the British army, there was no mention of our community,' said Abdul Razak bitterly, speaking of this event thirty years later,' and we were convinced that just because a few members of the Union of Malay Youth were helping and supporting the Japanese, as were some Chinese and Indians, that the British had written us off completely. In Pahang we saw them getting ready to leave us as they had already deserted the people of Kedah, Kelantan, Perlis and Penang — and we didn't want them back.'

The Japanese force advancing along the coast of Pahang occupied the port of Kuantan on December 30th and after heavy fighting during the course of the following few days was able also to take over the royal capital, Pekan. On January 9th the main body of defending troops began to withdraw towards the south and the local Volunteers, who had been serving with them, were given the choice of going home or of retreating into Johore. Most of these Pahang Malays decided to make for their villages to defend their own families; and there await the British counter-attack which they were assured would take place as soon as reinforcements, which were already on the way, reached Singapore. The less trusting peasant population watched sullenly but impotently as the 'protectors' departed. They had been told by the propagandists of the colonial government how the Japanese treated their prisoners. Now they were to be given the chance to find out if it were true.

Chapter Four
Japanese Occupation

As soon as news that the Japanese had captured Kuantan was received in Pekan, the Sultan, his family and his entourage which included some members of the *Dato Shahbandar's* family, left by river to seek refuge farther inland at Temerloh. Sometime later, they were joined there by Abdul Razak and his father, so that Dato Hussein, in his capacity of *Orang Kaya Indera Shahbandar,* could act as adviser to the Sultan in his delicate negotiations with the Occupation Forces over the future administration of Pahang.

After a brief stay in this temporary capital, Abdul Razak travelled on a further ten miles to the district of Semantan, an area that many years later he was to contest in Malaya's first general election, to the village where the members of his family had taken over two large wooden houses and the land that went with them. In this rural retreat Abdul Razak laboured in the fields and also organised and led a squad of vigilantes, who took over the protective functions of the disbanded police force; for after the evacuation of Pahang by the British and the consequent retreat to Singapore of their European officers, many locally recruited policemen had prudently taken off their uniforms and returned home to wait out events. Law and order then broke down and a brief reign of terror ensued during which bands of armed thugs engaged in an orgy of robbery, rape and murder, that did not end until after the fall of Singapore, when the Japanese could spare sufficient troops and military police to bring their newly occupied territories under effective control.

The British army had retired into Singapore on January 31st and then blown up part of the Causeway that linked the island with the mainland. At that time many people in the Malay States still believed that the British would eventually launch their promised counter-attack, for Singapore was of course impregnable, and despite the humiliating retreats of the past two months, some little of the illusory charisma of British power still remained. It was not long, however, before this misconception of invincibility was shattered for ever; for on February the 8th and 9th, after only three days of preparatory bombardment with heavy artillery, Japanese troops successfully landed in strength on the northern and north-western coasts of the impregnable island and immediately started a major drive inland. As soon as they had secured and repaired the Causeway, reinforcements with tanks and artillery poured across it, with the result that the weary defenders were overwhelmed and, on February 15th, forced into unconditional surrender. It was, as the Japanese soon made the rest of the world aware, one of the most disastrous defeats in British military history.

Not long after this capitulation, Japanese military police arrived in force in the Temerloh area and quickly put down the worst of the lawlessness. Although the cessation of gang violence was a great relief, a new terror now hung over the people, the fear of arbitrary arrest and detention by the dreaded *kempeitai*. One of the first persons in Temerloh to be arrested was Abdul Razak's father, for the Japanese authorities thought that Dato Hussein, with his very fair skin and bulky physique, looked far more like a European or Eurasian than a Malay. Only the timely intervention of a Japanese lady who was married to a Temerloh Malay saved him from interrogation, and perhaps torture, by the military police.

About a month later the Japanese, despite their underlying distrust of him, appointed Dato Hussein to their administrative service and he returned to his pre-invasion position as District Officer of Bentong. Things having quietened down in the country generally, Abdul Razak and those members of his family who were at Semantan decided to return to their homes near Pekan. All forms of motor transportation were by then under the control of the military authorities, however, and so they had no alternative but to travel by water, as their ancestors had done for a dozen generations before them. They therefore loaded all of their belongings on to a large raft and then set out on a tedious ten day journey down the Pahang River, working the clumsy craft by day and sleeping on the river bank at night.

For most of the remainder of 1942 Abdul Razak stayed in Jambu Langgar, living the life of a villager and earning his keep by planting and cultivating rice and by fishing. This kind of life, though undoubtedly safe and healthy, was rather too humdrum for the young and ambitious Razak and so, towards the end of the year, he travelled to Bentong to ask his father to find him a job. This he was unable to do immediately, as his Japanese superiors controlled all employment in the administration, and so Abdul Razak borrowed several hundred dollars and with the collaboration of a few friends started a weekly newspaper called the *Geraran Masa*, which may be roughly translated as 'Alter the Present'. It lasted for only four editions, however, for news, except for official edicts and pronunciamentos, was heavily censored; and the Japanese overtly suspicious of the motives of a son of Dato Hussein in control of a medium, however insignificant, of potential sedition and propaganda. The young man therefore found himself not only unemployed once more, but also heavily in debt.

At the time that he had arrived back in Bentong, Abdul Razak had been shocked at the change he saw in his father who, having lived for the better part of a year under the daily threat of arrest and imprisonment, had become almost a nervous wreck. In order to take some of the pressure off of him by lessening Japanese distrust of the family, the son began a serious study of the Nippon language and culture; a subterfuge which soon brought him the bonus of a clerk's job in the Bentong District Office.

During the first few months of their military occupation, before sufficient numbers of their own civil administrators arrived to take over most of the executive positions, the Japanese were dependent upon those locally recruited Asian civil servants who had remained at their posts to keep the Peninsula states running. At first many of these men, who had formerly been junior to even the most inexperienced expatriate Europeans, were promoted beyong their wildest expectations and so, not surprisingly, became firm supporters of the new imperialism. This enthusiasm waned, however, when they were just as quickly demoted. Thereafter, the Japanese found it necessary to seek less disenchanted and more reliable subordinates among people young enough to be trained to appreciate Nippon aims and culture.

In the scramble for acceptance which followed, for a government post could mean welcome personal and economic security, the Malays and Indians enjoyed a distinct advantage over the bulk of the Chinese, who were suspected of being sympathetic toward those Communist-led resistance groups who periodically emerged from the jungle to assassinate Japanese collaborators and sabotage installations. The ultimate ambition of any young man willing to serve the occupation authorities then became admission into the new sub-elite which could be gained only by graduation from the *Koa Kunrensho,* or Government Officers' Training Establishment.

As a Malay of superior education, Abdul Razak was soon selected by the local administration for training as an interpreter; and in January 1943 was sent to Singapore to join the third *Koa Kunrensho* for a six-month indoctrination course in the Japanese language, Nippon culture and Bushido. The principal of this 'college' was an elderly retired colonel, a typical martinet, who believed in lots of physical exercise and military training; and to Abdul Razak's disgust part of the latter consisted of marching with the ceremonial Japanese 'goose-step' and all too frequent forced marches of up to twenty miles in the tropical heat. There were compensations, however, for the students were accommodated in comfortable hostels sited in the camp grounds and were greatly privileged in the matter of rations.

As soon as Abdul Razak had completed his course he was sent back to Pahang and posted to a position with the Japanese administrative office at Temerloh, where later in the year he again came into contact with his friend from Raffles College days, Ghazali Shafie. On his return to Pahang from Singapore in December 1942, the latter had served for a short while in the Volunteer Corps and fearing reprisals after the rapid retreat of the British army, had gone to ground. Soon after the fall of Singapore, however, the Japanese military government in Pahang had adopted such a paternal attitude toward the Malays in general, that he had emerged and gone about the business of adapting to the new conditions of life.

In mid-1943 he too was selected for the *Koa Kunrensho,* from which he graduated after four months of training. Due to his proficiency in the Japanese language, he was at first given employment in Pahang as a school teacher; but finding this static life far from exciting, he obtained a transfer to the State Propaganda Department at Kuala Lipis, where he eventually became its most senior non-Japanese official. In this capacity he was able to move freely about Pahang and make contact with, and materially assist, his many local friends.

From September 1st, 1943, the Japanese imposed a strict censorship on all British, American, Chinese and Indian films; and so Ghazali Shafie found himself in charge of a cinema van, with which he toured the State's main towns and villages to give on-the-spot commentaries in English and Malay for Japanese and Filipino films that were considered to have propaganda value. He was always accompanied on these trips by a small circus of singers, musicians and cultural entertainers, and became so well known to the Japanese officials and police that they ceased to check his schedules or the identities of his companions. Whenever he gave a performance in Temerloh he lodged with Abdul Razak; and when he was in Bentong visited Dato Hussein to keep him informed of his son's activities.

PARA-MILITARY FORCES

During the course of their occupation of the Peninsula the Japanese tried, as part of their plan for keeping the local population in subjection, to adopt the old precept of 'divide and rule'. They used former Indian Army troops to augment their own internal security forces; and when it suited them, encouraged the Malays to terrorise the Chinese and vice versa. They lacked the finesse and guile of the former colonialists, however, and eventually succeeded in alienating almost everyone except the Malayan Indians, who were kept happy by promises of independence for the Indian sub-continent.

Even before the invasion of Malaya began, the Japanese had assembled in Thailand a small fifth column of Indians commanded by Major Fujiwara, one of their own intelligence officers. These dissidents later followed closely behind the advancing Japanese forces, disseminating propaganda among captured soldiers of the British-Indian army and recruiting civilians from the occupied towns to form anti-British Independence Leagues. Within a few days of invading the Peninsula, the Japanese appointed an Indian Army officer, Captain Mohan Singh, to organise and command an Indian National Army of the strength of one combat division. He was promoted overnight to the rank of general.

After the Malayan campaign ended, General Mohan Singh's command was extended to include all those Indians who had been taken prisoner-of-war, whether they supported his National Army or not. The whole movement soon disintegrated, however, for there were squabbles over leadership within the civilian Leagues; while in the army the recently promoted general paid the penalty of disagreeing on policy matter with his Japanese superiors and was arrested and imprisoned. His troops were then temporarily disbanded.

The arrival in Malaya of Subhas Chandra Bose, a highly respected nationalist who had escaped from India despite British attempts to imprison him, and who, upon reaching Europe had recruited Indian prisoners-of-war into the German army, brought the movement back to life. A provisional Liberation Government was set up and the National Army, with a new potential of three combat divisions, revived. It is doubtful, however, if many people in Malaya apart from the participating Indians ever took this poorly-equipped and ill-trained force very seriously; certainly Field Marshal Count Terauchi, supreme commander of the Japanese land forces in East Asia was not impressed with it as a field force, although it did serve a purpose both as an instrument of propaganda, and as a type of gendarmerie which could be entrusted with some garrison duties.

Towards the end of 1943, the Japanese authorities began the compulsory mobilization of local manpower to assist their own war effort and in December of that year announced the formation of a Labour Corps to be recruited throughout Malaya. In Pahang, for example, every group of about 250 people was required to provide 20 persons between the ages of fifteen and forty-five to serve in this Corps, which was placed under the control of the auxiliary police of each District [1]. It could be called upon to work for either the civil government or the local military command at any time. Only people like Abdul Razak and Ghazali Shafie, who were classified as being in essential work, were exempted.

Malayans, and especially Malays, had been recruited by the Japanese for service in auxiliary units, raised to assist their own forces with internal security and guard duties, from as early as 1942. On December 9th, 1943, however, the newspapers [2] announced that volunteers would also be accepted for two new organisations, the

Giyu-tai, consisting of local defence units who, on a part-time basis, would be responsible for maintaining order in their own districts; and the *Giyu-gun,* regular soldiers who were liable to have to serve anywhere within the Malay Peninsula. So popular was the latter force among the Malays, the newspapers claimed, that it caused a shortage of agricultural labour that was only corrected by bringing replacements from as far away as Java. These auxiliary forces, together with Indian National Army units, were kept fairly widely dispersed, however, while the Japanese prudently kept their own military formations concentrated in strategic areas from which they could easily crush any attempted revolt.

By the end of 1943 most of the Japanese leaders, civil as well as military, knew that they had lost the war and would not for much longer be able to hold on to their great conquests. They decided, therefore, to cause as much trouble in the occupied territories for the returning colonial powers as they could. To this end they began to encourage national independence movements and, as a preliminary step, Premier Tojo, in a speech to the Japanese Diet [3] that was widely disseminated by the occupation authorities, promised Malaya, Indonesia and Borneo participation in local politics. Accordingly, on October 3rd, 1943, the military administration in Malaya announced the formation of consultative councils at state and city levels [4], and that in future locally recruited personnel would play a more important part in the running of the country.

By this time, however, the great majority of the people in the country, including the Malays, had become disenchanted with the Japanese regime, the latter largely as a result of the enforced return to Siam of the four northern states of Kedah, Perlis, Trengganu and Kelantan; a bargain that had been made by the invaders in December 1941 to secure Siamese cooperation in the movement of troops towards the Malayan border. The transfer had, after much procrastination, taken place in August 1943. This betrayal of his race, together with the oppression and often senseless brutality that Abdul Razak had seen used against Malayans of all communities had completely disillusioned him; so that when early in 1945, he was approached by the representative of an underground anti-Japanese Malay Resistance Movement, he quickly indicated his willingness to join.

WATANIAH

This movement, which had the secret support of His Highness the Sultan of Pahang who eventually became its titular Colonel-in-Chief, was called *Wataniah,* from an Arabic word meaning 'Native Land'. It had been formed on a very small scale towards the end of 1942 by Yeop

Mahidin[5], one of Dato Hussein's assistants in the District Office at Bentong. At the time of the Japanese invasion, Yeop Mahidin had been the adjutant of the volunteer unit stationed at Raub; and he and his men, when disbanded by the retreating British, had buried their arms and uniforms and returned home to await the promised counter-attack, which of course never materialised. These buried weapons formed the basis of Wataniah's armament, which was later added to by salvaging guns and grenades that had been abandoned during the 1941 battles and by making lightning raids upon isolated Japanese and Indian National Army units.

In 1943 Yeop Mahidin was transferred from Bentong to Raub, where he was presented with greater opportunities to increase the scale and effectiveness of Wataniah's operations. He made his secret headquarters in the hills some twelve miles to the north of the town, at a place called Batu Malim. During the course of his employment, especially when making collections of rice from the outlying villages on behalf of the Japanese Administration, he was able to enter the jungle and make contact with, and also himself infiltrate, the Communist dominated Malayan Peoples' Anti-Japanese Army, the 6th regiment of which operated in the Raub area.

When the Japanese attacked the Peninsula the Malayan Communist Party, which was predominantly Chinese in membership, offered the colonial administration its total cooperation in fighting the common enemy. Somewhat reluctantly the British accepted this offer and more than a hundred guerillas, all specially selected by the Party from its own cadres, were trained in Singapore by army experts to organise and lead jungle warfare and sabotage squads capable of operating on the mainland behind the Japanese lines. Four squads of these trainees were already hidden in the jungle in different Malay States when Singapore capitulated; these, once they had been reinforced by volunteers supplied by the regional Communist organisations, became independent 'regiments' of the Malayan Peoples' Anti-Japanese Army, or MPAJA as it was more usually called. From time to time additional formations were recruited to serve in other states of the Peninsula; the 6th, or Pahang, regiment coming into being sometime in mid-1942. Each of these fighting units was backed by a number of clandestine civilian organisations that supplied money, recruits, weapons and food to their frontline comrades; and also, working through a network of spies who infiltrated every sector of the Japanese administration, acted as their eyes and ears.

The existence of Yeop Mahidin's undercover Malay force was never suspected by the Japanese, who right until the end of their occupation blamed the Chinese guerillas for its occasional raids and ambushes. Furthermore the Malay commander, who had good reason to be suspicious of the MPAJA's intentions toward his countrymen —

for the Communist Party that dominated it had let it be known that when the Japanese were defeated they intended to establish a Soviet-type Malayan Republic in which every person living in the Peninsula, regardless of racial origin, would automatically be entitled to citizenship — kept his own organisation and operations secret from the guerilla forces also.

Because of his position as a Japanese government official, it was not possible for Abdul Razak to do much active work for the movement, or to undertake training in the jungle, as his absence from his office would have led to investigation and discovery. He therefore contented himself with ferreting out information about enemy dispositions and police activities and passing it on to Wataniah, either through the agency of the peripatetic Ghazali Shafie, or some other Malay who could move freely about the state without arousing suspicion.

The distance between Malaya and the nearest Allied military formation equipped with radio being too great for the MPAJA's transmitters to carry, the British intelligence services, even though they had some European agents still active in the jungle, learned little about guerilla activities in the Peninsula until after the middle of 1943. From that time, however, a number of agents, both European and Chinese, were on various occasions landed from, and later taken off by, submarines operating from bases in Ceylon. Later still, several Britons with pre-war experience of Malayan conditions were sent to live in the jungle as liason officers with the established guerilla regiments; and these eventually negotiated an agreement with the overall leaders of the MPAJA whereby, in exchange for air-drops of arms and supplies, the Communist-led para-military forces would accept instructions from British Headquarters in Ceylon, so that the final effort to oust the Japanese should be coordinated. Being dependent upon such scanty information as these agents were able to supply, it seemed to those assessing the situation in London and invasion-army headquarters that only the Chinese were really resisting the enemy; for Indian activities in their National Army and Independence Leagues were known from monitored radio broadcasts, while the Malays were generally equated with the numerically unimportant fifth columnist Union of Malay Youth and the young men who, earning their living as others before them had done under the British, joined the foreign controlled defence forces. This misconception about the Malays was not corrected until the beginning of 1945, when the first officers from Force 136, the military contingent specifically charged with coordinating guerilla activities in Malaya, joined Wataniah in Pahang.[6]

When, in Malay villages, these officers first heard vague rumours of Wataniah, they at first doubted that it actually existed. Upon reporting what they had heard back to their headquarters in Ceylon, they were advised by Major D.J. Ambler, a pre-invasion headmaster of the Clifford School, Kuala Lipis, who was at that time attached to Force 136 as an adviser on Pahang affairs, to check the truth of this story with Ghazali Shafie, one of his former pupils. When, however, they found that their contact was working for the Japanese as Head of Propaganda for the whole State of Pahang, they immediately classified him as a traitor and decided to have him assassinated by the killer-squad attached to the guerillas' 6th regiment. Until matters were sorted out satisfactorily, this placed an added burden on the commander of Wataniah, the protection of his undercover men whose names he did not care to reveal to the Communists; for he soon discovered from his contacts in the MPAJA that the guerillas had a long death list, on which, incidentally, the name Abdul Razak appeared close to the top.

From the end of 1944 Allied aircraft began to make frequent bombing raids on strategic targets within the Peninsula and it became obvious, even in remote Pahang, that a counter-invasion was soon to be launched. Wataniah stepped up its preparations. By mid-1945 all of the members who could do so without arousing suspicion among the Japanese and their informers or the Communists had, on some pretext or other, entered the jungle to undergo group training in tactics and the use of weapons. By that time aircraft based in Ceylon could fly the round trip to Pahang and back, permitting air drops of arms and military supplies to the Force 136 men now stationed at the Wataniah headquarters at Batu Malim.

The Malay guerilla units still remained under cover and took little part in harassing the Japanese, for they had one paramount task that had been allotted to them by Force 136, preventing the Japanese from moving reinforcements across to the west from their east coast garrisons. At the appropriate time, it had been planned, they would assemble in the jungle and, as soon as the British seaborne assault began on the west coast of the Peninsula, cut and hold for as long as possible the Gap and Bentong roads along which the enemy would have to travel.

Excitement mounted among Wataniah members when, on May 11th, local newspapers informed them that three days earlier the Germans had surrendered unconditionally to the Allies; for now the whole weight of Anglo-American military power could be concentrated against the enemy in the Far East. By July 3rd, the same newspapers were giving prominence to a plan by the occupation authorities to evacuate from Singapore and South Johore all civilians not engaged in essential work; and on the 9th published details of a statement by a Japanese army spokesman in which he talked of defending Singapore to the last ditch. Thus the new battle for Malaya could start at any time, and so the undercover men of Wataniah were formally enrolled into the organisation and posted to their various units; Abdul Razak being given the rank of captain and command of the company at Bentong, to which town he had recently been posted.

The first news of the August 9th atomic bomb attack on Nagasaki appeared in Malayan newspapers two days later, when it was stated only that the Americans had dropped a bomb of extraordinary power on the city, causing immense destruction and many thousands of civilian casualties. An admission that the Soviet Union had entered the war against Japan was also included. The next day, General Itagaki, commander-in-chief of the armed forces in Malaya, publicly announced that the East Indies, which many people in the Peninsula took also to include Malaya, was shortly to be granted independence. On the 13th the expression 'atomic bomb' was used for the first time, when the newspapers somewhat belatedly published Japanese protests against its use on Hiroshima seven days before. The members of Wataniah knew then that the end could not be far off; although as an undefeated Japanese army still stood guard in Malaya, the country might yet have to face a terrible ordeal.

In mid-August the Sultan of Pahang was summoned by the Japanese to the State's administrative capital of Kuala Lipis, there to attend a conference which was to discuss some form of independence for Malaya, possibly as part of an Indonesian federation. He set out by car from Pekan on the 15th and on the way stopped, as was his habit, at the Ng Tiong Keat Tapioca Plantation to seek the latest war news, for there had been persistent rumours that the Japanese were negotiating a surrender with the Allies. At the plantation he was unable to get the confirmation he sought; but he was promised some fresh mutton if he would stop to pick it up on the way back — an offer that even royalty did not reject in those days of extreme shortages.

Meanwhile, radio messages had been received at Wataniah headquarters from the British in Ceylon indicating that a Japanese surrender was imminent. This information was supplemented by Abdul Razak and other undercover agents in the Japanese administration with doubly disturbing news: first, that the Japanese Malaya Command feared that their undefeated troops might run wild when ordered to surrender; and second, that the Communist dominated MPAJA, which was also aware of the impending surrender, was massing in strategic areas of the State ready to take advantage of the power vacuum to set up a Soviet-type Republic.

Following the atomic bomb attacks on Hiroshima and Nagasaki and the invasion of Manchuria by the Soviet Union, Japan had, on August 10th, though this was unknown at the time to the people of Malaya, offered to surrender if the Emperor were permitted to retain his throne. Their efforts at negotiation having been refused, the Japanese surrendered unconditionally on August 14th. Although this capitulation was proclaimed by the Emperor himself on the 15th, General Itagaki did not permit the news to be made public in Malaya until August 20th, when the Imperial Proclamation was printed in local newspapers.

A member of Wataniah, who was in Kuala Lipis at the time of the Sultan's arrival, was instructed by his headquarters to warn the Ruler that he might be in danger and to urge him to go into hiding in the jungle until after the Allied forces had landed and secured the country. He went to the house of the District Officer, where His Highness was staying, but was not permitted to see him, as the royal party suspected his claims to represent Wataniah as a trap set by the *Kempeitai*. He had therefore to be content with passing through Ungku Mahomed, the Sultan's A.D.C., a warning that should His Highness fall into Communist hands he might either be killed, or forced to aid their plans for a take-over of the State.

His warning was ignored, however, and the conference being over, the royal party, which consisted of Ungku Mahomed, his son Ungku Nazaruddin* who was His Highness's private secretary, the District Officer of Pekan and the Ruler's Chamberlain, set out for Pekan with the Sultan himself driving. As soon as Wataniah headquarters was informed, a radio message was sent to Ceylon advising them of the situation.

When the Sultan reached the Ng Tiong Keat plantation once again, he stopped to pick up the fresh meat and to allow his companions to take some refreshment in one of the shophouses close to the estate entrance. Before they had finished their business, however, they were approached by six armed members of Force 136, three Americans and three Nationalist Chinese under the command of Lieutenant Betoise who, after explaining the situation to His Highness, revealed that his orders, which had been radioed from Ceylon, were to take the whole party into the jungle and keep them there in a place of safety.

While they were inside the shophouse discussing the matter, a lorry-load of locally recruited Malay militiamen stopped to buy cigarettes. A confrontation between one of the non-Malay speaking Force 136 Nationalist Chinese and a militiaman, both seeking to use the same lavatory, led to an exchange of small arms fire and grenade throwing in which the royal party were unwilling participants.

When the militia finally broke off this contest and retreated, there was no further argument about the necessity of taking to the jungle and the whole party proceeded on foot to a camp that had been previously prepared. The next day the Japanese, who thought that His

---

* now Lt. General Tan Sri Ungku Nazaruddin DIMP, JMN, PJK, Malaysian Ambassador to the Netherlands.

Highness had been kidnapped by the Communists, sent out regular troops to investigate. These killed a number of innocent Chinese and caused the remainder of the estate workers in that area to flee into the jungle. The troops, unable to track down the hideout, mortared the area indiscriminately until nightfall, fortunately without exploding their bombs anywhere near the camp. Nevertheless, it was considered prudent to withdraw still deeper into the jungle. This added further to the discomfort of the ill-equipped royal party, who lost all contact with the outside world until early in September, when a messenger arrived with a letter from Colonel Headley of Force 136, that promised to have them moved to more comfortable quarters within the next few days. The messenger also brought for the Sultan a Wataniah uniform bearing the rank insignia of a colonel. His Highness was extremely moved by this gesture, but little realised the difficulty that the guerillas had had in getting at short notice one large enough for his considerable bulk.

In the meantime the Japanese, apparently in an attempt to ferment racial clashes, had posted notices in Malay claiming that the Sultan had been abducted and murdered by Chinese Communists. This effort was frustrated by the members of Wataniah, who under instruction from their headquarters followed the bill-posters around and tore down the inflammatory notices as soon as there were no Japanese in sight.

On September 8th, Captain Dorrity of Force 136 arrived at the camp and conducted the whole party to the main road to where Colonel Headley and a detachment of Wataniah in full uniform were waiting to escort the Sultan back to his capital. The Ruler, wearing his colonel's uniform, received a tumultuous welcome in every town and village through which he passed. The next day Colonel Spencer Chapman, of guerilla fame, travelled to Pekan from Kuantan to pay his respects to the Sultan on behalf of the Supreme Allied Commander for Southeast Asia, Admiral Lord Louis Mountbatten.

The Wataniah, backed by Gurkha paratroops of Force 136, took over the protection of the civil population of large areas of Pahang from the Japanese; and remained on the alert to frustrate any attempt by the MPAJA to seize control, until a detachment of regular troops was landed from destroyers at Kuantan. In November, 1945, the Wataniah paraded at the *Sa'adah* palace in Pekan where, following an inspection by the Sultan, they were entertained to a buffet dinner followed by dancing. They were finally disbanded on December 1st, 1945, at a parade in Kuala Lipis at which His Highness took the salute. Captain Abdul Razak was on parade and like every other member of the force, regardless of rank, received a gratuity of 350 Malayan dollars and a campaign ribbon.

Chapter Five
Post-War Problems

At the time that the war ended the Allied forces in India, Ceylon and Burma, under the overall command of Admiral Lord Louis Mountbatten, were preparing to launch a seaborne invasion of the Malay Peninsula. The plan, codenamed 'Zipper', called for the landing of a powerful force of infantry and armour on the beaches at Morib, roughly mid-way between Penang and Singapore and not far from Kuala Lumpur, under cover of carrier-borne aircraft of the British East Indies Fleet. This force, aided by Malayan guerilla units and parachute troops of Force 136, would first re-occupy the west-central and southern Malay States and then assault Singapore from the mainland as the Japanese had done in 1942.

Before this scheme could be put into operation, however, atomic bombs were dropped at Hiroshima and Nagasaki and these, together with Russia's entry into the war, caused the Japanese government first to seek peace terms and then to surrender unconditionally after these terms had been refused. At that time, however, the Allied Command felt that the Japanese army in Southeast Asia might well disobey its government's order to lay down its arms; and so the invasion was postponed while attempts were made to clarify the situation with the ailing Field Marshal Count Terauchi, Supreme Commander for the Southern Region, whose headquarters was then in Saigon. Contact was finally made on August 20th, six days after the official capitulation, and the surrender of his forces agreed upon.

Meanwhile, on August 19th General Douglas MacArthur, whom the Combined Chiefs of Staff had appointed to be Supreme Allied Commander for the whole Pacific Area had decreed that none of his junior commanders should accept the surrender of any enemy-held territory, invade it or attempt to re-occupy any part of it until after the formal articles of capitulation had been signed by the Emperor's representatives [1]. This order arrived too late to stop the British invasion fleet from sailing from its bases in Ceylon; and so this considerable force had to be maintained at sea until September 2nd, when the actual ceremony of surrender took place in Tokyo Bay on board the United States battleship *Missouri*.

With this formality out of the way, the re-occupation of the Malay Peninsula was at last begun. On September 2nd the capitulation of the local Japanese commanders at Penang was accepted aboard the British battleship *Nelson;* and the next day marines landed unopposed and took over the island. Then, preceded by Japanese minesweepers, part of the invasion fleet sailed down the Straits of Malacca and, on the morning of September 5th, army units began the re-occupation of Singapore. Three days later the main force landed at Morib and began to spread out through the Malay States.

Although the main towns were rapidly taken over, in many of the more remote parts of the Peninsula, especially in the east-coast states, anything from three to five weeks elapsed before British troops and officials arrived to enforce the directions of the Military Administration. During that perilous and violent interim period law and order quite often broke down completely, for the police had, in many places, disbanded themselves and gone into hiding, so that the only check to wholesale banditry, looting and murder was provided by a few Gurkha paratroops of Force 136 and the various guerilla units.

INTER-RACIAL CLASHES

As soon as the Emperor announced that the war had ended, Malaya Command withdrew all its scattered military, naval and police personnel who were Japanese subjects into a few garrison towns so that they would not be wiped out piecemeal by the Communists and other resistance fighters[2]. Lord Mountbatten then ordered the guerilla forces under his command to move into those areas vacated by the Japanese to guard installations, food depots and other state property liable to destruction or looting, until British forces arrived to relieve them. By the end of September almost all of the Peninsula had been taken over by the military; and the various guerilla formations, including Wataniah, incorporated temporarily as auxiliary units into the British army of liberation.

It did not at that time escape the notice of the military authorities, however, that although their troops received an enthusiastic welcome wherever they went, for not even the most fervent nationalist would have denied that a British regime was less oppressive than a Japanese one, in areas in which the population was predominantly Chinese the flags most commonly displayed were those of Russia or Nationalist China rather than the Union Jack. A little probing of the attitude of people in such places showed that during the long years of the Japanese Occupation they had been conditioned to expect that Chinese rather than British troops would, in the post-war period, take over the Malay States, Singapore and Penang; and to believe that the enemy forces there had been defeated by Communist-led Chinese guerillas and not by the Allies in the field[3].

Fortunately, from the point of view of those people in Malaya who were opposed to them politically, the MPAJA had been taken by surprise by the speed of the Japanese collapse; so that, although they were well disciplined and better armed than their enemies, when they tried to seize control of large areas of the Peninsula, their efforts were so poorly coordinated that they met with little success. Prudently they avoided any but minor confrontations with the defeated, but militarily still formidable, Japanese and instead turned their arms against the Malays, Indians and Nationalist Chinese. Using as their excuse accusations of collaboration with the Japanese or of assisting them as informers and mercenaries, they began hunting down and slaughtering former members of the locally recruited police and internal security services, most of whom were Malays or Indians; and in some areas, notably on Singapore Island, fought pitched battles with armed supporters of the *Kuomintang*.

In pursuit of their enemies, the Communists set up road blocks, stopped and searched trains and buses, and looted and burned whole villages. They did not hesitate also to use any degree of personal violence necessary to find out where those they sought were hiding, or to extort money for the upkeep of their forces. This ruthless and arrogant behaviour quickly brought retaliation; for although the Indians, except for the remnants of the 'National Army', were usually too weak effectively to resist, the Malays armed themselves and counter-attacked vigorously.

The most spectacular and also the most bloody of these inter-communal clashes began on August 21st, 1945, just after the Japanese had retired into their barracks inside the garrison towns and before British troops had landed to replace them. It started when Chinese Communists, spearheaded by units of the MPAJA tried to seize the Muar and Batu Pahat areas of Johore. Resistance to this aggression was led by a Malay District Officer named Onn bin Jaafar — a man destined later to wield great influence in Malayan politics — who mobilized thousands of his compatriots to fight back. The battle that ensued was bitter and conducted without mercy for women, children or the old and defenceless; and by the time it ended more than four hundred people had been killed and thousands more wounded or turned into homeless and penniless refugees.[4] This fighting spread into other states, especially in areas where many Chinese were concentrated, but Pahang, having a predominantly Malay population, was on this occasion spared; although inter-communal antipathy, as events were soon to show, was not absent but merely concealed beneath the surface calm.

Although Abdul Razak remained on the strength of Wataniah until it was disbanded on December 1st, 1945, the British Military Government considered that he would be more useful in an administrative position than as a soldier. He was therefore transferred into the civil service with the rank of Malay Officer on Probation, for despite the Japanese Occupation he had, on April 1st, 1943, the date on which he would have graduated from Raffles College had his three-year course not been interrupted by the invasion, automatically been promoted from Student-Probationer. There was an urgent need for junior civilian administrators and so he, and many other Malays whose formal education had been similarly curtailed, were allowed to sit the entrance examination to the Malay Administrative Service and, where successful, were given immediate postings. On September 8th, 1945, Abdul Razak became Acting Assistant District Officer, Raub, at a starting salary of 150 Malayan dollars a month. Five months later a tragedy occurred that he was never able to forget, for on one fateful day many of his old comrades from Wataniah were involved in a bloody race riot that brought them to the British Military Administration's Superior Court at Raub on charges that put them in danger of execution.

At that time Abdul Razak was due to undertake a tour of the Raub District for the purpose of collecting rent due on state lands, but was relieved of that task by his immediate superior, the Acting District Officer, one Encik Annuar. On February 11th, 1946, when he arrived at the village of Batu Malim, the wartime headquarters of Wataniah, Annuar found racial trouble brewing and religious fanatics inciting a mob to violence. The Acting District Officer tried repeatedly to persuade the hostile gathering to disperse, but the mob, many members of which were in various stages of religious ecstacy which induced them to believe that they were invulnerable, refused to be calmed. A few minutes after he had returned to the area headman's house to send off a messenger to collect reinforcements of police, Annuar heard the frenzied beating of the mosque drum, followed almost immediately by terrified shouts and screams.[5] When he tried to break up the riot that was then raging he was resisted, and as he had too few police available to help him, drove off to collect a more effective force. By the time that he returned with an adequate party of armed policemen, however, the fighting had ended and thirty Chinese and two Malays lay dead, while sixteen Chinese and ten Malays had been wounded.[6] His own career was an extra casualty. It might well have been Abdul Razak's.

On that ill-omened day there had been an open-air market in Batu Malim so that many of the people caught up in the bloody and senseless affray were from outside the area. One of the first officials to reach the scene of this riot was Ghazali Shafie, who was at that time seconded to the Indian Army in Malaya, for he happened to be passing through the village on official business. It was one of his unpleasant tasks to pull out of the river the dead body of one of his former school friends from Kuala Lipis, a Chinese who had been earning a precarious living as an itinerant hawker. Trouble between the local unit of the Communist dominated Malayan Peoples' Anti-Japanese Army and the Malay villagers, especially those who had served in Wataniah, was of long standing; and as usual innocent people were the chief sufferers in the clash.

For nearly two weeks the whole of the Raub area was in an uproar, with the bulk of the rural people, whether Malays or Chinese, going about armed. The police, who were badly demoralised because of the stigma they bore of having served the Japanese and who were less than impartial because of the hatred and fear they felt for those Chinese who had supported the MPAJA, were of little use in easing tension. It therefore fell mainly upon Abdul Razak, temporarily promoted to Acting District Officer, to prevent further bloodshed. This he did by touring every village and hamlet, accompanied by local community leaders of all races, reasoning and commiserating with the people and getting them to air their fears and frustrations. He was on the go each day until around midnight, slept in whatever accommodation the villagers chose to offer him, and was off again on tour the next morning soon after dawn.

Gradually the people calmed down and became less aggressive, although the root cause of their antipathy had not been eliminated. The immediate trouble, as Abdul Razak saw it, centred mainly around the Communist threat; but underlying this was a more fundamental problem that would surely lead to further intercommunal strife in the future: the problem of an economic imbalance among the various races; a pyramidal structure with the Europeans and Chinese at the top and the Malays buried firmly at the bottom of the pile.'Whenever our village people went into a town,' Abdul Razak was fond of saying when he discussed the problem in later years, 'they could not help noticing that everything seemed to be owned by the people whom they considered to be foreigners.'

On May 20th thirty-two persons, many of them mere youths, were arraigned before a military court and charged with being members of an unlawful assembly with intent to commit murder. The trial, which was presided over by a legally qualified army officer supported by two civilian assessors, lasted twenty-eight days and Abdul Razak, who was in court as often as his duties would permit, was fortunate to have been spared the harrowing experience of giving evidence against his former comrades-in-arms. The accused were defended by the distinguished lawyers Mr (later Dato) Rajasooria leading Encik (now T.Y.T. Tan Sri) Sardon bin Haji Jubir*. Throughout the period of the trial Sardon lodged with Abdul Razak and each evening the younger man, who had already made up his mind to qualify in law, acted the part of Devil's Advocate to help Sardon in

---

*now Governor of the State of Penang.

preparing his defence. Eventually, seven of the accused were acquitted and the remaining twenty-five sentenced to death. Upon appeal, a further two were acquitted and the sentences of the remainder commuted to terms in prison ranging from three to fifteen years.[7]

THE MALAYAN UNION

From the Malay point of view, however, the most significant and alarming event of the early post-war period was the announcement made by the British government in October 1945 of its intention to form a Malayan Union upon conditions which the indigenous people saw as an attempt to seize their country and hand it, and them, over to the more sophisticated and economically stronger Chinese and Indians. This plan had been worked out long before the Japanese were defeated, although its content were unknown to the people most directly concerned who, because their country was occupied by the enemy, could not in any case be consulted.

During the course of the war, and especially in the aftermath of humiliating defeats in the Far East, the home government had had to face up to the reality that, even should Britain eventually emerge victorious in war, the old-style Empire 'on which the sun never set' was a thing of the past. Having accepted this unpalatable fact, it had set out to formulate a series of schemes by means of which as much as possible might be salvaged from the debacle. One of these was concerned with the future of the economically important Malay Peninsula.

In April 1944 a basic plan, which had been drawn up by a special political committee of the British House of Commons, was endorsed by the War Cabinet[8]. Three months later the Colonial Office issued directions to those officers planning the military government which it was proposed to set up immediately after a successful counter-invasion had been launched in the Peninsula. In these it indicated that they should, as soon as practicable after the war had ended, form a Malayan Union which would consist of all nine Malay States, the island of Penang and the territory of Malacca, federated into a single administrative unit controlled by a central government nominated by the British Governor, or High Commissioner, who would actually wield the executive power. There was a further particularly important innovation mentioned, a new Malayan Union citizenship. This, it was made clear, was intended to ensure that every person, regardless of racial origin and creed, who could substantiate a claim 'by reason of birth or a suitable period of residence to belong to the country'[9], should have an equal right with all others to a share in the social and economic benefits and opportunities of the proposed Union and, eventually, in the election of its govern-

Post-War Problems 61

ment. Specifically excluded from the Union, however, was the island of Singapore, which the British hoped to retain as their premier military and naval base in the Far East. This was to become a separately administered Crown Colony.

In May 1945, as preparations for the invasion were nearing completion, Admiral Mountbatten had to decide the policy he should adopt in dealing with the various guerilla groups [10] who had by then agreed to accept his instructions in matters affecting the coordination of overall strategy, in return for arms and supplies. The chief difficulty lay in the assessment made by his intelligence advisers that if military plans became too dependent upon the cooperation of the MPAJA, it would be next to impossible for the British government to resist Chinese demands for equal rights in practically everything with the Malays; and that acceptance of this, if made public, could have the effect of driving the indigenous people actively to assist the Japanese in defending the Peninsula. The dilemma was whether to announce the terms of citizenship in the Malayan Union prematurely and so deny the Communists the chance to claim the prestige of having forced the colonial power to grant outstanding benefits to the Chinese and Indian communities; or suppress them, keep the support of the Malays until the reoccupation of the Peninsula was complete, and worry about Communist demands when, or if, they were presented. Early in June the British Chiefs of Staff, backed by the politicians at Westminster, reluctantly decided to pursue the latter course.

It was therefore not until the Secretary of State for the Colonies formally announced his government's intentions in the House of Commons on October 10th, 1945, that the Malays learned how they had been betrayed. The very next day Sir Harold MacMichael landed at Port Swettenham* from a British warship and established himself in Kuala Lumpur as the British government's Special Representative. He was there because although the Minister had said what his government intended to do, the action was in fact unconstitutional; under the Treaties existing between the individual Malay States and the British Crown, each Principality was a 'protectorate' and not a colony. Therefore, unless the change in the *status quo* was to be achieved by *force majeure,* a method already in bad odour in the post-war world, it was necessary to persuade each individual Ruler of a Malay State voluntarily to cede jurisdiction over his realm to the King of England.[11]

The Sultans, who had grown accustomed to accepting the advice of their British civil servants in all political matters, raised only tentative objections; and their subjects were, of course, not even invited to comment as their birth-right was put up for auction. As Captain

*now Port Klang.

Gammons put it some seven months later during a debate in the British House of Commons: [12]

> There was no consultation; there was no investigation; there was no Royal Commission; there was no Parliamentary mission. For some reason that I have never been able to understand, His Majesty's government decided to send out Sir Harold MacMichael to invite — and the word 'invite' in this connection means something quite different to what it means to most of us — to invite the nine Sultans to surrender all their powers to the King ...

By New Year's Day 1946 Sir Harold had successfully accomplished all that he had set out to achieve; and at the same time, although this was not necessarily part of his plan, he had also provided the catalyst needed to unify the Malays politically. Three months earlier when he had landed at Port Swettenham, the only Malay political organisations functioning, apart from the Malay Union of Singapore, were a few numerically insignificant left-wing extremist groups dedicated to the inclusion of Malaya within a Republic of Indonesia; but before he was half-way through his visit, militant editorials in vernacular newspapers such as *Utusan Melayu* and *Warta Negara* [13] had galvanised the Malays into action and led to the revival of those State Associations which had been banned by the Japanese occupation authorities. By the time that Sir Harold reached Pahang, that is at the beginning of November 1945, the State Association, once again with Dato Hussein as Vice-President and this time with his son Abdul Razak heading the Raub division, was cautioning the Sultan not to allow himself to be coerced into selling out his people. Despite this pressure a new Agreement, openly denounced by these advisers as detrimental to the interests of the Pahang Malays, was signed on November 2nd.

In Kelantan, where the Malays tended to respond more readily to the exhortations of their traditional leaders, especially those connected with the Islamic religion, opposition was strongest; and when the Special Representative reached the royal palace at Kota Bahru on December 15th, an estimated 10,000 belligerent citizens bearing pro-Malay and anti-Malayan Union placards, shouting slogans and beating gongs, marched in procession to the palace, there to make known their displeasure [14]. Emboldened by this display, the Sultan of Kelantan suggested that citizenship of the new Federation should be restricted to those residents able and willing to make use of the Malay language who were also prepared unconditionally to renounced all allegiance to their countries of origin. He also proposed an immediate end to all further immigration into any part of the Peninsula [15]. His suggestions were ignored.

These were mere skirmishes, however, compared to the storm of protest, both from the Rulers and their subjects, that followed the publication in London on January 22nd, 1946, of a White Paper which, for the first time, provided full details of the proposed future Constitution of the Malayan Union. The Sultan of Perak, for example, telegraphed the Secretary of State for the Colonies in London complaining that the White Paper 'instead of safeguarding the status and dignity of the Rulers completely deprives them of their sovereignty'.[16]; while the various State Associations let it be known that they intended forthwith to eschew parochial loyalties and interests and combine together to form a truly national organisation capable of defending the birthright of all Malays. This latter took some little time to accomplish, but at the beginning of March a Pan-Malayan Congress, attended by forty-one Malay Associations including Wataniah, met in Kuala Lumpur under the Chairmanship of that Onn bin Jaafar who had led the defence of Muar and Batu Pahat in the inter-communal fighting that followed the Japanese surrender, and passed a resolution that led to the birth of the United Malays National Organisation, or UMNO. It was to be through the future leadership of this party that Abdul Razak, who was present at the Congress as an observer on behalf of the Raub branch of the Malay Association of Pahang, was eventually to become Prime Minister.

On March 29th, three days before Sir Edward Gent was scheduled to be installed as first Governor of the new Malayan Union, the various Malay Associations, for UMNO did not officially come into existence until its Charter was adopted on May 11th, began their second Pan-Malayan Congress in Kuala Lumpur. The most important resolutions adopted that day called for a total Malay boycott of the Governor's installation; and refusal to take any part in the administration of the Union, including serving on the Malayan Union Advisory Council, the highest legislative body, to which some of them had already been nominated. The Congress also declared a state of national mourning, that was to be observed for a period of seven days. The next morning Onn bin Jaafar, at an audience with all nine of the Malay Rulers, informed them of these resolutions and told them in the bluntest language that it was the will of their people that they too should carry them out; and that if they failed to do so, their subjects would demand that they abdicate [17]. To show that this was no idle threat a huge crowd, most of them dressed in traditional mourning clothes, demonstrated outside the hotel where the Sultans were staying, calling upon them to appear and make a stand; and although they cheered and paid homage to this assembly of princes, the sheer size of the demonstration and the obvious intensity of their feelings were not lost on the, by then, frightened Rulers. They did not attend the ceremony of installation.

The political dangers that could arise from this boycott and the strength of the new Pan-Malayan movement that had enforced it did not fail to register on the British government; and within a few days it was announced from Westminster that two Members of Parliament, Lt. Colonel David Rees-Williams* of the Labour Party and Captain L.D. Gammons from the Conservative opposition, both of whom had lived and worked in Malaya before the war, would visit the country to meet the people and report their views on the Malayan Union for consideration by the home government. UMNO leaders decided to ensure that they should have no chance to misinterpret the feelings of the Malays.

Actually, the primary task of these two Members of Parliament was to visit Sarawak and assess the strength of opposition to the decision of the Rajah to cede that State to the British as a Crown Colony;[18] but their assignment in the area provided the then Secretary of State for the Colonies, George Hall, with an opportunity to obtain in addition an independent opinion of the situation in Malaya, which he had good reason to believe was rapidly becoming extremely dangerous. On their return from Sarawak the two M.P.'s arranged to meet the Rulers and the Malay nationalist leaders in Kuala Kangsar at the palace of the Sultan of Perak. In order better to assess the situation for themselves, by making contact with as large a cross-section of the ordinary people as possible, the two investigators went their separate ways, Rees-Williams starting at Penang in the north of the Peninsula and travelling south by car to the Perak capital, where he was joined by his associate who had made his way north by road from Singapore.[19]

Speaking some time later during a debate in the House of Commons, Captain Gammons said of his experiences *en route:*[20]

> The tour which I made .... was in some ways the most extraordinary experience I have had in my life. At literally every village there were banners across the road carrying slogans saying 'down with the MacMichael treaties. Up with the Malays'. In the town there were demonstrations with 5,000 to 10,000 people standing in front of us. But the most remarkable thing of all was the part the women were playing in this great national movement. In the 14 years I lived in Malaya I scarcely ever spoke to a Malay woman. But today they go up on to political platforms and make speeches .... That has all happened in the short space of six months ....

More correctly, of course, the emancipation of Malay women was begun during the Japanese Occupation when many were compulsorily mobilized by the military government to aid the war effort and, occasionally, to participate in 'patriotic' mass rallies, loyal demonstrations, and orgies of sycophantic speech-making.

Nevertheless, this hectic tour and the conference that followed it left the two M.P.'s in little doubt that unless the matter was quickly settled to the satisfaction of the Malays the Colonial Government could

---

*now the Rt. Hon. Lord Ogmore, P.C. T.D. P.M.N.

expect to have to contend with 'a most intense campaign of non-co-operation of the whole country, which would spread from the refusal to pay land rent down to the defection of the police force [21] '. In addition, the UMNO leaders did not hesitate to quote to them a statement made by a former British Parliamentary Under-Secretary of State for the Colonies, William G. Ormsby Gore, who in his Report on Malaya for 1928 had written: [22] 'Our position in any Malay State rests upon solemn treaty obligations, and, however great the changes may appear to have been since the dates when they were made, these changes have not in any way modified the fundamental status of these countries. They were, they are and they must remain 'Malay' States.'

That all of this manoeuvring had at least served some purpose was demonstrated early in July when the colonial government announced its intention eventually to replace the Malayan Union with a Malayan Federation and to amend the proposed terms under which citizenship might be obtained by those not considered indigenous to the area so as to make them more acceptable to the Malays. Three weeks later a Working Committee was set up to prepare a draft Constitution for this Federation; and its most notable feature was that, with the exception of a few expatriate civil servants, it was exclusively Malay in composition, and that these members were all moderate conservatives nominated either by the Rulers or by UMNO. This sudden return by government to its pre-war pro-Malay bias was brought about largely by a complete disenchantment with local socialist parties generally and the major non-Malay political organisations in particular, which, being generally controlled by radical or communist activists had, throughout the post-war period, consistently shown far more interest in stiring up strikes and other labour unrest than in accepting tuition in, and slow progress towards, constitutional reforms leading to self-government.

Having been successful in promoting a brief general strike in January 1946, the left-wing extremists had decided to see just how far they dared provoke the British Military Administration without paying too serious a penalty. They settled upon February 15th, the anniversary of the British surrender of Singapore to the Japanese, for the trial of strength; and on that day the Malayan Communist Party and its fellow-travellers, defying a direct government ban, organised simultaneous violent demonstrations all over Malaya. In the urban centres of Singapore, Penang and Johore Bahru, when the civil police attempted to disperse these illegal processions, they were attacked with sticks and other weapons, and pelted with stones and bottles; and so they, in order to avoid being overwhelmed, eventually resorted to the use of firearms, with the result that at least twenty people were killed and an undisclosed number wounded [23]. When the authorities learned of this, the army was ordered out to enforce the ban; and this unexpected show of strength and determination quickly brought defiance to an end. Such violence and disruption on the part of the non-Malays while plans for the new Malayan Union citizenship were still going forward, soon led the British to start considering whether they had not been too hasty in turning away from the more conservative Malays. Deciding that they had, they began quietly to reverse their position.

The Working Committee's constitutional proposals were published on December 24th, 1946, and these were, as might be expected considering the composition of the Committee, very favourable to the Malays. In an effort to minimise reaction from the other communities, the colonial authorities announced on the same day that these proposals would not, however, be considered by them until after any objections or amendments that the non-Malays wished to put forward had been heard. A Consultative Committee was quickly set up to deal with such suggestions, but there was little response, as the political associations of the non-Malays decided instead to combine their strength by forming a left-wing coalition to fight the proposed constitution with more direct action.

Limited as official discussion with the other communities was intended to be, the mere fact that it was even suggested caused consternation and anger in certain of the more aggressive factions of the Malays. Typical of this was the reaction of an overseas student organisation with which Abdul Razak was later to be closely associated, the Malay Society of Great Britain, which felt that the Working Committee's draft constitution should be put into effect without delay. On January 15th, 1974, the Society's President, Tunku Abdul Rahman, soon to become Abdul Razak's friend and, in course of time, his Prime Minister and Cabinet colleague, addressed the following letter of protest to the British Secretary of State for the Colonies: [24]

> On behalf of the Malay Society of Great Britain, I venture to submit certain observations in regard to the delay in giving effect to the Federation plan for Malaya.
> The members of our Society would emphasize that the present proposals .... were framed after many long hours of careful deliberation between ... the Rulers, the representatives of the United Malay National Organisation and ... the Governor-General and the Governor of the Malayan Union, in which the needs and requirements of all races domiciled in Malaya were impartially weighed and considered. The sacrifices made by the Rulers in respect of their sovereignty, and that made by the Malay representatives in respect to the wishes of the people they represent, for the common weal of all races, has reached the limit of conciliation and concession, if not gone beyond it.
> It is, therefore, with a feeling of consternation we heard of the decision of His Majesty's government ... that the proposals will again be submitted to non-Malays for their criticisms.

Post-War Problems 67

> We feel very strongly that in no case must any further demand be made upon us Malays to surrender any more of our rights and privileges, for to do so would amount to nothing short of a direct challenge upon our honour and birthright. It is needless to say that it would excite extreme opposition among the Malays throughout the length and breadth of Malaya.
>
> I would draw your attention to the fact that even the criticisms of the proposals for Federation already ventilated by non-Malays in their newspapers and utterances elsewhere, are driving the Malays out of the moderate organisation (UMNO) into the ranks of the extremists. It is not from any apprehension lest undue weight be attached to the heady and ill-digested views of non-Malays that we now make our appeal to you, but what we do fear is that further discussions between the representatives of His Majesty's government and the non-Malays will inevitably lead to the extension of inter-racial conflict.
>
> Until after the liberation from Japan, the policy of His Majesty's government, as manifested by every treaty, had always been to uphold the Malays as the indigenous population of the country, and we therefore submit that Great Britain is in honour bound to discharge her obligations to us. We would further stress that never at any time had non-Malays been flattered by any pretext on the part of His Majesty's Government to consult them as to the provisions of the treaties between His Majesty the King and Their Highness the Rulers, whether these treaties were State treaties, or the treaties constituting the original Federated Malay States ....

Despite these laments and misgivings the new Constitution, when its terms were published some seven months later, was a considerable victory for the Malays. Naturally there was for a time a backlash of ill-feeling from those who maintained that they had been deprived of their rights; a backlash that caused such unlikely partners as the Malayan Communist Party and the Chinese Chamber of Commerce to cooperate in staging a protest Pan-Malayan hartal, which due to Malay and Muslim Indian opposition was only partly successful; and the latter to threaten that its members would refuse to serve on any government board, or assist in any other way with the administration of the new Federation. Unmoved either by this threat, or by economic pressure when it was applied, the British government inaugurated the Federation of Malaya on February 1st, 1948.

FOR WANT OF LATIN

In the meantime, however, Abdul Razak had applied to the government of the Malayan Union for a scholarship to study law at the University of London; and on July 13th, 1946, this application was approved by the Director of Education and two days later was confirmed by the Chief

Secretary who, in his report, commented favourably on the young man's wartime service in Wataniah. Abdul Razak's elation was short-lived, however, for on the 20th of that month it was discovered that he did not possess the qualification in Latin necessary to enter the University. Because of this his scholarship was postponed for a year; a procedure that did not make him any better disposed toward British officialdom. There being no suitable Latin course available at Raffles College, to which it was at first suggested that he should return, he had no alternative but to study privately in his spare time; occasionally travelling over to Kuala Lipis for a lesson from his District Officer.

Despite these difficulties, Abdul Razak passed the London Matriculation Examination in Latin in May 1947 and three months later, it being by then uncertain whether or not a place could be found for him at the University, signed an Agreement to enter Lincoln's Inn of Court to study for the Bar. On August 27th, flush with a £10 allowance for expenses on the voyage, he sailed from Singapore aboard the troopship *Scythia*; being accommodated, along with other male students *en route* for the United Kingdom, in a 24-berth dormitory. There were a number of interesting people on board, including Kwa Geok Choo, a Chinese girl student — a Queen's scholar bound for Girton College Cambridge — who was destined later to become the wife of Lee Kuan Yew, the future Prime Minister of Singapore.

This was the first time that Abdul Razak had ever been out of Malaya and so he thoroughly enjoyed the time ashore during the few days that the ship stayed at Bombay, waiting to pick up troops who were being sent back to the United Kingdom. There he and the other students were entertained and shown around by their Bombay counterparts; and were able to savour the joy and nationalist fervour of an ex-colonial territory that had as recently as August 15th attained independence. It was a joy that was somewhat overshadowed, however, by news of the pitched battles between Hindus and Muslims that had followed the partition of the sub-continent into the two Dominions of India and Pakistan; and which had resulted in the uprooting and exchange of some two million refugees. To Abdul Razak it was a grim reminder of the ever-present danger of communal clashes in his own country; a problem the solution to which would, he knew, have to be found before the shield of British law enforcement could safely be dispensed with.

The *Scythia* stopped briefly at Aden, then continued by way of the Suez Canal and the Mediterranean to Liverpool, where Abdul Razak disembarked on October 1st. That afternoon he travelled on a special boat train to London, and was met at Euston Station by a few old friends, themselves students, who escorted him to the somewhat dreary hostel where he was to spend his first few nights in Britain.

Chapter Six
Student in London

Due to the Japanese Occupation, Abdul Razak had fallen badly behind in his education; and although this made it necessary for him to study harder than he would normally have done, the two and a half years that he spent in the United Kingdom as a student was still one of the happiest and most carefree periods of his life. There, he was faced with none of the administrative and social problems that had plagued him as a District Officer, and despite the range and complexity of the courses he felt driven to undertake, he still found plenty of time to indulge his love of sport and to associate with, and try to understand the motivation of, a wide cross-section of the British people. Nor were his efforts at career building confined solely to the academic field, for at the same time he also obtained a useful grounding in politics, and acquired a more sophisticated and tolerant outlook on life than would have been possible had his experience been only of his own country.

The study of law seems to have presented Abdul Razak with few problems, for he passed his final examination to become a barrister in less than eighteen months, although due to the vagaries of the British system, he was then supposed to wait for anything up to a further year and a half before being 'called to the Bar'. So as not to waste any opportunity of advancing his career during this latter period, he enrolled at the University of London for the external B.Sc course in economics. Here fortune turned against him, for although he passed his intermediate examinations without difficulty, the early death of his father, which necessitated a return to Malaya to take control of his family's affairs before the full three years of his scholarship had expired, prevented him from obtaining his degree. In 1949 he did, however, manage to enter Cambridge University and successfully complete the Second Devonshire Course in economics and public administration; gaining knowledge that was later to be of great practical value to him although at the time, as he now freely admits, he enrolled mainly in order to obtain the extra allowance of 21 shillings a day, a windfall for a 27 years-old student living on a grant of £310 a year.

He followed the usual pattern of life of an overseas student of the period, starting off by living in drab, restrictive boarding houses and moving quite quickly, as he found companions suited to his temperament, into a series of shared flats; noisy and mildly bohemian establishments that soon became centres of Malay, and later Malayan, student activity. In the evenings, and especially at the weekends, Abdul Razak and his friends gathered at one or other of the local pubs which, like the British people with whom they mixed, they soon came to regard more as social clubs than as places intended primarily for drinking. There they were able to meet with people of many social types and differing opinions, get into arguments and play darts, all for the price of a couple of soft drinks.

During the greater part of his stay, Abdul Razak shared his flat with another Malay law student, Taib Andak, whose continued friendship was, several years in the future, to provide him with the opportunity to meet the girl who later became his wife. Taib, who had been studying longer in Britain, was called to the Bar and returned to Malaya earlier than Abdul Razak; and so the present Sultan of Perak, then Raja Muda* Idris, moved into the flat in his place and rapidly made of it an open house to which any Malayan was welcome to drop in at any time of the day or night.

The Perak prince did most of the cooking for their guests, an art in which he excelled, while the undomesticated Abdul Razak was relegated to the less glamorous positions of dish-washer and general factotum. Because of the noise he was seldom able to study in the flat, for when Raja Idris wasn't entertaining, usually with the radiogram going at full blast, he was practicing on his guitar. There were many compensations, however, not the least being that the exuberant prince had a new Jaguar car and was willing to play the part of royal chauffeur to any Malay who would join him in having an uninhibited good time. By student standards at least, he also received a very large allowance; and was generous in using it to entertain his close personal friends at places like the Astor nightclub, where Edmundo Ross was currently the star attraction. The music was great and Abdul Razak was particularly fond of dancing there, although several of his more outspoken friends left him in no doubt that they felt that he had little natural aptitude for it, or even a feeling for the rhythm.

POLITICS IN BRITAIN

Abdul Razak's social life soon began to reflect his growing interest in politics. First he became the Secretary of the Malay Society of Great Britain, of which the Kedah prince Tunku Abdul Rahman was President, and then helped to form a similar association which, as it was open to Malayan students of all ethnic groups, would, it was hoped, promote inter-racial harmony. Abdul Razak soon became concerned, however, because the majority of Malay students stuck resolutely to their own

*heir apparent.

Association and showed little inclination to participate in the activities of the multi-racial organisation. He attributed this lack of interest mainly to a condition imposed by the colonial government of his country when these two societies had been formed; this was that neither should be used for any political purpose whatsoever, or for the open discussion of controversial matters. This embargo meant that much of their use as a medium for resolving racial and social antipathies was made abortive. He therefore called a meeting at his flat at which he and a number of friends with similar interests founded a Malayan Forum, a debating society intended, as he later put it, 'to bring together Malayan students regardless of their racial origin and social background and encourage them to take a personal interest in the political development of their own country'. By this latter he meant, of course, not only the Federation of Malaya, but also Singapore.

It was in this Forum that Abdul Razak was to meet and try out his debating skill with, and sometimes against, such embryo political leaders as Goh Keng Swee, a future Finance Minister of the State of Singapore, budding diplomats like Maurice Baker* and Fred Arulanandom, in time to become a leading advocate in the higher courts of Malaysia and eventually a judge. Later on, such distinguished contemporaries as Lee Kuan Yew and Toh Chin Chye, respectively the future Prime Minister and Deputy Prime Minister of an independent Singapore, served their apprenticeship in this same Forum. A radical element, then generally absent among the Malayans, was supplied by students and lecturers from the London School of Economics and by guest speakers from the Labour Party; so that participants had the opportunity to learn at first hand, and to dispute if they felt like it, the opinions of such controversial political celebrities as Professor Laski and the fanatically left-wing socialist member of the British Parliament, Fenner Brockway. For its part, the Malayan government, showing rare tolerance, decided that this Forum was not an official student organisation and so turned a blind eye to its unequivocally nationalistic and anti-colonial bias.

On February 1st, 1948, the Malay Society of Great Britain, of which Abdul Razak was still Secretary, celebrated Federation of Malaya Day and with it the demise of the detested Malayan Union, with a dinner at Chez Auguste, the members' favourite Soho restaurant, which provided appetizing food at prices students could afford, had a dance floor and, even more important, made no cover charge. For Abdul Razak there was another event to celebrate, for his father, Dato Hussein, had been nominated for what was then the nearest that Malaya possessed to a local Parliament, the Federal Legislative Council.

---

*sometime High Commissioner for Singapore in Malaysia.

Only a few months later, however, Abdul Razak began to receive in his letters from home disturbing news of a large-scale Communist inspired insurrection that was subjecting his people to terrorism of a most vicious kind, arson, extortion and murder. These excesses had been met, after some hesitation on the part of the colonial government, with measures that included the declaration of a State of Emergency and the passing of special regulations that gave the civil police unprecedented powers of arrest, search and detention without trial, and extended the list of crimes for which death was the penalty to include the unauthorised possession of weapons, ammunition or explosives. As the situation worsened, military reinforcements were despatched from Britain and her remaining colonies; and the Malayan people settled down once again to endure the ever-present fear of mutilation or sudden death that they had thought had ended three years before with the defeat of Japan. Worst of all, as Dato Hussein informed his son, all of the submerged inter-communal hatreds and jealousy were now threatening to burst forth, due largely to the racial composition of the fighting forces of the main protagonists, for the great majority of the terrorists were Chinese, while the bulk of the police, and a considerable proportion of the other security forces, were Malay.

On September 29th Abdul Razak and his friend Tunku Abdul Rahman were, in their capacity of leaders of the student community, invited to Malaya House to attend a reception in honour of Sir Henry Gurney, the new High Commissioner of the Federation of Malaya appointed to replace Sir Edward Gent who, some two and a half months earlier had been killed in an air crash over London while flying in to report to the home government on his handling of the Communist rebellion. The two students had had little choice except to obey this official summons, although the appointment was looked upon as something of an insult by the majority of Malayan Muslims, for Sir Henry had earlier played an important part in the political moves by which the British had disengaged from a Palestine which, on May 14th 1948, had become the new State of Israel; an involvement, as certain Malay newspapers had been quick to point out, hardly likely to make him popular with the pro-Arab majority of the people he was being sent out to govern.[1]

Abdul Razak now became very serious about politics and not only studied the British system in theory, but as often as possible went to Parliament to see it in action. Upon returning from any interesting debate in the House, he would practice making his own political speeches, either enrolling Taib Andak to serve as a Chamber of one; or, without benefit of an audience, retire to Taib's bedroom, which was well equipped with wall-mirrors, so as to be able to study and criticise his own actions while orating.

Student in London

Despite his aristocratic heritage Abdul Razak, perhaps because his early years had been spent working with the ordinary village people in the rice fields, felt himself drawn politically toward social democracy and so, when the opportunity presented itself, he joined both the British Labour Party and the Fabian Society and also, in his spare time, voluntarily attended lectures given by some of the more progressive thinkers from the London School of Economics. This was mainly because he felt that a socialist government in Britain would be more sympathetic than a Conservative one towards independence for Malaya; although it was from the Conservatives that, in less than a decade, he and his colleagues who were to form the first free Malayan government were, on behalf of the country, to receive it. But as Abdul Razak put it at the time: 'I had read Churchill's earlier speeches about India's advance toward self-government and heard him as Leader of the Opposition pontificating in Parliament before and after she had won her independence; and I thought then that I saw in him an arch-imperialist who would fight to the last ditch rather than countenance any further fragmentation of the British Empire'.

He was thinking, perhaps, of Winston Churchill's famous, or from the Asian point of view notorious, speech in the House of Commons in 1931 during the course of which he described the Indian nationalist leader Gandhi as: 'a seditious Middle Temple lawyer, now posing as a fakir of a type well known in the East, striding half-naked up the steps of the Viceregal Palace, while he is still organising and conducting a defiant campaign of civil disobedience, there to negotiate and parley on equal terms with the representative of the King-Emperor'[2]. This and his classification of Gandhi and Nehru as 'evil and malignant Brahmins[3]' had seemed to indicated not only a contempt for anyone who did not possess a white skin, but also an unwillingness to believe that any Asian could possibly be fit to administer and control the destiny of his own country — an attitude hardly in line with the thinking of a young man who, if only in his daydreams, already saw himself as a potential leader of a free and independent nation.

So it is not surprising that in Abdul Razak's opinion these reactionary and vituperative outbursts, which he was at that time still too politically immature to recognise as mere oratorical embellishments, compared unfavourably with the attitude and actions of Mr. Clement Attlee, who since mid-1945 had been Prime Minister of the British socialist government. Early in 1940 he, while still Leader of the Labour Opposition — that is before he joined Winston Churchill's wartime coalition government as Deputy Prime Minister — had said in a special radio broadcast when dealing with German claims for colonies and pretensions to racial superiority:

We have accepted to a large extent the principle that all colonial territories should be held under trusteeship for the native inhabitants. We have gone a long way to giving self-government to the people of India. We have relinquished our hold on Egypt and Irak .... If we want to persuade others that we wish for a world free from imperialist domination (by the Nazis), we must put ourselves right. We must press forward with the policy of extending self-government wherever, that is practical. We must abandon any claim to special rights (over others). We must be prepared to bring all our colonial territories under the mandatory principle and to extend and widen the scope of international control. We must rid ourselves of any taint of imperialism. Only so can we put ourselves into a position to ask for a world organised on the democratic principle.[4]

He had later put these theories into practice by granting independence to India, Pakistan, Ceylon and Burma — so why not to Malaya?

The personal friendship between Tunku Abdul Rahman and the Labour M.P. David Rees Williams, towards whom Malays generally were well disposed as they felt that he had helped to end the Malayan Union, brought the Kedah prince and Abdul Razak into social contact with many of the leading lights of the world of politics, whom they met at his house in South Croydon when they were invited over for a social evening. Although at that time rice, the basis of most Malayan dishes, was extremely difficult to obtain in austerity Britain, David Rees Williams occasionally received some as a gift from friends in New York. Whenever that happened, he invited the Tunku to bring Abdul Razak and a few of their mutual friends across to cook and eat some real Malayan food. All of the culinary arrangements being handled by the gifted Tunku who, despite complaints that many of the necessary spicey ingredients were unobtainable in such a barbaric country, always managed to turn out a splendid meal for them.

David Rees Williams, or Lord Ogmore to give him his present title, remembers the Abdul Razak of those days as 'a quiet, studious young man of kindly and cheerful disposition' to whom he and his wife took an immediate liking.[5] He was, though, rather shy in company and it usually took a long time to draw him out on political questions. Once launched on the subject, however, he told them that one of the most important things that he had learned during his stay in Britain was the value to any country of a national unity and loyalty based largely upon the possession of a common culture and the use of a single dominant language. This was something that his own multi-racial homeland, Malaya, lacked; and was the basic cause, he believed, of the continuing inter-communal hatreds and divisions that could easily provide the excuse needed by reactionary elements to retain physical control of that dollar-earning capacity of the Peninsula that was so important to the British economy.

Student in London　　　　　　　　　　　　　　　　　　　　75

The general elections held in February 1950, gave Abdul Razak a chance to enjoy a democratic privilege in the United Kingdom that, paradoxically, was denied him by the British in his own country, the right to help elect the government. He voted Labour. Then, anxious as always to add to his political and social experiences and knowledge, he obtained permission to witness the counting of votes at the Town Hall in Chelsea. The whole election was an exceptionally interesting experience for a budding politician, for who next should govern was not decided until almost all of the results had been declared. In the event, the final count gave Labour, the party he supported, a majority of only seven in a Chamber of six hundred and twenty-five seats.

INDONESIAN NATIONALISM

In the years immediately following the end of the Second World War many outlawed nationalists who had succeeded in escaping from the colonial authorities in their own countries sought sanctuary in London, from where they could continue their political propaganda without fear of arbitrary detention. Numbered among these refugees were Dr Subandrio, the official Representative of the Indonesian Republic at that time in conflict with the Dutch, and the adopted children of the Prime Minister of that disputed territory, Des Alwi and Mimi Shahrir. These escapees often found themselves in serious financial difficulties and so Abdul Razak and the other Malay students, feeling close to them through ties of race, custom and religion, went out of their way to help and support them in any manner possible.

The Indonesians had been struggling against Dutch colonial rule since the seventeenth century; but it was not until the Japanese occupied the country during World War Two that there had seemed to be any real chance of them eventually regaining their full independence. At the time of the Japanese invasion many of the nationalist leaders like Hatta, Shahrir and Sukarno were under detention or serving prison sentences; but as soon as the campaign was over, most of them were released by the military administration, which needed their cooperation in keeping the occupied territories peaceful, so that more troops could be released to serve at the war fronts. Some like Sukarno and Hatta collaborated wholeheartedly; while others, notably Shahrir, went underground and opposed the Japanese with the same fervour that they had previously displayed in fighting the Dutch.

In mid 1945, with the Allies advancing on all fronts, the Japanese military administration at last decided to grant independence to Indonesia, mainly in the hope that the guerilla forces then operating against them would, through ambush and sabotage, delay and disrupt any army attempting to re-occupy the archipelago. Just before the Emperor gave the signal for the war to end, Sukarno and Hatta were summoned to Saigon to meet the Commander-in-Chief of the Southern Armies, Field Marshal Count Terauchi, who granted them independence, although stipulating that it would not be effective until he chose to make it so by a formal proclamation. On August 17th, 1945, two days after the Japanese had capitulated, Sukarno and Hatta, realising that only by presenting the Allies with a *fait accompli* had they a chance of stopping the now victorious Allies from handing their country back to the Dutch, unilaterally declared Indonesia to be an independent republic.

In the Peninsula a substantial number of Malays, particularly those who feared reprisals because they had been active in collaborating with the Japanese, received this declaration with enthusiasm. They immediately demanded that Malaya be permitted to join the new Republic; but although this plea gained the support of Sukarno, who felt that the Federation would be strengthened, both economically and militarily, if it controlled both shores of the Malacca Straits, it was rejected by a majority of the Revolutionary Council, which thought that it would be disastrous to provoke the British and the Dutch simultaneously. The latter, not surprisingly, refused to recognise the Indonesian Republic and, being at that time themselves militarily impotent, called upon their allies to regain their lost colonies for them. British and Dutch troops began landing at Batavia on September 29th.

As early as October 12th, 1945, the Dutch, reluctantly yielding to pressure from their more powerful allies, had offered the Indonesians not independence, but a form of self-government as a dominion under the Crown of Holland. Negotiations took place, but as the Dutch were merely marking time until they could assemble sufficient military strength to crush any resistance once they were left on their own, while the rebels were determined to accept nothing short of complete independence, little real progress was made. Despite the slow but methodical reoccupation of the main urban areas of the country by Allied troops, the embryo Republic continued to exist with Sukarno as President and, from November 13th 1945, with Shahrir as its first Prime Minister. Protracted wrangling and intermittent guerilla warfare continued throughout 1946, until the Dutch, faced with the imminent withdrawal of all British military forces from the Indonesian islands, were forced finally to recognise the Republic as having jurisdiction over Java, Sumatra and Madura. They did manage to retain some vestiges of control over these areas, however, by bringing into being an unstable federation, called the United States of Indonesia, that combined their remaining territories in the Archipelago, Southern Borneo, the island of Celebes, Sunda and the Moluccas, with the Republic in a commonwealth that recognised the Dutch Queen as its titular sovereign.

The more extreme elements among Indonesian nationalists would have nothing to do with this compromise agreement, however, and kept up their guerilla attacks on the Dutch, who were forced to act more and more oppressively in order to exist. In June 1947 Shahrir, anticipating that open warfare would soon result, resigned in protest and then, as a precaution, sent his adopted son, Des Alwi, to London, where he joined the staff of the Indonesian Representative's office in Knightsbridge and lodged with Dr Subandrio and his wife.

Abdul Razak first met Des Alwi at a students' party and the two men soon became close friends as well as collaborators in the cause of Indonesian independence. By that time all money being sent from Indonesia to support Dr Subandrio had been cut off by the Dutch and he and his staff found themselves existing on charity. Some of this money came from the profits which resulted from concerts organised by Malay and Indonesian students, who were aided by a few left-wing British sympathisers with show-business connections, and who were able to arrange theatre accommodation and get programmes printed free. It is ironic, therefore, that this same Dr Subandrio should later have become one of the most bitter opponents of Malaysia at a time when Abdul Razak was, as his country's Minister of Defence, charged with its security from Indonesian aggression.

EUROPEAN HOLIDAY

While he was still a student, Abdul Razak made a point of sight-seeing extensively within the United Kingdom and also, despite the strict currency regulations then in force, of visiting as many places in Europe as he could. He managed to cover a lot of territory in France, Belgium, Holland, Switzerland and Italy, travelling third class by rail and living in student hostels in order to make his money go farther. In the summer of 1949 he and Des Alwi planned a new and more ambitious excursion to the Continent for a party of Malayan and Indonesian students; but just before they were due to start, the official Agent for Malaya caused a modification of their plans by inviting him and Tunku Jaffar* to represent their country at the World Assembly of Youth that was due soon to meet in Brussels.

On the day of departure the whole party assembled at Abdul Razak's flat where, having given up their lodgings in order to find money to pay for the trip, they were to leave their belongings. They took the train to Harwich and then proceeded by boat to the Hook of Holland. The amount of sterling that could be taken out of the country was strictly limited and so, like almost everyone else travelling abroad at that time, they distributed a few extra pound notes illegally throughout their

*now His Highness The Ruler of the State of Negeri Sembilan.

clothing and hoped for the best. From the Hook they went by train to Amsterdam, where they were able to book rooms in a student-workers hostel for the equivalent of about two shillings a person a night. Then, with their base secured, they got in touch with some of Des Alwi's relatives who had a house there, and so solved most of their food problems. This left the bulk of their money free to be spent on more entertaining things.

They soon also made contact with a number of local students, both Dutch and Indonesian, and over the evening *rijstaffel,* a gargantuan meal based on rice and curry, argued interminably about the rights and wrongs, as they saw them, of Indonesian independence. Few of the Dutch students were in favour of giving up the East Indies and often, in the heat of the moment, condemned the whole independence movement as a communist plot to take over the Archipelago. The Indonesians, on the other hand, claimed that it was the extreme conservatism of the Dutch that had caused many of their countrymen who had studied in Holland to associate with the extreme left, as the Communists and their fellow-travellers seemed to be the only Europeans willing to support them in their struggle.

Their next stop was in Brussels, for the whole group had packed up and accompanied Abdul Razak and Tunku Jaffar there, although they had no part to play in the conference. The delegates, being guests of the Belgian government, were accommodated in a school hostel; and as there were plenty of empty rooms, for all the pupils were away on holiday, the rest of the Malayan party moved in uninvited, glad to be able to obtain lodgings and breakfast free. This was a proud occasion for Abdul Razak, for it was the first time that he had had the opportunity of addressing an international audience made up of delegates from some thirty countries. After the Assembly's Charter, which had been drafted the year before, had been ratified, he spoke on the importance of the State providing adequate facilities aimed at making the increasing leisure of young people productive and interesting, so that they became less susceptible to the counter-attractions of crime and violence.

As soon as the conference ended, however, the school hostel was closed; which meant that the Malayans had to spend their last night in Belgium at a cheap hotel. The next morning they left by train for Paris, where they booked in at a third class hotel in the students' quarter, not far from the Sorbonne, so that they could eat cheaply at the University canteen. Most of the party decided to economise even further by sharing rooms; and so Abdul Razak found himself doubling up with Des Alwi, which gave him an extra 400 old francs a day to spend on entertainment. Such rooms were equipped with neither baths nor showers; and indeed the occupants were supposed to pay an extra 100 francs every time they used the corridor bathrooms, which were at all times kept securely locked. Fortunately, however, the privileged Tunku Jaffar had a room with a private bath and so one by one, every day, members of the party surreptitiously made use of that.

While in Paris they were joined by Raja Idris, also the Crown Prince of Pahang*, and Taib Andak and his wife Zainab. The presence of Taib's wife at first tended to restrict their freedom of action, or at least Taib's, until he hit upon the idea of taking her window-shopping every day so that she was too tired to go out again in the evenings. This left them free to visit their favourite night-spot, Le Naturalist in the Place Pigalle, which fortunately imposed no cover charge and where, once again for the price of a few drinks, they could dance until the early hours of the morning and enjoy an excellent, and for the times quite daring, floor-show. On one occasion Des Alwi and the Crown Prince of Pahang stayed on at the nightclub until 4 am and then invited some of the performers out to breakfast. The bill was so high that Des Alwi had to leave the prince as hostage while he took a taxi back to the hotel to raise funds. There he woke Abdul Razak, who was acting as their common treasurer, and stifled his objections by threatening him that if he didn't produce the money 'the heir apparent of your State will go to the Bastille and your father will have to explain to the Sultan how it happened'. He got the money.

At the end of their stay in Paris, Abdul Razak and a number of the others decided to revisit Holland, which they had found to be cheaper than most other places on the Continent. Des Alwi went on ahead to prepare his relatives for the shock of their return, while the Crown Prince of Pahang and Raja Idris were sent back to the United Kingdom. Then the rest of the party set out for Holland by train. They had not realised, however, that transit visas were necessary for Belgium even though they were not stopping there; and so at the frontier they were thrown off the train and told to return to Paris. As most of their little store of money had gone on rail fares, for they had expected to be able to borrow some from Des Alwi's family in Holland, several of them were in an embarrassing position. By pooling their resources, however, the entire party eventually got to Calais and across to Dover, though they lived mainly on French bread and cheese on the way. Back in London, an exasperated Abdul Razak, blowing off student hot air, threatened that if ever he became politically powerful when Malaya was independent, he would oppose diplomatic relations with Belgium. Many years later, as Deputy Prime Minister of Malaysia, he was jokingly to relate this story to the Belgium Ambassador at the conclusion of a ceremony at which he was awarded that country's highest Order of Chivalry.

*now His Highness The Sultan of Pahang.

DATO HUSSEIN'S DEATH

Early in 1950 Dato Hussein was admitted to hospital in Kuala Lumpur and Taib Andak, who was a frequent visitor, sent regular reports on his condition to his son in England. At the beginning of May Abdul Razak had his first and only experience of precognition, the premonition of his father's death; for one night he dreamt that the eye-glasses of his spectacles suddenly broke away from the side pieces and, although they remained *in situ,* everything went black and for a moment or two he was unable to see through them. When he awoke this dream was still in his mind and, as much as he told himself that it was nonsense, he could not lose the feeling that his father, for whom he had a great admiration and affection although as a child he had not seen very much of him, had died at the very moment that the eye-glasses had broken. The next day the dreaded cable arrived from Malaya as expected. His carefree student days were over; for his inheritance carried with it responsibilities to his family and to his State; and so it was necessary for him to return at once to Pahang, there to settle his father's estate and his own future.

Part Two

The Road to Power

Chapter Seven
UMNO and the Alliance

Abdul Razak left London for Malaya by air on May 6th, 1950. Normally, as he still ranked only as a Malay Officer on Probation, he would have been expected to return by sea but, being anxious to reach Pahang as quickly as possible, he decided to gamble that the Treasury would not bill him for the £75 difference in the two fares. In those days the flight proceeded in leisurely fashion with night stop-overs at Cairo and Karachi, so that it was not until late in the afternoon of May 8th that his plane touched down at Kallang Airport in Singapore. There Taib Andak and some of his other friends were waiting to take him to Johore Bahru, where he was to stay until the next morning. As the communist insurrection, which officialdom chose to refer to as 'The Emergency', was then at the peak of its senseless viciousness, it was dangerous to travel far at night, for the terrorists all too often shot-up or ambushed cars and sometimes even tried to derail trains.

He was lucky, however, and in daylight completed the journey to Kuala Lipis, the capital of his home State, without incident. When he reported for duty, as he was bound to do before even visiting his family home, he was posted without delay to the vacant position of Assistant State Secretary, for there was a considerable shortage of administrative officers at that time, especially those with legal qualifications. With this appointment came promotion to the Malayan Civil Service, an advancement that carried considerable prestige. He was fortunate, too, in that because his early arrival suited the colonial government's convenience, he was excused repaying the debt of £75 excess fare that he had incurred.

One disappointment that Abdul Razak had to suffer, however, was that as the Sultan of Pahang was abroad at the time that he reached Kuala Lipis, he was left in doubt as to whether or not he would inherit his late father's title. The passing of this to the eldest son was not automatic, but depended upon the decision of the Sultan in Council as to whom among the male members of the former holder's family was the most suitable successor. By tradition a particular *keris*, a short stabbing weapon presented to one of the earlier nobles by a former Sultan, is returned to the Ruler whenever the title falls vacant. Whichever member of the family is called to the palace to receive back this *keris* then becomes the title-holder for life. Following the Sultan's return, this honour was conferred upon Abdul Razak who, on November 1st, 1950, was officially installed as the tenth *Orang Kaya Indera Shahbandar*.

U.M.N.O.

Although civil servants were, in the colonial period, generally discouraged from playing too active a role in politics, Abdul Razak soon found himself becoming more and more involved in the affairs of the premier Malay party, the United Malays National Organisation (UMNO); the Kuala Lipis branch of which he had joined soon after his return to Pahang. His promotion into the top echelon of the party came as a complete surprise to him, however, for it took place while he was enjoying a quiet weekend in Kuala Lumpur. On the Saturday afternoon, having nothing in particular to do, he went to the Sultan Sulaiman Club and casually attended the Annual General Meeting of the UMNO national youth movement. There, to his astonishment, he heard himself being proposed for election to the position of Youth Leader, an office that carried with it automatic advancement to a Vice-Presidency of the Party, in place of Hussein Onn, son of the UMNO President, who had recently become the Party's Secretary-General. Although his own wishes had not been consulted, he was duly elected; and so was presented with a politically significant power-base that was, and indeed still is, considered one of the major stepping-stones leading to the pinnacle of the Party's hierarchy. This was shown to be so in August 1951 when Abdul Razak, who was then only 29 years old, was elected, unopposed, to be Deputy President of UMNO. It was a position that he was to continue to hold until January 23rd, 1970, the day after he succeeded Tunku Abdul Rahman as Prime Minister of Malaysia.

While Abdul Razak had been away in Britain, UMNO had grown into a powerful and efficient organisation accepted by the great majority of moderate Malays as the champion of their rights and the promoter of their political and racial aspirations; and by the colonial authorities, albeit reluctantly, as the likely future government of the country. This may possibly have encouraged the Party's President, Dato Onn to take the unfortunate steps that he did; actions that eventually consigned him to the political wilderness and unexpectedly gave Abdul Razak's friend, Tunku Abdul Rahman, the leadership of UMNO.

By mid-1949 Dato Onn had begun to veer away from communal politics and see himself instead as the head of a multi-racial party with sufficient support to ensure him of the future leadership of his emerging nation. Despite intense opposition from its more conservative elements, he put forward proposals that would eventually have turned UMNO from a Malay into a Malayan party; and urged the acceptance of a more liberal policy towards citizenship in order to gain the confidence and support of the moderate Chinese and Indians. This was a bold step to take and also one frought with considerable danger, as Dato Onn was soon to find out. For a time, however, the near adulation which so many Malays accorded him, helped to maintain his dominant position; but as he continued supporting the claims of the non-Malays, opposition within UMNO mounted until, on a forced vote, his plans were totally rejected. Dato Onn did not stay to argue, he resigned; an action which left the Party split in its loyalties and without an effective leader. He then waited patiently until the reaction that he had expected, and indeed gambled upon, set in and temporarily won for him a considerable tactical success; for on July 27th, 1950, some thousands of rank-and-file Party members assembled and marched in procession to his house in Johore Bahru, where they noisily exhorted him to take back the Presidency. After a brief show of reluctance, he allowed himself to be persuaded to do so.

Despite his usual political astuteness, however, Dato Onn seriously misinterpreted this gesture, mistaking a demonstration of gratitude for his past dynamic leadership for overwhelming public support of his new, more controversial policies. He therefore continued trying to bulldoze through his virtually unacceptable demand that UMNO should agree to support a more liberal citizenship policy and when this requirement was rejected by the Party executive, resigned once more, this time adding a threat that if necessary he would form a new multi-racial party of his own. Confident that this concealed threat to poach members from UMNO and so split the Malay vote would cause his opponents to capitulate, he then sat back and waited; but this time he had gone too far and his former hold over the Malay masses was soon shown to have largely disappeared. There was no spontaneous grass-roots revolt in his favour; and his resignation was allowed to stand.

The United Malays National Organisation now had to find a new leader who, should Dato Onn's recruitment threat become a reality, possessed sufficient charisma to keep the majority of Malays loyal to the Party. Of necessity he had also to be acceptable to the British; for it was obvious that whoever was selected would, in the near future, have to treat with the colonial authorities for the gradual hand-over of executive power; and thereafter accept increasing responsibility as the country advanced slowly from power-sharing to self-government and finally to complete independence. After some severe heart-searching, for all were politically ambitious, each member of the executive modestly came to the conclusion that he was as yet too inexperienced to undertake the task; and it remained for Abdul Razak to suggest as a candidate someone who, although as untried in politics as the rest of them, possessed certain advantages stemming from his family background, royal upbringing and amiable and extrovert temperament. His choice, which was unanimously agreed upon, was his close personal friend Tunku Abdul Rahman, the former President of the Malay Society of Great Britain.

At seven o'clock the next morning Abdul Razak led a small delegation to the Kedah prince's house to seek his acceptance of their nomination. This was the Muslim month of Ramdzan, however, during which Malays observe a religious fast throughout the day and, being able to eat and drink only during the hours of darkness, prefer, if it is a holiday, to sleep late; and so the normally genial and easy-going Tunku was unusually terse when woken so early. At first Tunku Abdul Rahman, who was at that time employed as a Deputy Public Prosecutor in the Attorney-General's office in Kuala Lumpur, was reluctant to accept and instead urged Abdul Razak himself to lead the Party, stating that if he would agree to do so he, Tunku, would give him his full support and backing. Eventually, however, Abdul Razak, after an appeal on patriotic grounds, managed to persuade the older man to stand for election. He did so, and won handsomely, at the next session of the full UMNO Assembly; which at the same time also unanimously elected Abdul Razak as his Deputy. They made an effective and formidable team, with the courtly and affable Tunku as front man and Abdul Razak serving as the Party's top organiser, the managerial power behind the throne.

In February 1951 Abdul Razak was nominated a member of Malaya's Federal Legislative Council, the embryo Parliament in which he was to serve his ministerial apprenticeship. Although councils empowered to pass legislation had existed in a number of the Malay States from the closing decades of the nineteenth century, it was not until 1909 that a Federal Council, serving the four Federated Malay States of Pahang, Perak, Selangor and Negri Sembilan was constituted. This latter consisted of the four Sultans of the participating States, plus nine nominated members, most of whom were government officials. In 1927 the Rulers, for reasons of prestige and protocol, withdrew from this Council and were each replaced by a representative of their own choice. After the war a new enlarged Federal Legislative Council was established, which was intended to represent the whole country with the exception of Singapore. From early in this post-war period until his death in 1950, the member nominated for Pahang was Dato Hussein; it was to his vacant seat that his son, Abdul Razak, succeeded some ten months later.

In 1948 the number of nominated members comprising the Federal Legislative Council was increased to seventy-five, so that representatives of industry and labour could be included; which meant that for the first time the unofficial, or non-government nominees, formed a majority. In April 1951 a further significant step toward self-government was taken with the introduction of an apprentice system whereby nine of the Council members were given some degree of ministerial responsibility for particular government departments. These 'Ministers', together with two further non-official members who were without specific portfolios, the British High Commissioner (Governor), his Deputy, the Chief Secretary to the Government, the

UMNO and the Alliance 87

Financial Secretary and the Attorney-General, the last five all being colonial officials, then formed a rudimentary Cabinet, which was known as the Federal Executive Council.

MARRIAGE — MALAY STYLE

The years from 1951 to 1955 were intensely busy ones for Abdul Razak, for in addition to his civil service responsibilities he had regularly to attend meetings of the Legislative Council or the UMNO executive in Kuala Lumpur, and to run the ever-expanding youth section of his Party. The strain of this was in no way lessened by the activities of the Malayan Communist Party, for at that time Pahang had the doubtful distinction of being the only State in the Federation in which a predominantly Malay guerilla regiment operated. This was commanded by a cousin of Yeop Mahidin, Abdul Razak's former commanding officer of Wataniah days; and included a liquidation squad that was notorious for its viciousness toward Malays who supported the Administration. Because of this, whenever Abdul Razak had to undertake the dangerous journey by road from his office in Kuala Lipis to the Federal Capital, Kuala Lumpur, in his old Morris Oxford, he dressed in bush-jacket, khaki slacks and a songkok*, so that if stopped on the way by terrorists he could claim that he was merely a driver taking the car into the next State in order to pick up his employer. Fortunately for him he never had to put this subterfuge to the test, for the nearest that he ever came to being caught in an ambush was on a September day in 1952, when he was on his way to Johore Bahru where he was to be married. He and his mother were travelling by car when just outside Bentong, where for so many years his late father had been the District Officer, they found the road blocked and armed khaki-clad figures crouching in the undergrowth. It was only a joint military-police exercise, however, and they suffered nothing worse than a minor fright.

Abdul Razak first met his future wife, Rahah binte Haji Noah, during a visit to UMNO headquarters which, in Dato Onn's time as President, was located at Johore Bahru. One day, when he was staying at the house of Taib Andak, his friend surprised and intrigued him by saying that in following the instructions given to him by Dato Hussein, just before he died, he had looked out a suitable bride for him. She was, Taib added, still only a schoolgirl of eighteen, but a good many young men about the town already had their eyes on her, for she was not only extremely attractive, but also intelligent and, for a Malay girl of the period, exceptionally sophisticated. After such a build up, naturally Abdul Razak wanted to know when he could meet this paragon; and was

*Malay cap.

told that as she was studying at the Convent of the Holy Infant Jesus, they would first park outside the school gates so that he could get a good look at her as she went by. Fortunately they had a ready-made excuse, for Taib's daughter was a junior at the same Convent, which meant that they could pretend that they were waiting to collect her. Abdul Razak has always been able to think on his feet and make snap decisions; he saw Rahah walk through the Convent gates and made one there and then.

In 1952 Malay weddings were no casual Registry Office affairs to be organised by the participants, nor indeed are they today, for they were and are, serious matters that must be attended to with all the pomp and circumstance that custom demands. First Taib, acting in place of a member of Abdul Razak's family, all of whom lived far away in other States, had to discuss his principal's qualifications with Haji Noah, who was Chairman of the Johore State UMNO and a member of both the Federation Legislative and the Johore State Councils as well as Rahah's father, and then negotiate the amount of the marriage settlement. When his had been agreed, Abdul Razak was formally presented to his future parents-in-law. They accepted him; and he next went through a ceremony of betrothal to Rahah. At the end of this, the provisional date for the wedding was fixed; and the female members of the bride's family, for by custom the ceremony had to be held at the father-in-law's house, began to plan and prepare for the great occasion.

In the evening of the day set for the wedding, Abdul Razak headed a small procession that walked from Taib's house to that of the bride, bearing on silver trays a number of traditional gifts together with the bridegroom's contribution towards the expenses. This latter was traditionally a thousand and one dollars, consisting of uncirculated currency notes made up into the model of a peacock, to the beak of which the gold ring was attached. Haji Noah's house was gaily decorated for the occasion and crowded with distinguished guests who had come to witness the ceremony. In the largest room in the house a colourful three-tiered dais, topped with two throne-like chairs had been constructed; but on this occasion the bridegroom sat not upon this raised platform, but upon an embroidered mat at the base of it, while the trays containing the presents and the currency peacock were laid in a row down the centre of the room. After these traditional gifts had been accepted by the family, they were passed to the rear of the house where Rahah waited unseen, for she had no part to play except at the very end of the ceremony.

Abdul Razak then turned to face the registrar of Muslim marriages who was seated on his right. After delivering a formal prayer and address, this official took the bridegroom by the right hand and declared: "Abdul Razak son of Hussein, I bestow on you in marriage Rahah, daughter of Haji Noah ....". In reply, Abdul Razak merely declared that he accepted Rahah as his wife and, by law, they were married. After receiving the congratulations of all those present, the bridegroom was escorted to the back of the house, where he formally touched his bride on the forehead as a sign that they were united. He then took a meal with the male members of his wife's family, a celebration from which Rahah was, of course, excluded; and later returned to Taib's house to spend the night. If all this seems less than romantic, then it should be said that although Muslims may, in certain circumstances which are laid down in the Quran[1], or condoned by custom, possess up to four wives at any one time, Abdul Razak never married any other woman, and that he and his wife, blessed by *Allah* with five sons, lived contentedly together for nearly a quarter of a century.

The main ceremony of the marriage, the *bersanding* or enthronement, for the bride and groom are as *Rani* and *Rajah* for a day, had yet to be undertaken, however, and was scheduled for the most auspicious period in the Muslim week, a Thursday evening after the sunset prayer. As soon as Abdul Razak had been carefully dressed in traditional Malay costume, his female relatives and their friends hurried ahead to announce his imminent arrival to the waiting guests. Preceded by a group of youths beating out a rhythm on small drums, the bridegroom and his escort marched in procession to the front of Haji Noah's house, where they were halted by the usual 'marriage sentinels' who, after a little harmless horseplay and chaff permitted them to enter the compound.

Abdul Razak then went inside the house and took his place on the three-tiered dais in the seat on the right of his wife, who was already enthroned there. By custom they had to sit motionless and poker-faced while their friends resorted to every trick they could think of to make them smile. Then, a number of the distinguished guests, including the Regent of Johore and his wife, the Chief Ministers of Pahang and Johore, and the British Adviser to Johore, were invited on to the dais to sprinkle the bridal pair with yellow rice and rose water; a ritual intended to ensure their future happiness and good fortune. Finally everyone went home, taking with them as a parting gift small porcelain flower baskets each containing the Malay symbol of fertility, a hard-boiled egg.[2]

A few days later while Abdul Razak was enjoying his honeymoon on Penang Island, a telegram arrived from Sir Gerald Templer, High Commissioner of the Federation of Malaya, who occasionally liked playing practical jokes on his officers, informing him that his leave was cancelled and that he was to go immediately to the Cameron Highlands, in Pahang State, and prepare an official report on the fly situation. This was a reference to the result of the Chinese farmers in the area using on their smallholdings a cheap fertilizer made from prawn dust, which bred a self-perpetuating plague of two-winged insects that soon invaded the hill-station's many hotels, leave-centres and holiday bungalows. Normally a direct order from Sir Gerald, who was not noted for either his tolerance or his forbearance, was not something to be ignored even while honeymooning, but Abdul Razak decided to risk assuming that it was intended as a joke and merely replied: 'you can have Cameron Highlands either as a holiday resort or for vegetable gardening — not both'.

A CHANGE OF CAPITAL

Abdul Razak and his wife set up house in Kuala Lipis, where their first child Mahommed Najib, named after President Naguib of Egypt, was born on the 23rd of July, 1953; and their second son, Ahmad Johari, on November 29th, 1954. For much of that period Abdul Razak, who had been promoted State Secretary of Pahang, was concerned with the administrative difficulties of moving the State Capital from Kuala Lipis, inconveniently situated right in the interior of the country, to the more practical site of Kuantan on the coast, which was only about 20 miles away from the royal capital of Pekan. The latter town had been the centre of government from time immemorial until the establishment of the British Protectorate, when Hugh Clifford had demanded that it be moved to Kuala Lipis; and had been spent the remainder of his tenure of office regretting his impetuousness. Since that time various officials had gone through the motions of evaluating alternative sites, but until Abdul Razak took over, no one had prepared a detailed report clearly listing the points for and against each place suggested. Despite this, General Sir Gerald Templer, while approving a move, insisted that it should be to the equally unsuitable town of Temerloh. When Abdul Razak persisted with the claims of Kuantan, Sir Gerald flew into a temper and told him: 'I want you to go to Temerloh, but it you want to go to hell — go to hell!'

The seat of government was officially moved to the coastal port of Kuantan on August 27th, 1955. By that time, Abdul Razak had been promoted to Acting Chief Minister of Pahang; and one of the last duties that he performed in the old capital was to declare the entire Kuala Lipis region, with the exception of the Cameron Highlands, a white area, or one free of Communist terrorists and so no longer subject to curfew. This decision was taken against the advice of the local military commander and the chief police officer of the State, but turned out to be the correct one; for it led to no resurgence of terrorist activity, but rather to a de-escalation of fear and tension.

In celebration of his recent promotion and victory in moving the capital to Kuantan, Abdul Razak had, as a surprise for his wife, had a new house built there. Just as it was completed, however, he decided to contest a seat in the first ever general elections to be held in Malaya and so, knowing that if he were successful it would mean giving up the civil service in order to concentrate all of his time on politics, he dared not

UMNO and the Alliance

immediately tell his wife of the new house in case she should insist that he stick to the safety of government service.

BIRTH OF THE ALLIANCE

As early as September 1950, the Federal Legislative Council had passed a Bill which authorised the introduction of elections at Municipal and lower levels. The first Municipal elections were held at Penang and Malacca toward the end of 1951, but were fought mainly on parochial issues. The election held in Kuala Lumpur, the campaign for which started at the beginning of 1952, was of much greater interest, however, for it resulted in a surprise alliance of two communal parties, one Malay and the other Chinese, that was to have tremendous impact on the political future of the country.

On September 16th, 1951, Dato Onn at last launched his long awaited multi-racial political association, the Independence of Malaya Party (IMP). He did so in the confident expectation that it would enjoy the full support of the Malayan Chinese Association (MCA)* — which had been formed in February 1949 with the avowed intention of protecting the interests of the Chinese community against an escalation of aggressive Malay nationalism — and the Malayan Indian Congress (MIC). He hoped, too, to pick up at least sufficient Malay support to permit a little political window-dressing; for the all-out opposition not only of UMNO, but also of the Rulers, who feared that the IMP would strive to erode even further their few remaining sovereign powers, had already precluded the possibility of any substantial indigenous participation. Unfortunately for Dato Onn, however, right at the beginning he made yet another egregious blunder that cost him and his party dear, for at the inauguration ceremony he failed to invite on to the platform as a guest of honour the influential, and easily provoked, Colonel H.S. Lee, a powerful force in the Selangor MCA, who soon afterward laid plans for his downfall.

For his first showdown with UMNO Dato Onn picked the Municipal elections due to be held in the Federal Capital, Kuala Lumpur, an urban centre where the majority of voters were non-Malays; for a success there would not only establish him as a national leader in Malayan eyes, but also demonstrate to the British the advisability of including such a broadly-based organisation in any future negotiations for self-government. Some five weeks before polling day, however, the Selangor State branches of UMNO and the MCA unexpectedly, and as it later transpired without prior consultation with their respective party national executives, announced that they were to form a temporary

---

*It had also been formed to provide some social and welfare assistance to those Chinese resettled in the New Villages.

electoral alliance. This move, although it lacked high level backing, was outstandingly successful, for the new alliance won nine of the twelve seats available — six going to the MCA and three to UMNO — while the IMP managed to secure only two. Despite the restricted list of voters involved and the few seats fought, the significance of the results was not lost on the various community leaders standing watching on the sidelines; for analysis showed that all the Chinese and Malay candidates standing on the IMP ticket had been defeated and that the Party's two successes had both been in constituencies where Indians formed a majority of voters.[3] This meant that a communal stand, though perhaps tempered by compromise and cooperation was in; and political integration was out. Acting upon this intelligence appreciation, the executive leaders of UMNO and the MCA quickly adopted the brainchild of their Selangor branches and held talks to consider extending the alliance, perhaps even to the extent of making it a permanent electoral feature.

Despite their disparate interests, for some time the two parties to this political alliance worked closely together and indeed at one point achieved such rapport that the richer Chinese organisation even announced its intention to donate half a million dollars to a welfare fund, to be administered jointly with UMNO, that was to be set up to improve the lot of the poorer Malays.[4] This never materialised, however, for after this first honeymoon period, communal interests, notably in the field of education, began sharply to diverge; with the inevitable result that disenchantment rapidly set in.

There was at that time no official Malayan language; and education was carried on mainly on a communal basis with instruction given, according to the type of school chosen, in either Malay, English, Chinese or Tamil. As the colonial authorities wished to promote and extend the use of English, but recognised Malay as the language of the indigenous peoples, the bulk of government subsidies went to schools teaching in one or other of these two languages. Chinese and Tamil schools, on the other hand, were almost entirely privately financed and controlled. During the early 1950's, however the Legislative Council Education Committee, of which Abdul Razak was a member, accepted the report of a Royal Commission that recommended, among other things, that a new education policy should be worked out that would ensure the gradual phasing out of private communal institutions, which should be replaced by national schools using a common syllabus taught in either Malay or English. This caused wide-spread consternation among the non-Malays, who saw in it an attempt to deny their children the right to their own language and culture and to turn them into pseudo-Malays; a sensitive issue that has plagued Malayan and Malaysian politics ever since.

UMNO and the Alliance

Their divergent interests notwithstanding, the two partners in the Alliance realised that they needed each other's cooperation if the country, when finally independent, was to be governed without continual inter-racial strife; and despite the fulminations of fanatics on either side, gradually worked out compromise solutions to their main problems. So successful were they, on the surface anyway, that by the beginning of 1953 they were in a position to exert the pressure of their combined strength on the colonial government to hold Federal elections in the following year. The result of this was that in mid-July the British High Commissioner set up a Working Committee, the UMNO members of which included Abdul Razak and Tunku Abdul Rahman, to decide whether such an advance was really feasible. Early in 1954 this Committee reported that, in its joint opinion, it was; and after due consideration the colonial government announced that elections would take place, not in 1954, but in mid-1955, and that in the new Legislative Council fifty two of the ninety eight Members would be elected.

Although this could be considered an unprecedented constitutional step forward, for no other British colonial territory had gone directly from a wholly nominated Legislative Assembly to one with an elected majority, UMNO was dissatisfied. Its leaders felt that not even the Alliance could hope to secure fifty of the elected seats; and so in the introduction of any progressive legislation would be likely to find themselves obstructed by the nominated members, few of whom could be expected to be sympathetic toward their aims. They therefore demanded a larger proportion of elected seats; and when this was refused sent a delegation, headed by Tunku Abdul Rahman and including Abdul Razak, who had hurriedly been recalled from the United States where he was touring on a State Department 'leadership' grant, to the United Kingdom to deal with the home government direct.

At first Oliver Lyttleton, the Secretary of State for the Colonies, refused to see this delegation, but by the time it reached London David Rees Williams had, at the request of his friend Tunku Abdul Rahman, arranged the meeting. The Secretary of State remained adamant on the proportion of elected members, however, and in mid-May the members of the delegation, less Abdul Razak who stayed behind to clear up a few points connected with some of the minor concessions that they had won, returned to Malaya to report to their respective parties. Meanwhile, in London, Abdul Razak, with the help of David Rees Williams, had opened an UMNO/MCA 'Merdeka' (freedom) Bureau, from which it was intended to disseminate propaganda advocating rapid independence for Malaya.

When, at the end of August, Abdul Razak arrived back in Malaya, he found that the UMNO/MCA Alliance had instructed all its members serving on any government sponsored legislative body to resign in protest at the refusal to meet their demands. Although a large number of them had done so, with disastrous results to the administration of the country, the colonial government remained unmoved. Later, however, Sir Donald MacGillivray, who had replaced Sir Gerald Templer as High Commissioner, met with Tunku Abdul Rahman and assured him that certain of the nominated seats in the Federal Council, which it had been intended should be reserved for government officers, would instead be filled only in agreement with the leader of the majority party in the Chamber [5]. This olive branch was accepted; and Alliance members were once more permitted to serve on the various executive and legislative councils.

Early in March 1955 the government announced that Nomination Day for the first-ever Federal Elections would be on Wednesday June 15th, and Polling Day on July 27th. This early warning was welcomed by all parties, for it gave them plenty of time to prepare their campaigns. Abdul Razak was invited by the Alliance, which by then also included the Malayan Indian Congress, to contest the Semantan constituency of his home state of Pahang; and so, as he was a government official, in order to do so he had to seek permission to retire on pension.

Chapter Eight
Minister of Education

Although to Abdul Razak and the other leaders of UMNO the concept of a multi-racial Alliance seemed to hold the greatest promise for future political stability, the presence of their Chinese and Indian partners proved to be more of an embarrassment than a help in the country's first general election. This was because Malays formed nearly eighty-five per cent. of the one and a quarter million persons then eligible to vote, while non-Malays made up a majority of electors in only two of the fifty-two constituencies to be contested. Despite these known statistics, however, the more chauvinistic elements in both the MCA and the MIC were adamant in demanding the selection of many more candidates from their communal organisations than their electoral strength warranted, which left to UMNO the difficult task of persuading large numbers of Malays not only to support Alliance policies, but also, in some constituencies, perhaps to vote for non-Muslim Chinese or Indian candidates in preference to members of their own race standing for other parties.

This put a considerable strain upon the somewhat tenuous coalition, for an influential pressure group within UMNO, taking a rather short-sighted view of the situation, wished the party either to go it alone, or at least to field Malays in all but two or three of the constituencies. The party's leaders, who were better able to appreciate the long-term benefits of the coalition however, pointed out that if all of the non-Malays who were eligible to do so had registered as voters, they would have formed at least one fifth of the total electorate; and even more important, as nearly three-quarters of those Chinese and Indians who were already Federal citizens were below voting age,[1] the strength of both communities would inevitably be far greater in any future election.

Eventually, they won over their more conservative compatriots to their way of thinking and the MCA, representing at best a Chinese community that accounted for 11 per cent. of the total electorate, was offered the chance to fight ten seats against the six to which its likely contribution toward success might more nearly have entitled it; while the MIC, as in no constituency did Indians form more than 15 per cent. of the total voters,[2] was allocated none. On second thoughts, however, it was realised that the greatest threat to an UMNO victory was that these two parties might combine with Party Negara, Dato Onn's latest political venture, to form an alternative multi-racial coalition. Finally, therefore, it was agreed that the MCA should contest fifteen constituencies and the MIC two.

Except for the Alliance which was fighting every constituency, only Party Negara and its ally the National Association of Perak, which together were fielding thirty nine candidates, had any hope of winning a majority of the seats being contested. Party Negara had been launched in 1964 after Dato Onn, finding himself deserted by the Chinese, had abandoned his multi-racial Independence of Malaya Party and returned to communalism. His new party, although nominally also non-communal, was in fact almost totally Malay orientated, for it was his intention that it should eventually replace UMNO in the Alliance. He therefore based his election manifesto and appeal to the voters mainly upon independence by 1960 and the use of Malay as the sole official language of the country.

The Alliance was able to better this, however, for its own manifesto promised to fight for independence by 1959 and quickly to end the Communist-inspired insurrection that was disrupting the life of the country and delaying its economic advancement. This document also gave notice of a feature with which Abdul Razak was particularly associated, the party's intention to introduce a new and comprehensive education policy that, while it would make Malay, which was to be the sole national language, a compulsory subject in all government schools, would nevertheless still permit those parents who wished to do so to have the greater part of their children's education conducted in the language of their own choice. This support for the language upon which their livelihood depended, successfully won over the bulk of the ordinary Malay schoolteachers — who had tended in their frustration vociferously to support other, more militantly nationalistic political parties — while the concession on other teaching media reduced the opposition of many moderate Chinese and Indians. In order to show the village people that they too had not been forgotten, plans for large-scale governmental spending on rural development were announced; while the votes of civil servants were sought through promises of the rapid Malayanisation of national, state and quasi-government services.

One other party that caused some concern to UMNO was the Pan-Malayan Islamic Party (PMIP) which, because of its strong religious associations, was influential in the rural areas. This party, which campaigned mainly in the northern states, played upon the fears of the economically under-privileged Malay communities in those areas that exploitation, particularly by the Chinese, would increase after the British had left; and tried also to persuade them that it was contrary to the teachings of their religion to cooperate politically with non-Muslims, as UMNO was then doing. These were the tactics which Abdul Razak had to combat in his own constituency of Semantan, which covered roughly one third of his home state of Pahang.

ELECTED MEMBER

One of the disadvantages of having to campaign in Semantan was that a very large part of the constituency was still covered with jungle, the depths of which provided a safe refuge from where units of the 10th (Malay) Regiment of the communist guerilla army made occasional sorties. The majority of these men were not, in fact, real communists, but rather disgruntled local boys opposed to the Colonial Administration because they felt that under it their race was being deliberately impoverished and deprived of its birthright for the benefit of others. They were not alone in this view and so enjoyed such widespread support, or at least tolerance, in the surrounding countryside, that they were able frequently to visit their families and friends with little fear of being betrayed to the security forces.

As Abdul Razak moved around that area electioneering, he knew that sometimes there must have been armed guerillas included among his audience, listening to what he had to say about the amnesty that the Alliance proposed to offer them were it returned to power. This did not make for easy speaking. After the election was over, when he was working to get these Malays out of the jungle and back into their villages, one of them told him: 'we could have shot you many times, but we felt it was just possible that you meant what you were saying and one day would try to help us'. Starting in 1960, when he became Minister of National and Rural Development, Abdul Razak was to repay that forbearance.

There were at that time 20,004 registered voters in the Semantan constituency, of whom 17,944 were Malays, 1938 Chinese, 113 Indians and the remaining 9 of other racial origins;[3] and Abdul Razak, travelling out of Temerloh, his campaign headquarters, by boat and train, for there were few motor-roads, visited as many of them as he possibly could. The result, when declared, was impressive:

Dato Abdul Razak bin Hussein (Alliance)	14,094
Mohommed Yassin bin Mohommed Salleh (PMIP)	1,999
majority	12,095

Seven out of every eight of the eighty-two and a half per cent. of the registered electors who voted, chose Abdul Razak. His PMIP opponent, on the other hand, lost his deposit.

ALLIANCE VICTORY

For the Alliance this election was an outstanding success, for it won 51 out of the 52 seats it contested, losing only Krian in Perak to the PMIP, and that by only 450 votes. Furthermore, its candidates received more than eighty per cent. of the total votes cast; and in every constituency in which they were successful obtained more than twice the number of votes given to those opposing them.[4] This election also brought about a further step in the emancipation of Malay women, for when Cik Halimanton binte Abdul Majid, the wife of a District Officer, won the Ulu Selangor seat for the Alliance, she became the first woman ever to serve Malaya in the Legislative Council.

The most important aspect of the Alliance victory was undoubtedly the revelation that despite their sometimes dangerous preoccupation with questions of race, language, culture and religion, the different communities in Malaya could be persuaded to cooperate politically. As the High Commissioner put it on August 31st in his official address at the opening of the first session of the new Legislative Council[5], 'in an electorate which was 84 per cent. Malay, there being only two constituencies in which the Malay electors were outnumbered by non-Malays, seventeen non-Malays were returned to elected seats. This is a very happy augury for the future, and surely a sign that a united Malayan nation is not the idle dream that some may think it to be.'

It was a sign too that full internal self-government followed by absolute independence could not long be delayed, for one of the two remaining excuses for withholding this, the inability of Malayans to unite in order to govern themselves, had been shown to have no substance. This left only the communist-inspired insurrection to be overcome; and as the party behind the newly elected government had already pledged itself to offer the insurgents an amnesty, it seemed likely that even this last impediment would soon be removed. It was with a feeling of great optimism therefore that the Alliance prepared to take office, for its leaders had yet to learn that the Malayan Communist Party was as bitterly opposed to what it considered a right-wing local government as it had been toward the occupying colonial power.

*****   *****   *****

The Alliance Government, with Tunku Abdul Rahman at its head, consisted of ten Ministers, of whom six were Malays, three Chinese and one an Indian. Abdul Razak held the appointment of Minister of Education; and at thirty-three was the youngest member of the Cabinet. He had been given this post, which was certain to prove a 'hot seat' subject to attack from every community, because he had already begun to emerge as the party's chief trouble-shooter. For the same reason he was also appointed to be Parliamentary Chief Whip, a post that demands a strict disciplinarian who nevertheless has a reputation among members for impartiality and who is able to keep his temper under provocation.

SUBVERSION IN THE SCHOOLS

The most immediate task that Abdul Razak had to tackle upon taking over responsibility for the Department of Education, was the problem of subversion in Chinese schools. Many of these had for several years been heavily infiltrated by members of the Malayan Communist Party, or their fellow-travellers, who had then used gullible students in the dissemination of their political propaganda. Such communist infiltrators had been far more successful in promoting subversive activities in Singapore than in the Federation of Malaya, however, for there students, particularly those from Chinese secondary schools, had played an active role in fermenting industrial unrest, strikes and riots.

When, therefore, Abdul Razak learned from the Special Branch of the Malayan Police that many of the large number of Chinese children intending to visit Singapore during the school holidays were believed to have as their primary objective contact with extremist student political elements in the Crown Colony, he instructed the Director of Education to issue a strong warning to the managers of Chinese schools throughout the Federation. The directive that was duly circulated concluded with the caution that,

> if it should later appear to the Government that acts of indiscipline or other conduct improper to school pupils result from these visits, then the Government will be forced to take drastic action ... and would like to issue this warning to Managers that they must either take every precaution to avoid the contamination of their pupils by undesirable elements or, if they are unable to ensure this proper control, to discourage these visits which may well lead to undesirable manifestations in the schools under their control.[6]

Whether caused by contact with political forces in Singapore or not, such an undesirable manifestation occurred in the following year at Penang when students at a Chinese High School, the headmaster of which had been murdered by left-wing extremists some three and a half years earlier, attempted to subvert the authority of the managers and staff, on the pretext of protesting against the recent expulsion of two pupils and the suspension of a school magazine. The dissidents, abetted by boys from other local Chinese schools, assaulted and abused teachers, sang pro-communist songs, chanted revolutionary slogans, and finally barricaded the main building and took other measures for defence as soon as the police were called in to subdue them.

When Abdul Razak arrived in Penang by air from the Federal Capital, he found that pupils from other schools, who wished to take no part in this political demonstration, but had merely been sitting examinations in the main hall, were being detained against their will;

and that parents were being forcibly restrained from removing their sons from the school premises. He therefore instructed the police to inform the dissidents that the school had been closed under the Emergency Regulations and then to order them to disperse. When it became obvious that the ringleaders intended to continue their defiance even in the face of a direct government order, the police cleared the school by the use of tear gas, but made no arrests.

THE RAZAK REPORT ON EDUCATION

Later, Abdul Razak personally assured delegates attending the annual conference of the National Union of Teachers that they need not fear that such disciplinary measures in any way presaged an attack on the Chinese school system as a whole, for he conceived it be a most important part of his duties, he said, to 'explore the needs and aspirations of the people of the various races in the country and to formulate an educational policy which will be acceptable to all .....'[7]. In order to achieve this purpose he had, only a month after his appointment as Minister of Education, set up a Committee which consisted of fifteen of his fellow members of the Federal Legislative Council, with himself as Chairman. Its main terms of reference were: 'to examine the present education policy ... and to recommend any alterations or adaptions that are necessary with a view to establishing a national system of education acceptable to the people of the Federation as a whole; which will satisfy their needs and promote their cultural, social, economic and political development as a nation; having regard to the intention to make Malay the national language of the country, whilst preserving and sustaining the growth of the languages and cultures of other communities living in the country'.[8]

This Committee, which held its first meeting at the end of September 1955, decided to invite every association and individual in any way connected with education to submit suggestions to aid it in its investigations; and also formed sub-committees to examine and compare the educational systems then operative in the Philippines, India, Ceylon, Burma, Indonesia and Hong Kong.[9] Its recommendations, which became known generally as *The Razak Report,* were published at the beginning of May 1956 and presented by Abdul Razak for acceptance by the Federal Legislative Council a fortnight later.[10]

Abdul Razak began his speech, the most important so far in his Parliamentary career, by tracing the history of education in the Peninsula from the foundation of the first English-language school in 1816 in the British Settlement of Penang. Thereafter, he told the Council, English remained the sole medium of instruction in government sponsored schools until the 1860's when a start was made in providing elementary tuition for a few Malays in their own language. The early Chinese, Indian and Arabic schools, the latter teaching mainly subjects connected with the Islamic religion, were private ventures the media of instruction at which were usually the dialects of founding philanthropists or of clan associations. This diversification and communal fragmentation inevitably led to a complex pattern in which schools with no common syllabus, varying standards of efficiency, and with teaching carried on in a multiplicity of languages and dialects, had unwittingly helped to forge communal insularity, economic inequalities, and racial animosities.

He then turned to the recommendations of his own Committee and its suggestions for solving the main issue that had confronted it, the eventual introduction of an integrated national system of education, based upon a common syllabus and predicated upon the modern needs of a multi-racial society. He and his colleagues felt, he told the House, that the first move should be to establish two broad categories of primary school: Standard Primary Schools with the national language, Malay, as the medium of instruction; and Standard-type Primary Schools in which the chief teaching medium would be the Chinese national language, *Kuo Yu,* or Tamil, or English. In the Standard Primary Schools, English would be a compulsory subject and Chinese or Tamil taught if there were fifteen or more children among the students whose parents wished them to learn one or more of those languages. Malay and English would be compulsory subjects in all Standard-type Primary Schools, no matter what the principal language of instruction was.

The Committee, he made clear, also wished to establish national-type secondary schools in which all pupils would follow a common syllabus that was orientated toward life as it existed in Malaya and designed to equip them to sit standard final examinations. Malay and English would be compulsory subjects, but it was hoped that sufficient flexibility could be incorporated into the system so that other languages might be used whenever considered desirable. At the same time, the authorities also proposed to introduce a new Federation of Malaya Lower Certificate of Education to be sat for on the completion of three years in these secondary schools and a National Certificate of Education to be taken at the end of the secondary course.

Abdul Razak next brought up one of the potentially most controversial subjects he had until then had to deal with, the establishment of secondary schools teaching their entire curricula in the national language, Malay. The truth of the matter was that there were at that time far too few schoolteachers suitably qualified to staff such schools even if they had existed; but the available teachers steadfastly refused to face this unpalatable fact and instead continued their powerful political lobby to force the issue through. The best that Abdul Razak could offer them, however, was a firm promise that such schools would be established as soon as practicable.

In an effort further to placate Malay public opinion he then went on to outline his plans for the provision of religious instruction in the new schools. If there were more than fifteen Muslim pupils in any school, he declared, instruction in Islamic subjects would be taught them at government expense. These same schools might also, if they chose to do so, offer similar facilities to students belonging to other religions, but in this case the expense of such a service would have to be met from sources other than public funds. Although he did not at the time raise the question, Abdul Razak was already working upon a further controversial issue connected with religion, the modernisation of the syllabus followed in Islamic schools. Having himself been brought up in a village where half of his early education had been in subjects connected with the Muslim religion, he realised only too well the difficulties faced by such pupils in later obtaining employment in a modern, mundane society. At the same time, as a politician, he had to take into consideration the feelings of traditionalist parents and, particularly, those teachers whose livelihood came from such schools and who often wielded considerable power in rural areas where they were also local religious leaders.

Finally, he dealt with a subject of great importance to a developing nation, technical education. This was to be promoted at three levels: first, by the establishment of trade schools for pupils who had completed a full primary school course; second, through the media of technical institutes specifically designed for students who had completed a minimum of three years of secondary education; and, thirdly, in technical colleges which would provide courses suitable for those who had successfully completed a full secondary education.

Abdul Razak ended his address with a plea for unity and tolerance, something that experience had taught him his Report was, in the circumstances, hardly likely to receive.

> As I have said ...., [he wound up], it is not anticipated that a Report on such a controversial and delicate subject as education will please everyone. But this Report was formulated by fifteen Members of this Council of all communities who unanimously endorsed the recommendations without reservation. It was in a spirit of give and take and sense of duty to this country as a whole that Members of the Committee were able to reach complete agreement ....
>
> .... this country is undergoing a period of ... transition. Political freedom and full nationhood are just around the corner. Therefore, as Malaya enters this .... new period in her history, let us give our children ideals and loyalties to which they can stretch their hands and which can promise them a happy and contended future ....

STORMY PASSAGE

After debating this Bill with great vigour for several hours, the Chamber passed it without dissent; although the MCA members present must have feared that certain parts of it, especially those connected with the national language and the general move away from China-orientated subjects, would generate considerable anger and opposition within their own community. Nor were their fears groundless, for almost immediately a bitter attack was launched on the Report by both the United Chinese School Teachers' Association and the All-Malaya Chinese Schools Management Association,[11] who were soon joined by several other militant communal organisations. So violent did this opposition in fact become, that the MCA, although it had already agreed to support a pro-Malay education policy in return for a less stringent UMNO policy on citizenship for non-Malays,[12] was forced to backpedal sharply and indulge in a little histrionic horse-trading with the senior partner of the Alliance until it eventually won the useless but face-saving concession that the basic structure on which the future education system was to be built would be reviewed after the 1959 general elections.

Another section of the Report that came under heavy fire, especially in Chinese schools, was that relating to age limits for students. Because of the interruption to normal education during the Japanese military occupation of the country, over-age students had been accepted in most schools; but this, eleven years after the cessation of hostilities, Abdul Razak proposed to abolish. This was in order to alleviate the acute shortage of school places brought about by a rapidly expanding population. Although not specially introduced to counter their activities, this measure was nevertheless a severe blow to the communists, who had become adept at infiltrating Chinese schools with their fellow-travellers masquerading as students.[13]

Opposition to the education policy was by no means confined to the Chinese community, however, for a powerful Malay language lobby, spearheaded by schoolteachers and backed by sections of the vernacular press, deplored what they called 'the statutory recognition of English and other languages'[14] aimed at devaluing the worth of a Malay education. The indignation of the bulk of the former subsided to some extent as soon as they began to realize the opportunities that would automatically be open to them when every non-Malay-language school needed at least one teacher to instruct in the national language.

TOWARDS INDEPENDENCE

Important as these internal problems were, however, during the latter part of 1955 they became overshadowed by the far greater issue of the possibility of the nation quickly attaining its independence from

Britain. Even while the Razak Report was in course of preparation, Abdul Razak was making arrangements to join other members of the Alliance government and representatives of the Malay Rulers in a mission to London, to begin preliminary negotiations on the terms of agreement.

Chapter Nine
Independence

As progress towards independence gathered momentum, the Malay Rulers, who had at first embraced the movement with enthusiasm, began to have serious second thoughts. The fate of their Indian counterparts had been a severe shock to all the remaining royal families holding office in dependent territories; for it had shown them what their likely end might well be as soon as their colonial backers had been replaced by popular governments of their own people. This led to an escalating estrangement between the UMNO leadership on the one hand, and the Princes and their traditionalist aristocratic advisers on the other, which in the second half of 1955 ended in direct confrontation, fortunately soon followed by compromise and agreement.

The detonator that set off this political explosion was activated on September 17th, 1955, by the octogenarian Sultan Ibrahim of Johore who, in a Diamond Jubilee speech, called indirectly but unmistakably for a continuation of British rule. This led UMNO leaders to fear that other Sultans, seeking to protect the continuity of their dynasties, might provide the colonial government with an excuse to maintain military and economic control over the country by direct invitation of the Rulers of individual States. Reacting quickly to this perhaps not very real threat, for the British had long before turned resolutely away from imperialism, the Alliance government pledged itself, in return for outright royal support for rapid advancement toward self-government and independence, to protect the Princes' rights and privileges by including them in the country's new Constitution. The Sultans, who had been left in no doubt that failure to accept this offer could only strengthen the hand of those radical elements among their subjects who advocated a Federal Republic, capitulated gracefully.

Right at the end of August 1955, just after the Alliance government had taken office, an official visit to Malaya by Alan Lennox Boyd, Secretary of State for the Colonies in Anthony Eden's British Conservative government, had afforded an ideal opportunity for a direct request for immediate top-level discussions on further moves towards the handing over of power. This approach was successful, for later in the year the British government agreed to meet two delegations, one to be appointed by the elected Malayan government and the other by the Malay Rulers, at a Conference to be held in London in January 1956.

LANCASTER HOUSE

Tunku Abdul Rahman personally headed the Alliance delegation, which consisted of Abdul Razak, by then already widely recognised as the Chief Minister's eventual successor; Dr Ismail bin Abdul Rahman, the Minister for Natural Resources; and Colonel H.S. Lee, the Minister of Transport and an important figure in the policy-making hierarchy of the Malayan Chinese Association. The Rulers were represented by the Chief Ministers of the States of Perak and Selangor and the Deputy Chief Minister of Johore, together with a former Chief Minister of Kelantan, the legally qualified Dato Nik Kamil, who was also to act as adviser on matters affecting the Treaties still in existence between the individual Sultans and the British Crown. These negotiators were accompanied by the then Secretary-General of the Alliance, Mr T.H. Tan, who was to act as secretary to the first delegation; and by Abdul Kadir Samsuddin*, who was to perform the same office for the representatives of the Rulers.

On New Year's Day the ten of them sailed from Singapore in an ordinary passenger liner *en route* for Karachi, from where they were scheduled to fly to London. This sea trip had been included for the sole purpose of providing the members of the two groups with ample time, in pleasant and relaxed circumstances, to sort out their differences; so that when in London they could operate from a position of greater strength by presenting their demands from a united people. By the time that the ship berthed at Karachi, they had tentatively reached agreement on nearly everything; and so had become more nearly one unified party than two separate delegations. Nor was their optimism lessened upon arrival at London Airport, for while walking through the reception lounge with Sir John Martin, the Permanent Under-Secretary to the Colonial Office who had met them, he replied to Abdul Razak's casual, 'Are you going to make things difficult for us?' — by saying: 'No, we are going to give it to you on a golden platter'. Unfortunately this chance exchange was overheard and later reported in the Malayan press. It became a verbal brickbat with which the opposition parties were, for some years, occasionally to pelt the Alliance.

Once settled in the British capital, the Malayan party found that David Rees Williams, a Labour Member of Parliament who had accepted an invitation to advise them on constitutional matters,[1] had already made all the necessary arrangements and contacts on their behalf and organised a political lobby in their support. The series of talks that were to decide the future of Malaya opened on January 18th in Lancaster House, with the Colonial Secretary himself in the chair. They were held in an atmosphere of great cordiality, mainly because Alan

---

*now Tan Sri Abdul Kadir Samsuddin P.S.M., J.M.N., Chief Secretary to the Government.

Independence

Lennox Boyd made it clear from the very beginning that he was there to reach an amicable agreement, not to procrastinate. The negotiations for the transfer of power, including control of Malaya's finances, economic affairs and internal security, were concluded without much difficulty; and as an added act of good faith, the Colonial Secretary also agreed to withdraw all British Advisers to the various Sultans, some of whom were suspected by the Alliance leaders of working covertly to oppose independence, and make provision for their duties to be taken over by the elected government. With these concessions in hand, the Malayans readily agreed that for a trial period, while they were gaining experience in government, responsibility for foreign affairs and defence against agression from outside the country should remain the prerogative of the colonial High Commissioner.

One brief period of disenchantment did occur, however, when the delegation demanded a set and unalterable date for the granting of complete independence. This the Colonial Secretary declined to give, basing his refusal on two continuing current dangers to internal stability, the communist-inspired insurrection and the ever-present possibility of a renewal of inter-communal strife. The delegates, while agreeing that a British military presence would be essential for some time if the communist guerillas were ever to be defeated, nevertheless pointed out that if the ordinary Asian people were to be won back from extremism they, who had been elected as a multi-racial political coalition and so could justly claim to be representatives of all communities living in the country, were in a far better position to resolve such problems than the British. Despite the weight of their arguments, this particular meeting ended in deadlock; but negotiations continued at an unofficial level until, on February 8th, it was agreed that Malaya should become completely independent on August 31st, 1957; two years earlier than had been promised in the Alliance election manifesto.

TRIUMPHAL RETURN

A week later Tunku Abdul Rahman, Abdul Razak and the other delegates left London by air for Malaya where, news of their success having preceded them, they were assured of an enthusiastic reception. They took the opportunity to break their journey in Cairo in order to confer briefly with the Egyptian nationalist leader Colonel Nasser, who was then an heroic figure among anti-colonialists, and to accept his congratulations; and then flew on to Singapore where, following a welcome night's rest, they took an internal flight to Malacca where a huge crowd, the greater part of which had spent the previous night sleeping in the open air, was waiting to cheer them. This particular venue was an appropriate choice for the public announcement of the date of independence, because it was on the site of this town that, nearly four and a half centuries earlier, the first fortified European colony had been established in the Peninsula. It was a great moment for Tunku Abdul Rahman as he was acclaimed by the crowd as the architect of independence, and Abdul Razak, who throughout the entire series of talks had deliberately maintained a low profile in relation to his chief, was happy to help applaud him.

In April, when full internal self-government brought the allocating of even more prestigious political positions within the power of the Alliance government, Abdul Razak was content to remain as Minister of Education; while Colonel H.S. Lee took the key post of Minister of Finance; Commerce and Industry went to Dr Ismail; and Tunku Abdul Rahman himself took on the added responsibility of internal security.

THE REID COMMISSION

Some time before travelling to London for the Conference, the Alliance leaders had decided that the country would be better served if the Constitution to be adopted at independence were formulated by a Commission of outside experts not subject to the same communal stresses and pressures as Malayans would inevitably be. Abdul Razak was therefore elected Chairman of a Committee formed to work out the full details of this proposal; and was later responsible for presenting them for discussion during the talks at Lancaster House. After this plan had been approved, nominations for membership were invited from several already independent Commonwealth countries; and from the names submitted, Lord Reid, a legal peer, was selected as Chairman; with Sir Ivor Jennings, Master of Trinity Hall, Cambridge; Sir William McKell, a former Governor-General of Australia; and Justices B. Malik and Abdul Hamid, from India and Pakistan respectively, to assist him.[2]

The greatest problem facing this Commission was to include measures for forging a common Malayan nationality from a number of separate communities dissimilar in culture, language and religion. Difficulty arose chiefly through the demands put forward by the Malays that certain safeguards for their race should be written into the Constitution; privileges which the other communities held to be excessive. These rights were, the Malay leaders claimed, designed solely to shield them from economic exploitation by the richer and more sophisticated immigrant races; and to protect their religion, language and culture, which was that of the indigenous people. Among other things, they required that certain areas of land should be held by Malays only; that a quota of jobs in the public services, and especially the armed forces and the police, should be reserved for them; that they should receive precedence in the issue of some licenses, for example in commercial ventures connected with the transportation of goods and passengers; and also that they be given many more scholarships and greater finan-

Independence

cial aid for education generally. There was also the position of the Sultans to entrench; and the protection of the legislative and executive powers of their various participating States vis-a-vis a necessarily strong Federal government.

Nor were the non-Malays backward in pushing the claims of their communities, for they saw in this Commission, which held public sessions in every State of the Federation, an opportunity to win back the inalienable rights of citizenship which they had been promised after the defeat of Japan and which, they felt, had been denied them through the weakness of the colonial authorities in the face of rampant Malay nationalism. For a time this issue of citizenship caused a substantial part of the membership of the Malayan Chinese Association to advocate a break with the Alliance, for many of the more aggressive leaders felt that appeasement of UMNO had already gone too far. In the end, however, moderation prevailed and the three partners to the coalition were able to submit a single set of proposals for the new Constitution, although as a concession to their members' feelings, both the MCA and the MIC were permitted to express to the Commission their wish for a more liberal citizenship policy. Abdul Razak, who on behalf of the government was responsible for ensuring cooperation with the Commission, found Lord Reid very easy to get on with, although his wife was a very different proposition. She was so fussy about the accommodation provided for her, that she soon had Federal House so well furnished and confortable that when the aristocratic couple departed, Abdul Razak and his family moved in.

CONSTITUTIONAL WORKING COMMITTEE

As soon as the recommendations of the Reid Commission were made available, the High Commissioner set up a Working Committee, with himself as Chairman, and the Chief Secretary to the Government, the Attorney-General, Abdul Razak and three other members of the ruling Alliance, plus four representatives nominated by the Rulers, as members, to prepare a draft formula for the consideration of the British government. In its final form this draft, which was eventually accepted by both main parties to the independence agreement, provided a compromise solution generally beneficial to all communities living in the Federation, in that, while including many of the privileges that the Malays had demanded and preserving the position of the Sultans, it had also made easier the acquisition of Federal citizenship by members of the other races. As had been expected, Malay was designated the sole national and official language, although as a further concession to the wishes of the other communities, it was written in that English might continue in official use for a further ten years.

The draft also included the provisions necessary for transforming Malaya into a Constitutional Monarchy; and for the establishment of a bicameral Parliament. The problem of adequately protecting the rights of the individual Sultans had been overcome by the adoption of an ingenious scheme whereby the nine Rulers, in conference, were every five years to elect one of their number to serve as Head of State, or Paramount Ruler (*Yang di-Pertuan Agung*). Parliament, which was to be based largely upon the Westminster model, was to consist of a wholly elected Lower House; and an Upper Chamber, to be called the Senate, the members of which were to be nominated, some by the individual participating States and some by the Head of State acting on the advice of his Prime Minister. As by that time it was already too late to prepare new electoral rolls in time for late 1957, elections for both the Federal Parliament and the various State Legislatures were postponed until 1959.[3]

As the date upon which Malaya would officially be freed from colonial rule approached, Abdul Razak was appointed to head two important Committees: the first to plan and supervise the preparation of the Merdeka (Independence) Stadium, where the actual hand-over of power was to take place; and the second to organise the nation-wide celebrations that were to follow.

INDEPENDENCE — AUGUST 31st, 1957

On the evening preceding Independence Day, many thousands of Malayans of all racial origins assembled in the heart of Kuala Lumpur, on the playing fields in front of the Selangor State Secretariat, to await the flag raising ceremony that was due to take place during the first few minutes of August 31st. A little before midnight Tunku Abdul Rahman, Abdul Razak, V.T. Sambanthan and Tan Cheng Lock, representing the three organisation comprising the Alliance government, took their places on a raised dais facing two flagpoles, one of which bore a flag, the Union Jack. As the twelfth stroke of midnight sounded from the clocktower on the State Secretariat building, the Union Jack was slowly lowered; and at the same time, on the other pole, the flag of the Federation of Malaya was hoisted. Although the British still remained in Singapore the rest of the Peninsula was, from that moment and for the first time since 1511, free of colonial domination. It had all been done in a very gentlemanly fashion, far too much so for some of the more radical Malays who, with the example of Indonesia in their minds, felt that independence was of little value unless it had been fought for. What had been taken from them by force, should be recovered by force. But the great majority of Malayans wanted no part of unnecessary violence, and were sufficiently happy with what their leaders had won for them.

Independence

When, after enjoying little more than four hours sleep, Abdul Razak awoke later that same morning, he found that it was pouring with rain; which meant that he had quickly to decide whether or not the formal ceremony marking the surrender of suzerainty, that was due shortly to be enacted at the newly opened Merdeka Stadium, should take place. On arrival at the Stadium, he found that Sir Gerald Templer, a former High Commissioner of the Federation who had been specially invited for the occasion, had reached there before him. Sir Gerald, never a placid man, then became so agitated at the prospect of a cancellation, that Abdul Razak thought it best to calm him with a stiff whisky and a firm promise that the postponement he was about the order would be for only one hour. Fortunately the rain soon stopped and the ceremony was able to proceed as planned.

Assembled on a huge dais raised in the centre of the Merdeka Stadium, were nine sovereign Malay Princes; one of them, the Ruler of Negri Sembilan, recently elected as Malaya's first king; the Duke of Gloucester, who was representing Britain's Queen Elizabeth; Tunku Abdul Rahman and Sir Donald MacGillivray, the retiring High Commissioner. The British royal duke formally handed over the constitutional documents of the transfer of sovereignty to the Malay prince, Tunku Abdul Rahman; and another territory of the nearly defunct British Empire was eligible to apply for membership of the Commonwealth as a free and equal partner.

THE COMMUNIST REBELLION

Shortly after independence Tunku Abdul Rahman, who had automatically become the new nation's first Prime Minister, re-organized his government. Abdul Razak was appointed Deputy Prime Minister and also given the key portfolios of Defence and Internal Security. His inclination was rather to accept responsibility for national and rural development, for there was an ambitious Five-Year Economic Development Plan waiting to be implemented, but he realised that priority must instead be given to ending the Communist-inspired insurrection, so that scarce resources of money, manpower and expertise could, as soon as possible, be put to better use in advancing the country's social progress.

In 1948, when the Malayan Communist Party suddenly switched tactics from causing labour unrest and organising political subversion to assassination and outright guerilla warfare, the Colonial Authorities, though they had not lacked early warning, were nevertheless caught unprepared. Their police forces were undermanned and of low morale due to the stigma that remained of actions taken during the Japanese Occupation; while because of continuing large-scale demobilization of the British war-time army, the local garrison had been run down to a dangerously low level. Nor were the guerillas lacking in popular support, at least among the Chinese community, many of whom, either through fear of reprisals or because of a feeling that communism offered them better prospects for the future, helped them by providing food, shelter, intelligence and money and by disseminating political propaganda. By the early 1950's, however, when nearly half a million Chinese peasants and labourers had been resettled in restricted and protected New Villages; and the security forces, both military and civilian, had been heavily reinforced, the tide of battle inevitably began to turn in favour of the 'big battalions'.

Probably the greatest single turning point in this undeclared war occurred as the result of an ambush in which, on October 6th, 1951, Sir Henry Gurney, the then High Commissioner of the Federation, was killed when on his way to the Fraser's Hill holiday resort. Although it is extremely unlikely that the Communists knew whom they were ambushing, such a blow to British prestige could not be allowed to pass unchallenged; and so the dynamic and ruthlessly efficient General Sir Gerald Templer was sent out in his place. Sir Gerald, who not surprisingly was more skilled in military matters than in administering civilians, had as his deputy Sir Donald MacGillivray to assist and advise him; and between them, and in combination, they not only effectively employed the considerable force of arms available to them, but, with even more success, won the support and cooperation of the great majority of the local people. By 1954, when the High Commissioner's tour of duty ended, large areas of the more developed and heavily populated parts of the country had already been freed from terrorism, and the guerillas forced to retreat into the inhospitable depths of the densest jungles.

When the Alliance won the 1955 Legislative Council elections, it became obvious to the policy-makers of the Malayan Communist Party that independence could not be long delayed and that their best tactic for the future would be to negotiate with the new government a legal basis for their party, while keeping their strength intact until the British forces had been withdrawn. They asked for a truce; and in December Tunku Abdul Rahman, together with David Marshall, the Chief Minister of Singapore and Tan Cheng Lock the leader of the MCA, met with Chin Peng, the Party's Secretary-General, at Baling close to the border with Thailand. Negotiations proved abortive, however, for the Malayan and Singapore governments declined to recognise the legality of the Communist Party and Chin Peng refused to surrender on any other terms. So the truce ended and the struggle continued.

By the time independence was achieved, only two really bad areas of the country remained to be cleared of terrorists, although these were vast in extent and of considerable economic importance. They covered the greater part of the State of Johore and the whole of the western side of the Peninsula from north of Kuala Lumpur to the frontier with Thai-

Independence

land. This then was the situation when Abdul Razak took over as Minister of Defence. He quickly decided that the time for half measures was over and that, if necessary, the whole resources of the nation should be mobilized in a final effort to defeat the remaining insurgents.

In pursuance of this policy, a Proclamation was issued by the Paramount Ruler on June 1st, 1958, that required all male citizens of the Federation of Malaya who were within certain age groups to register for national service. Speaking in defence of this by no means universally popular measure during the course of an official broadcast over the State radio network, Abdul Razak said:[4]

> It must not be thought that the attainment of Merdeka last year was the end of our struggle; it was indeed only the opening stage ... (for) it is the duty and responsibility of all of us to see that the ideals for which we have struggled are maintained and jealously guarded ... Consequently, we consider it only prudent that registration of young men of the ages 17 to 28 should now take place in order that we may assess the reservoir of manpower on which we can draw in the event of a sudden emergency .... Citizenship carries with it responsibilities as well as privileges. It is the duty of all of us to answer the call of our country, to serve her and defend her with all of our might and if necessary with our lives ....

One of the worst areas of communist terrorism in the entire country was that of Yong Peng in Johore, especially the 'cowboy' town from which it took its name. This place had, on more than one occasion, been described by General Templer as 'that bloody village'. So when, in August 1958, that part of north Johore was at last declared free from terrorism and so a 'white area', Abdul Razak telegraphed to the former High Commissioner: 'I have declared your bloody village white'. Despite the end of active resistance there, Yong Peng remained unrepentent, for when Abdul Razak publicly made the announcement that ended the daily curfew, less than 100 people turned out to hear him. He told those that were there: 'although we are making this place 'white', it is not because of any help from you'.[5]

In the preceding month Abdul Razak had been able to promise the people living in the area between Kuala Lumpur and Ipoh that all of this territory would soon be declared 'white', due to a break-up of the communist forces formerly operating there, which had led to the surrender over the past few months of no less than 118 terrorists. The starting point of this substantial success had occurred on October 15th, 1957, when a European civilian, who was driving along the main road close to Tapah, was stopped by five uniformed terrorists who, instead of shooting him, asked him to take them to the nearest police station.[6] They later told the police that they, and others still in the jungle, wished to surrender. They also offered to assist in the elimination of those communists who were determined to carry on the fight. With these renegades to help them, the security forces succeeded, over a period of about seven months, in disposing of fourteen separate terrorist units, either by killing or capturing those serving in them. The guerillas who surrendered brought in with them a total of 180 weapons, 80 hand grenades and 18,000 rounds of ammunition.[7]

Despite continuing successes of this kind, the Alliance government decided that as there were still some 1300 terrorist operating from hideouts in the jungle, the Emergency Regulations would have to be extended for a further year. In a speech to this effect delivered in the Legislative Council during August, 1958, Abdul Razak said:[8]

> It would give me today the greatest satisfaction if I could say to the House that the Emergency Regulations are no longer required. There is nothing that this Government would like better than to see the State of Emergency ended so that the resources and energies of the country and the administration could be fully directed into constructive purposes for the prosperity of this country. However, armed terrorists are still at large and powers must be retained to enable the necessary ... measures to be taken to stamp them out once and for all.
>
> The remaining 1300 terrorists are mostly operating in Johore, in central and north Perak, in Kedah and in the Thai border areas ....

Abdul Razak then went on to say that he appreciated that Members might wonder why, as the communists had now been confined to a few specific areas, the whole country should still be covered by these, admittedly, unpopular Regulations. It was necessary, however, that the government should have immediately available the means of combating any sudden revival of terrorism or subversive activity in areas already declared 'white'. He reminded them that they were under attack not only from the actual terrorists who operated from hideouts in the jungle, but also by would-be assassins and saboteurs who sought to spread fear and disruption and by propagandists whose main objective was to turn one community against another.

Abdul Razak next produced a captured terrorist secret document,[9] dated June 1st, 1958, which showed that the Malayan Communist Party, having all but lost the shooting war, was preparing to infiltrate certain of the socialist political parties as the first step towards establishing a legal, but covertly communist dominated, left-wing coalition or united front. This paper, he told them, also listed the tactics to be followed in fighting the forthcoming elections, which basically were to form a combined opposition to defeat Alliance candidates and by the use of intimidation and gangs of rowdy schoolchildren to disrupt their meetings. The essence of this was contained in sections (b) and (c) which stated:[10]

The overall method is to make good use of the election campaign period to call upon the masses; ... and active elements of the public to carry out large-scale propaganda openly and constitutionally by using their legal status. Through the influence of the organised masses we approach their relatives and appeal to them to vote in favour of those candidates who are regarded by us as progressive elements. We may also use the students' defiance of the education policy and urge their guardians not to vote for the Alliance. When possible we may assemble ... the masses ... to take part in the propaganda campaign organised by the progressive parties' candidates and appeal to the public to cast a blank vote, or abandon their voting right, when in their constituency only Alliance candidates and none from other political parties are contesting the elections.

.... to boycott all election rallies organised by ... Alliance candidates or instigate the children and students to create disturbances and boo them .... Any sort of disturbance will serve the purpose ....

Such disruptive elements, Abdul Razak made clear, risked detention without trial under the Emergency Regulations; and their presence in the community was one of the main reasons why such safeguards, which in other circumstances might well be considered undemocratic, must be retained.

It has often been suggested, [said Abdul Razak] that persons should not be arrested and detained unless they can be tried in a court of law. This is, to my mind, to misunderstand the whole purpose of detention in times of emergency. A person is detained not because he has committed an offence but because there are reasonable grounds to suppose that if he is not detained he will be likely to assist the enemies of society and imperil the safety of the State. In an emergency situation it would clearly be most dangerous to allow a person of known subversive tendencies and associations to have unfettered freedom until such time as he happens to be found out in the committing of an offence.

Such a situation was deemed to have arisen on October 1st when, according to an Alliance government press release,[11] it had become necessary for the police to arrest more than a hundred people who had been actively, but clandestinely, assisting the efforts of the Malayan Communist Party. At the same time the Socialist Youth League had been declared an illegal organisation and some left-wing publications banned throughout the Federation. These actions caused a storm of protest and two days later Abdul Razak had to issue his own press statement in order to defend himself against an allegation made by the Chairman of the Labour Party that these arrests had been aimed not at preserving the State from subversion, but rather at crippling the socialist opposition at a time when every party was preparing to fight the forthcoming Parliamentary and State elections;[12] and another by the leader of the Peoples' Progressive Party that the arrests were aimed at so frightening people that a new and tougher Bill for the preservation of public order could be bulldozed through the Legislative assembly.

> These allegations have no basis, [Abdul Razak declared angrily] there is no truth in them at all. The police action against suspected subversive elements was carried out without any political motive. The arrests made were of people who are known to be supporting the cause of the Communist Party of Malaya .... The fact that some of the arrested persons were officials and members of political organisations is merely incidental. I would not hesitate to take similar action against any member of the Alliance Party if he were found to be involved in subversive activities.
> The government has given repeated warnings. It will not relax its vigilance against subversion in the Federation .... The jungle war against the Communist terrorists is easing, but the menace of subversion seems to be growing. The government has kept a close eye on these activities for some time, but it did not act until October 1st, to make sure that there was enough evidence for the arrests to be made .... We shall continue to take action until all subversive activities have been ended for good.

This exchange of accusations and counter-allegations, threats and counterthreats, may be considered as the opening barrage in what was to turn out to be an acrimonious and savagely-fought series of elections. From the very beginning it was obvious that the Alliance could expect much tougher opposition than it had encountered in 1955; and so in mid-1958, with plenty of time still in hand, the leaders of the coalition set up a special committee, with trouble-shooter Abdul Razak as its Chairman, to plan an electoral strategy common to all three participating organizations. He was later also appointed to head two other important committees: the first charged with the preparation of a single Alliance Manifesto; and the second, an UMNO only committee, to decide the tactics to be employed in each individual constituency that the party intended to contest.

Chapter Ten
The 1959 Elections

On April 16th, 1959, Abdul Razak temporarily took over from Tunku Abdul Rahman the position of Prime Minister of Malaya; and the next day had the pleasant duty of signing the Treaty of Friendship with Indonesia that he had sponsored during an official visit to that country the year before. As he was putting his signature to the document, Abdul Razak said to Dr Djuanda, the Indonesian Premier who was the other signatory, 'With the signing of this Treaty we have achieved a desire which has been in our hearts for a long time — to re-establish with our brothers in Indonesia the close relationship that was severed by Western colonialism'.[1]

TROUBLE WITHIN THE ALLIANCE

Abdul Razak's promotion had not occurred because the fifty six year-old Tunku showed the slightest inclination to retire, but was rather designed first to permit the older man to take a well-earned rest and then to leave him free of official duties so as to be able to devote the whole of his time and energy to preparing the Alliance for the forthcoming election campaign. The political pundits were quick to read into this move, however, a purely imaginary coup by the hard-liners of UMNO which, they claimed, was aimed at permanently replacing the liberal-minded Kedah Prince with the tougher and less flexible Abdul Razak, as a prelude to insisting on a more Malay-orientated Alliance policy. Such rumours and speculations did nothing at all to strengthen goodwill among the various parties to the coalition which, due to the divergent interests of the various communities represented, was already suffering a number of severe stresses and strains. In fact, as the crucial election period approached, there were many indications that the Alliance might collapse altogether.

The principal weakness was in the Malayan Chinese Association, a right-wing, business-orientated political organisation which, since its formation in 1949, had seldom really reflected the needs and aspirations of the bulk of ordinary members of the community it claimed to represent. Due to the existing citizenship laws, it was also, despite its superior financial and intellectual resources, electorally weak in comparison with UMNO which, to the chagrin of the majority of Chinese, completely dominated policy within the Alliance. In the 1955 elections the Malays had been calculatingly generous and the MCA, while representing at best 11 per cent. of the registered voters, had been able to secure fifteen out of the fifty one seats taken by the Alliance. It was feared, however, that the Malays' beneficence might not long continue.²

The Chinese responded to this threat, real or imagined, by electing younger and more dynamic and at the same time more communally inclined leaders to replace the older, conservative, moderates who for many years had controlled the MCA; until, in 1958, even Tan Cheng Lock, founder of the party and long-time personal friend and confidant of Tunku Abdul Rahman, Abdul Razak and other Malay leaders, was deposed by Dr Lim Chong Eu, who became the new President. With this change of leadership came also an abrupt switch of policy; the most controversial aspect of which was withdrawal of support from previously agreed areas of cooperation such as the working of the education policy earlier formulated by Abdul Razak and the recognition of Malay rights and privileges. Soon, too, the new MCA leaders sought to re-introduce the sensitive issue of Singapore's eventual incorporation into the Federation, a proposal that the Malays viewed with concern, particularly as the percentage of Chinese eligible to vote was steadily increasing towards the point when, if as a community they chose to cooperate with Indian political organisations, they could well pose a threat to Malay hegemony.

RIOTS AT PANGKOR

Less than three weeks after he had taken over the Premiership, Abdul Razak was faced with an outbreak of inter-communal rioting on the island of Pangkor, off the coast of Perak, which threatened to aggravate still further the tensions already evolving between UMNO and the MCA. For a long time Chinese and Malay criminal hooligans, employed as enforcers by the protection racketeers operating on the island, had been quarrelling over the allocation of gang territories. They chose to clash over the not very controversial issue that a Malay boy had fallen in love with and decided to court a Chinese girl; and because Sino-Malay antipathy always lurks dangerously just beneath the surface of tranquility, the resultant fist-fight threatened to escalate into a miniature civil war.

The ordinary islanders, unaware of the true origin and implications of the dispute but automatically assuming it to be an attack by one race on the other, involved themselves until a general, though at that stage unarmed, melée developed on communal lines. During the course of this completely unnecessary disturbance three Malays were injured and a considerable amount of property damaged. The Malays, who had had the worst of this first encounter, were forced to retreat; but soon returned with reinforcements who were armed with machetes and various other weapons. They were met by a force of similarly equipped Chinese and only the timely intervention of a strong force of armed police, who had been brought over from the mainland, averted serious bloodshed.

The next day the local Islamic religious leader called a number of the more influential Malays to the mosque to plan for the defence of their community. Soon, however, news of this meeting spread and the Chinese, feeling that it was inimical to their safety, armed themselves once again and advanced to within a few yards of the mosque's compound, where they remained passively watching events.[3] Being fearful that they were about to be attacked, several of the Malays slipped out through the rear of the building to fetch knives and machetes from nearby houses. Soon after their return with these weapons, these would-be warriors, together with reinforcements from the village who had secretly entered the mosque with them, rushed out and assaulted the Chinese, driving them away after a short but lively engagement. Thoroughly aroused by this successful skirmish, the Malays then set fire to a Clan Association building and a number of Chinese houses in the vicinity of the mosque[4]. This provoked a spirited counter-attack, in the course of which one Malay was killed and five more injured and one Chinese killed and two injured. The trouble then rapidly spread around the island, with both sides attacking indiscriminately people of the opposite community, injuring them and destroying their property.

News of this fighting caused considerable inter-racial tension on the Perak mainland, and only the arrival of the Prime Minister in person headed off a series of bloody riots. Two hundred extra armed policemen, including members of a specialist Federal riot squad, were immediately sent over to Pangkor; where Abdul Razak, who had accompanied them, undertook a tour that covered almost every habitation on the island, addressing members of both communities, appealing for calm and tolerance, and explaining to them how they had been duped into fighting each other when there was absolutely no reason to do so. In order to give the people time to cool down and at the same time keep them apart, he then imposed a dusk to dawn curfew; and within a couple of days the island had returned to its normal peaceful state.[5]

THE 1959 STATE ELECTIONS

A little over two weeks after this well publicised inter-communal conflict had ended, elections for the first two of the eleven State Legislatures had to be fought. Fortunately, the remaining electoral contests were spread over the next five weeks, thereby giving time for racial and religious hatreds to die down. Nevertheless, whether sparked off by this or for some other reason, large numbers of voters transferred their political allegiance to organisations primarily supporting the advancement of their own particular communities: the Malays turning to the ultra-religious Pan-Malayan Islamic Party and former supporters of the MCA and the MIC deserting them for the predominantly non-Malay Socialist Front and the Peoples Progressive Party. When all the State election results had been declared the Alliance, although it had won nearly three-quarters of the seats contested, 207 out of 282, had secured little more than 55 per cent. of the total votes cast; and would have won far fewer seats had the opposition parties presented a united front.

In Kelantan, where the PMIP and Dato Onn's Party Negara had been in a good position to exploit UMNO's weakness of being in alliance with the Chinese, the ruling party had done very badly, winning only two out of the thirty seats available and so losing control of the State government. This was a bitter defeat which Abdul Razak was, at the post-mortem that inevitably followed the elections, to lay at the door of haughty and ill-mannered local party officials who had lost touch with reality and their peasant origins. Trengganu, too, was a disaster, for there the Alliance won only seven seats against thirteen for the PIMP and four for Party Negara.

While Abdul Razak and the UMNO leadership saw this political reverse as the direct result of too openly appeasing the other communities at the expense of their own, there were many in the MCA and the MIC who feared that it presaged an upsurge of belligerent and uncompromising Malay nationalism — a feeling that was strengthened by the tougher attitude adopted by the senior partner to the allocation to the Chinese and Indian organisations of constituencies to be fought in the forthcoming Parliamentary elections. The more extreme among UMNO members, on the other hand, after pointing out that in far too many of the State constituencies the Chinese and Indians seemed to have preferred the Socialist Front and the Peoples Progressive Party to the MCA and the MIC, argued that UMNO would stand a better chance of winning at Federal level either by going it alone or as part of a new coalition of Malay-only parties.

It was at this point that Abdul Razak, who felt that it would be a mistake to prejudice his own position for the future by appearing to side too openly with other communities, called in Tunku Abdul Rahman, whose views on the value of maintaining the coalition were well known, to calm down the extremists. This the Tunku did by repeating a theme that he had used some months earlier in similar circumstances over the distribution of State constituencies; that although the candidates from the MCA and the MIC would for some years be a burden to UMNO in any election campaign, the Malays owed them their support, first because they had lost that of their own communities mainly through backing the multi-racial coalition; and also because the British would

The 1959 Elections

not have granted independence so quickly or so easily without the assurance, which the coalition provided, that there would be a sharing of power among the three main racial groups.

THE 1959 PARLIAMENTARY ELECTIONS

Despite Tunku Abdul Rahman's plea for moderation, the UMNO hardliners got their way to the extent that when the 104 constituencies to be contested in the Federal elections were allocated on a communal party basis, 74 went to the Malays, 28 to the MCA and 2 to the MIC[6] This the leaders of the MCA, who estimated that at that time Chinese made up 35 per cent. of the registered voters, flatly refused to accept; and indicated to the Tunku, who was in overall command of the Alliance election strategy, that unless their share of seats was substantially increased, the party would immediately withdraw from the coalition. This in itself might not have precipitated a crisis, for such threats had been flying around for a long time, had the MCA leadership not gone on to back their claim by suggesting that UMNO, in order to regain popularity with its own community, was considering altering the Constitution to the detriment of the other races,[7] who therefore needed sufficient seats in Parliament to make this impossible by denying the Malays, in any combination of political parties, the necessary two-thirds majority to push such a Bill through the House.

At this point the UMNO leaders decided that they had had enough and authorised Tunku Abdul Rahman to inform Dr Lim Chong Eu that they accepted that the MCA, as a party, was no longer a participant in the coalition, but that UMNO and the MIC, plus any individual members of the MCA who cared to join with them, would still fight the election as the Alliance. After a series of urgent discussion held secretly at Abdul Razak's house a compromise was reached, however, whereby, in consideration of being re-admitted into the Alliance, the MCA agreed to abide by the decision of the Tunku and his advisers not only as to the number of seats that should be allotted to them, but also which particular individuals should be nominated to contest them. Those responsible for this abortive revolt, realising how unlikely it was that in the foreseeable future they would be offered responsible positions in any Alliance government, resigned; and Dr Lim Chong Eu, the party's President, soon followed them.[8] Eventually the leaders of UMNO relented to some extent, voluntarily giving up five of their constitituencies, three of which were re-allocated to the MCA and two to the MIC.

On June 27th the Legislative Council, a left-over from Colonial times in that many of its members had been nominated for their positions, was finally dissolved, so as to make way for a new, fully elected Lower House of Parliament. Nomination Day for the Federal Elections came eighteen days later, when 259 candidates were put forward to contest 104 seats. Of these, 104 represented the Alliance, 58 the Pan-Malayan Islamic Party, 38 the Socialist Front, 19 the Peoples Progressive Party, 9 Dato Onn's Party Negara and 2 the Malayan Party. There were also 29 independents.

For this election Abdul Razak had moved to a different constituency, that of Pekan, named after the royal capital of his home State, which covered roughly the same area of Pahang that his ancestors had once administered on behalf of the Sultan. He knew that although his position as *Orang Kaya Indera Shahbandar* would give him, in some ways, a considerable advantage in what was still largely a feudal society, rank also had its obligations. Because of this every village and hamlet would expect him to pay a personal visit; and the voters, should he fail to live up to their expectations, might well feel sufficiently slighted to wish to teach him a lesson in humility by electing his opponent. So, despite the difficulties of travel in those days when motor roads were still few, and the other calls upon his time as head of the interim government, he undertook a whirlwind tour of the constituency, using the extensive river system as his chief mode of transportation; and every day tramping inland for many miles along dusty tracks in the tropical heat. When the time came to visit the fishermen of Pulau Tioman, a large island remote from the coast of Pahang, there were storm warnings already posted at the customs house, but knowing that if he missed this opportunity he would not have another chance to put his political message over to the people living there, he accepted the risk and discomfort and took a small boat across.

Then, as later, Abdul Razak showed that he did not possess the natural attributes of an impromtu speaker; nor the inclination or skill to indulge in histrionics or extravagant feats of oratory. His speeches were usually prepared well beforehand and learned practically by heart — for he was gifted with an outstanding memory — so that they were repeated *ad infinitum* at every stopping place during a tour. He made no attempt to rouse a crowd with impassioned appeals or to sway it with roaring rhetoric; but rather concentrated upon putting his case through logical argument couched in language simple enough to be understood by everyone, yet avoiding any hint of condescension. Many felt justified in criticising his style; but for him it worked.

In this critical campaign Abdul Razak's wife, Datin Rahah, proved a tremendous help to him, travelling separately about the constituency with her companions from the UMNO women's organisation and winning over to his cause the housewives who, in rural Malay families, wield considerable influence. When he had to rush off to strengthen the Alliance effort in Kelantan and Trengganu, she held the fort in Pekan, carrying the campaign to the most remote villages and proving that Malay women were undoubtedly a force to be reckoned with in Malayan politics.

The 1959 Elections

The opposition, as the State elections had only too clearly demonstrated, was very much stronger and better organised than that faced in 1955. In Pahang, for example, the intensely religious and completely chauvinistic PMIP was so determined to extend its influence into this middle belt State, that it had deviated from its professed beliefs to the extent of forming an electoral pact with the Socialist Front — an organisation that was normally anathema to its members — in order to avoid splitting the anti-Alliance vote. By this arrangement each party fought only three of the six available seats, but actively campaigned for its unlikely ally in the other three. The PMIP concentrated its main effort in areas where the religiously-minded rural Malays were strongest; while the Socialist Front contested Bentong, where Chinese voters outnumbered the Malays;[9] Raub, where the combined voting power of the Chinese and Indians was nearly equal to that of the Malays; and Temerloh — where it fielded a Malay candidate — which was a new constituency formed out of the more urbanised portion of Abdul Razak's former seat of Semantan. In none of the six seats contested was either opposition party successful, however, although all three of the Socialist Front candidates did well enough to give the Alliance a fright, and make its Malay leaders glad that they had made large-scale economic aid for rural development their main platform in this election, for it was in the hamlets and villages that they had picked up most of their votes.

The result in Pekan, where Abdul Razak won without difficulty, was:

Dato Abdul Razak bin Hussein (Alliance)	8,811
Mohammed Ariff bin Abas (PMIP)	2,593
majority	6,218

In the other East Coast states the results were very different, however, for in Kelantan the PMIP won nine out of the ten available Parliamentary seats, all by very substantial majorities, and lost the tenth to an Alliance candidate by a marginal 466 votes in a registered electorate of nearly 23,000; and in Trengganu took four of the six seats, a fifth going to Dato Onn — whose electoral campaign the PMIP practically ran — and the sixth to an Alliance candidate who anyway was unopposed. In both of these states the PMIP made great play with religious slogans and quotations and was particularly effective in turning voters away from UMNO because of its alleged support, in some parts of the country, for infidel Chinese standing against Muslim candidates of other parties. It also gained credit with the credulous by advocating the formation of a theocratic state that would eventually join with Indonesia and other Muslim areas of Southeast Asia to form a Pan-Islamic Federation; and, an issue that won it widespread support, especially in Kelantan, by demanding the incorporation into Malaya, by force if necessary, of those provinces of South Thailand in which Muslims predominated.

So serious indeed did this attempt to influence Muslim voters through their religion become, that at one point it was considered necessary for the Paramount Ruler and the Sultans of the individual states, acting as leaders of Islam in their own communities, jointly to issue a statement that made it clear that under the Constitution every registered voter was entitled to vote for any candidate he chose, regardless of that person's religion, race or party. This statement ended with the unequivocal pronouncement that 'the choice of a candidate from any party has no connection whatsoever with the faith and religion of Islam'.[10]

In the more developed and sophisticated West Coast states of the Peninsula the only real opposition to the Alliance came from either the Socialist Front or the Peoples Progressive Party. The first of these was a combination of the supposedly non-communal, though factually Chinese-orientated Labour Party and the almost exclusively Malay Party Rakyat. These two organisations which had little in common except for rather extreme left-wing tendencies including republicanism, had banded together solely in order to offer the electorate a multi-racial alternative to the Alliance. The second was another Chinese-orientated party, again nominally non-communal because part of its leadership and a minority of its members were Ceylon Tamils or Indians, that had little following outside of the State of Perak. In addition there were, of course, a number of those dissidents who had resigned from the MCA standing as independents, but these lacked the support of any properly organised vote-catching machine and so had to depend largely upon personal charisma for any chance of success.

Until 1954 the Labour Party had consisted only of a few loosely affiliated regional socialist political groups, each largely the propaganda vehicle of a particular leading trade unionist. Even when reconstituted as a single party, centrally controlled, it did badly in the 1955 elections; for the leadership, which was largely Indian, offered non-communal policies that had little appeal for the bulk of Chinese voters and none at all for the Malays. Following this electoral fiasco, however, the party moved sharply to the left and thereafter gathered some non-Malay support by championing the cause of Chinese and Indian education and culture. This platform eventually brought into the party a substantial number of dissidents who had resigned from the MCA and the MIC because of the support, however grudging, of those organisations for Abdul Razak's controversial new education policy.

The Parti Rakyat, which stood well to the political left of any of the other Malay political parties, was led by the dynamic and aristocratic Ahmad Boestamam, who for seven years, from 1948 when the Communist insurrection started until his release in 1955, had been imprisoned by the Colonial authorities for alleged subversive activities. In the interim period after the Second World War had ended and before

The 1959 Elections

British troops re-occupied the Peninsula, Boestamam, as the leader of an authorised Malay political organisation, had, with the blessing of the capitulated Japanese army of occupation, sought to issue a joint declaration of independence with Sukarno, that was intended to bring about the union of the two States into a Greater Indonesian Republic. When this venture failed to achieve large-scale support from either the Malay or Indonesian masses, he became a founder member of the Malay Nationalist Party, which tried to demand immediate independence for Malaya from Britain. Again failing to make any headway, Boestamam, in February 1946, inaugurated the Awakened Youth Corps (API), a violently revolutionary offshoot of the more stable Malay Nationalist Party, that openly advocated insurrection as a means of attaining political freedom. It was due to the activities of this militant faction that he was arrested and imprisoned.

A few months after his release he formed the Parti Rakyat, to replace the by then defunct Malay Nationalist Party. It gained little support in comparison with the well-established Malay parties, however, for both the PMIP and UMNO took pains to persuade Muslim voters that its aims were contrary to the teachings of Islam.[11] This caused Boestamam temporarily to abandon his fiercely communal approach to politics, to the extent that he even accepted a few radical Chinese into the party. This did nothing much to enhance the appeal of his party for the Chinese and Indians, but merely lost him support within his own community. In the 1959 Parliamentary elections the Parti Rakyat candidates were therefore unsuccessful in predominantly Malay constituencies, although due entirely to their association with the Labour Party in the Socialist Front, they were elected in two areas where Chinese and Indian voters were in the majority.

The left wing Perak Progressive Party was founded in January 1953 by two brothers of Ceylon Tamil origin — S.P. and D.R. Seenivasagam. In 1954 this new party, which had by that time become much more conservative in its policies, formed an electoral coalition with the Alliance in Perak. This marriage of convenience lasted only until 1955, when the interests of the Seenivasagam brothers and other party leaders were found to differ greatly from those of their opposite numbers on the Alliance over nominations for the first Federal Legislative Council elections. After breaking with the Alliance, the PPP contested two seats on its own, but as its policy, not surprisingly, differed very little from that of its former ally, the voters rejected its candidates. Following a further heavy defeat in the Perak State elections, the party's leaders realised that they faced a bleak political future unless substantial Chinese support could be obtained; and so adopted a pronounced pro-Chinese attitude toward education, citizenship and the use of communal languages. In 1956, the organisation's name was changed to the Peoples Progressive Party (PPP).

When all the Parliamentary election results had been declared, the Alliance was found to have won 74 of the 104 seats, the PMIP 13, the Socialist Front 8, the PPP 4, the Malayan Party and Dato Onn's Party Negara 1 each, and independents 3. Abdul Razak then resigned as Prime Minister and, on August 21st, Tunku Abdul Rahman was sworn in to take his place. Next day the Tunku presented to the Paramount Ruler his new Cabinet, in which Abdul Razak was again Deputy Prime Minister and Minister responsible for both defence and internal security.

Just over a week later, on the second anniversary of the country's independence, Abdul Razak was awarded the highest honour that the Federation could bestow on a commoner; he became a Grand Knight of the Most Distinguished Order of Defender of the Realm and was thereafter entitled to be styled Tun Abdul Razak.

The Malay school at Langgar where Abdul Razak received his early education and (below) the Malay College at Kuala Kangsar.

Plate 1

Plate 8

The Malay school at Langgar where Abdul Razak received his early education and (below) the Malay College at Kuala Kangsar.

Abdul Razak (second row extreme right) with a group of Malay College prefects in 1938; and (seated second from the left) as captain of his House in 1939.

Plate 2

Students in London 1948. With Abdul Razak (centre) are, on his right, F.C. Arulanandom (now Mr. Justice Arulanandom) and, on his left, Taib Andak (now Tan Sri Taib Andak, Chairman of Malayan Banking); below, a group of Malayan and Indonesian students, Abdul Razak (standing extreme left) and Des Alwee (standing second from right).

Plate 3

A Malayan Students Association Dinner in London. Abdul Razak is seated second from the left and opposite to him (extreme right) is Lee Kuan Yew, future Prime Minister of Singapore.

Abdul Razak speaking at the opening of Malaya Hall in London in 1949. Seated on his left are Sultan Ibrahim of Johore and the Duchess of Kent.

A photograph taken when Abdul Razak was called to the Bar in London in 1950 and (below) when he was called to the Malaysian Bar in Kuala Lumpur in 1975.

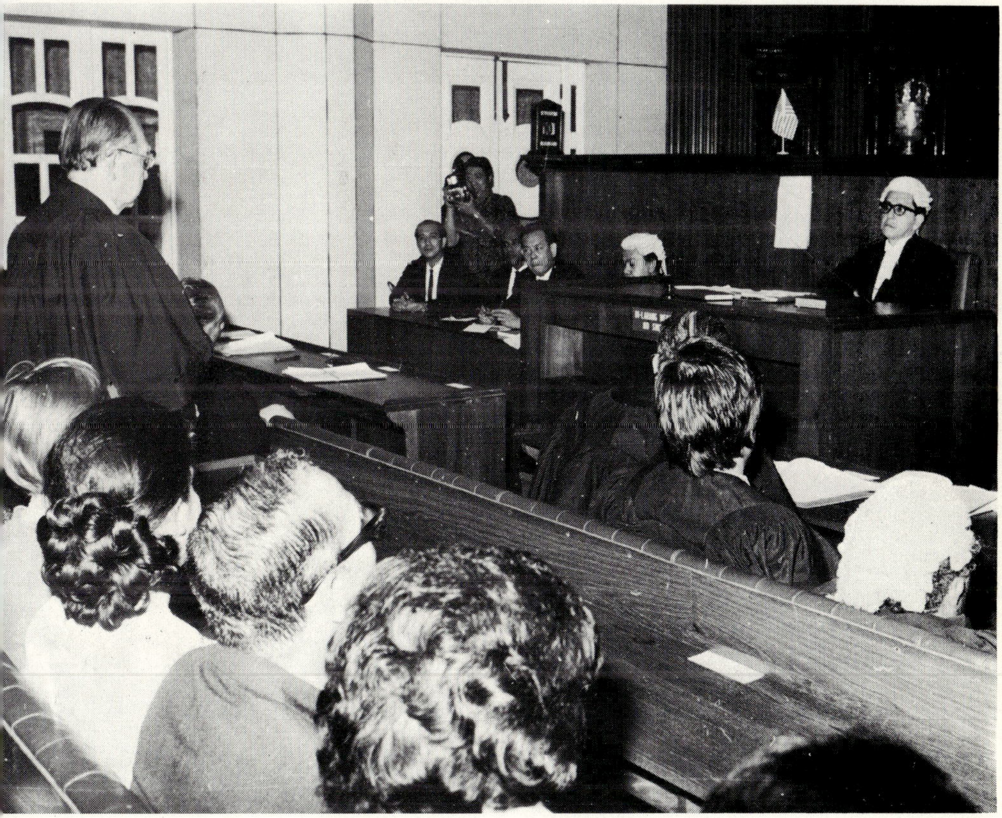

Abdul Razak and his bride, Rahah binte Haji Noah.

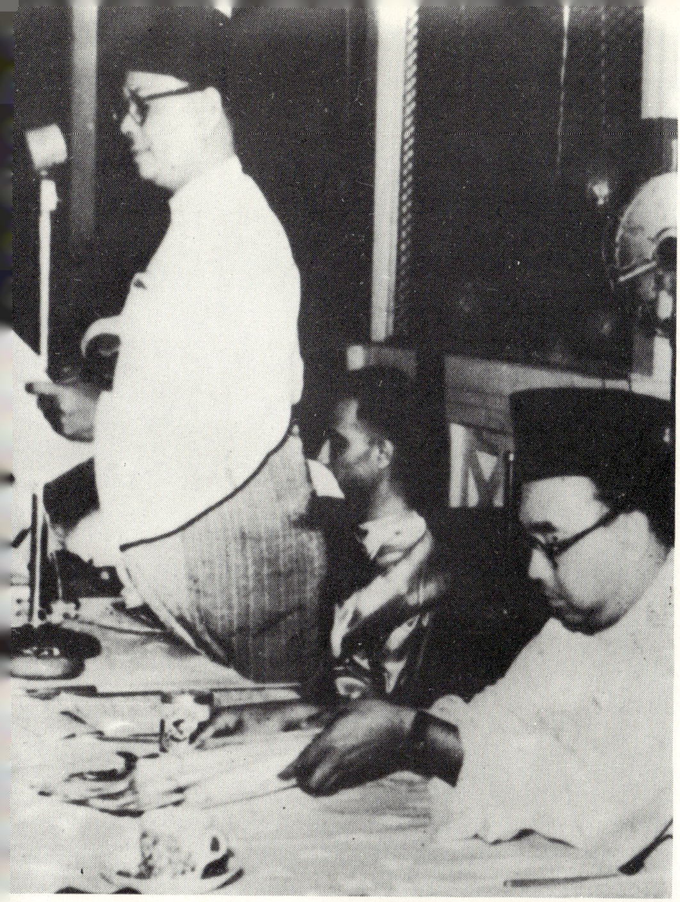

The UMNO General Assembly August 1951. Tunku Abdul Rahman speaking, with Abdul Razak seated on his left.
Below, a meeting of the Committee which produced the Razak Report on Education 1955.

Plate 7

Plate 8

Top left: As Deputy Prime Minister attending the Commonwealth Prime Ministers Conference in London 1962, Abdul Razak is behind Robert Menzies (Australia). Seated on Queen Elizabeth's right are Eric Williams (Trinidad), Pandit Nehru (India) J.G. Diefenbaker (Canada). On her left are Robert Menzies, Ayub Khan (Pakistan) and Harold MacMillan (Great Britain).
Bottom left: Abdul Razak as Prime Minister at the 1972 Commonwealth Prime Ministers Conference held in Singapore.
Below: With President Sukarno on Abdul Razak's visit to Jakarta in 1959.

Plate 9

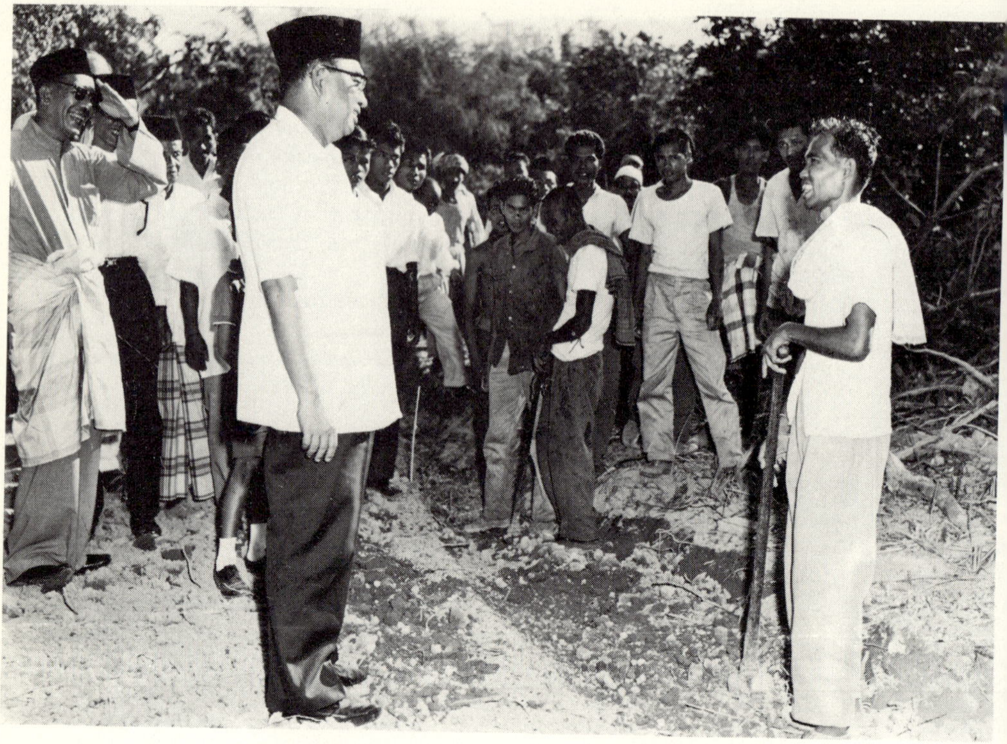

Visiting a land development scheme as Minister of Rural Development and in the Johore State Operations Room.

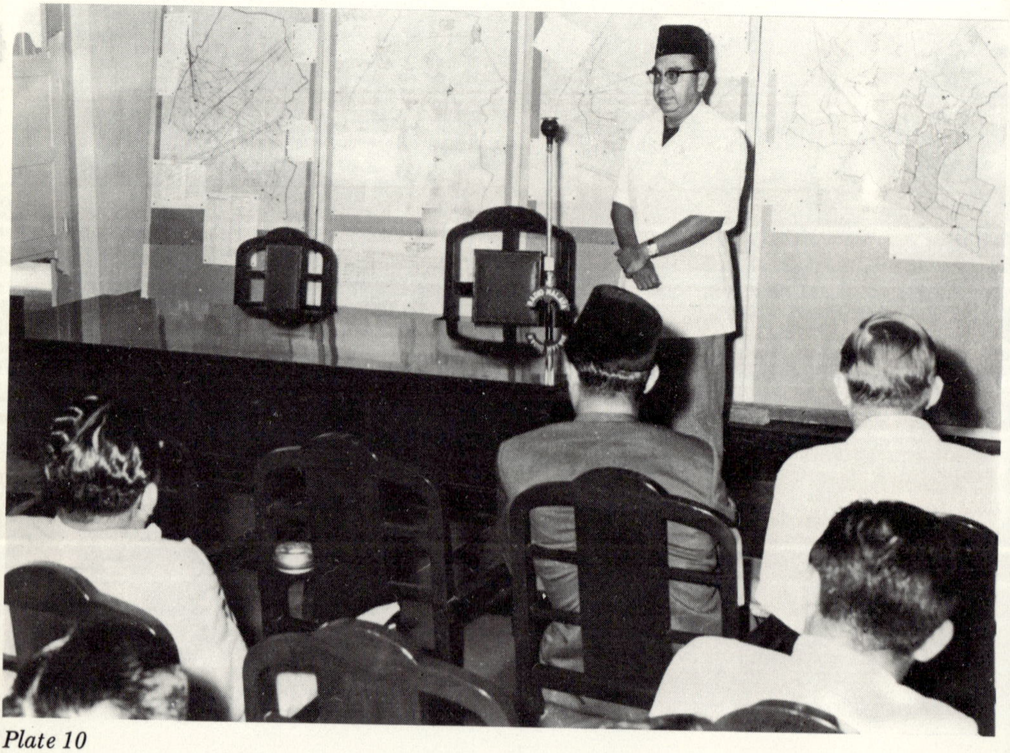

Plate 10

As Minister of Defence Abdul Razak visited Harold Wilson, British Prime Minister in 1964. Below, with United States President, Lyndon Johnson, on the latter's visit to Malaysia in 1966.

Plate 11

Presenting degrees as Chancellor of the National University.
Below: Abdul Razak's first Cabinet after becoming Prime Minister, with his deputy, Tun Dr. Ismail, on his right.

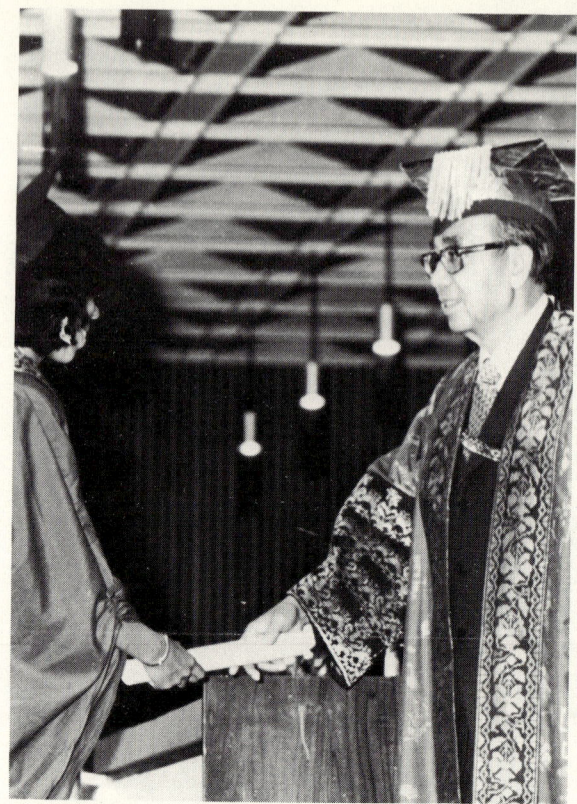

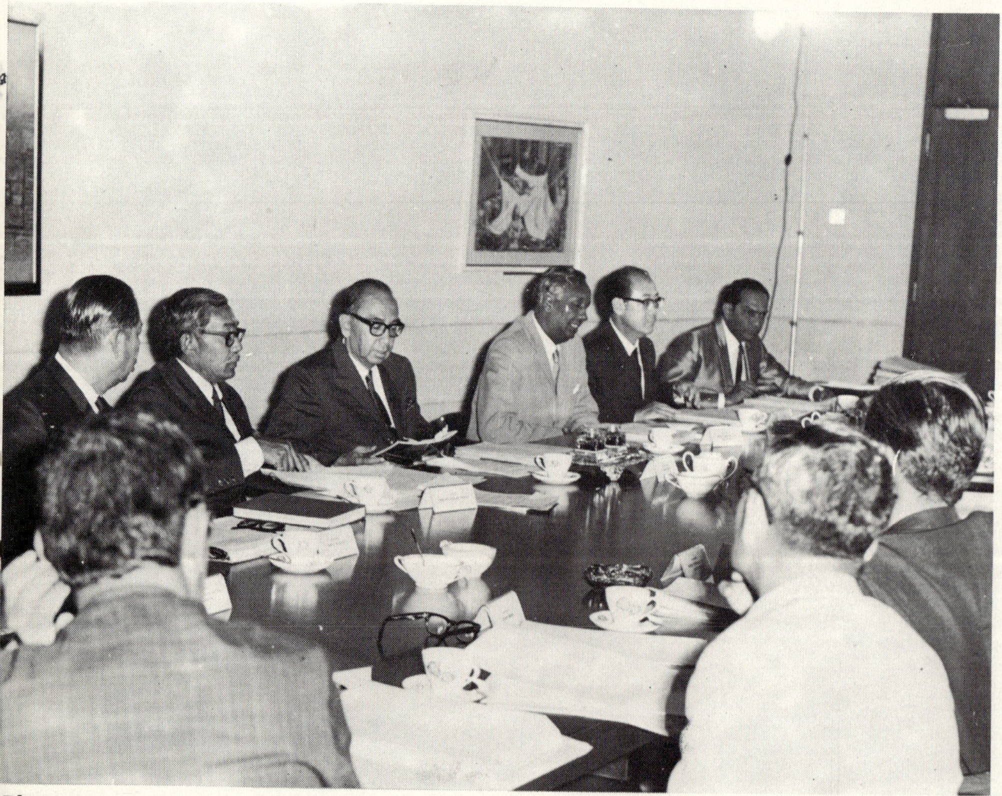

Plate 12

Addressing an election rally during the 1974 General Election and (below) addressing the UMNO General Assembly as its President in 1975. Seated in the front row, second from left, is the present Prime Minister of Malaysia Datuk Hussein Onn.

Plate 13

Meeting Chairman Mao Tse-tung when Abdul Razak became the first South East Asian statesman to visit China in 1974.
Below: his last overseas visit in November 1975, shortly before he died, was to hold discussions with President Suharto of Indonesia.

Playing golf with Tunku Abdul Rahman, and (right) being introduced to the Pakistan team during the World Cup hokey tournament in Kuala Lumpur in 1975.

Abdul Razak and his family. The eldest of his five sons, Mohd. Najib, was returned unopposed to his father's Parliamentary seat in the by-election following his father's death.

Chapter Eleven
National and Rural Development

By the time that the newly elected Alliance government took office; more than three-quarters of the country had been freed from the fear of communist terrorist attacks and it had become obvious that as far as the great majority of the ordinary people was concerned, the Emergency would soon be at an end. Desirable as they found this to be, Abdul Razak and his Cabinet colleagues feared that with the official end to this insurrection, new socio-political dangers and inter-communal hatreds might well appear to destroy the benefits of peace; for the economic imbalance existing between the main ethnic groups, a point of friction that underlay most of the ever-present, though generally dormant, antipathy between Malays and Chinese, had unwittingly been aggravated by the efforts of both the Colonial authorities and the first post-independence Alliance government to turn the numerous Chinese squatters living in the rural areas away from communism.

NEW VILLAGES

In order to protect these unfortunate people from the intimidation and extortion to which they were particularly vulnerable first General Briggs and then General Sir Gerald Templer, had, during the early 1950's, moved them into New Villages where, behind barbed wire patrolled by armed guards, they were comparatively free from molestation. Such an uprooting, which few at first desired, could only lead, unless the people involved were well compensated for the inconvenience, to further estrangement between the squatters and the government. The communists were not slow to utilize this opportunity for propaganda; and in order to refute their charges of racial discrimination and oppression, it became necessary to provide, and even more important to be seen to provide, better amenities within the New Villages than the former squatters could ever have hoped to enjoy outside the restricting wire.

To this end the houses into which they were moved, all of which were of course newly built, were equipped with electricity and running water — a by no means automatic feature of rural housing at the time — and were situated conveniently close to newly erected schools and recreation centres and to the central markets. Cultivatable land, already mechanically cleared and drained, was available outside the wire, but within protective range of the security forces. This VIP treatment had placed the Chinese villagers in a most advantageous position when compared with the lot of the majority of the rural Malays; for after paying for the Emergency and this extravagant resettlement, the Colonial government was left with insufficient funds to provide equivalent social benefits for the indigenous people. Incensed by such discrimination, especially when it continued after the attainment of independence, the Malay peasants who at that time held the balance of voting power had, during the course of the 1959 elections, made it clear to the Alliance leaders that they could expect little electoral support in the future if this imbalance were not quickly rectified.

MINISTER OF NATIONAL AND RURAL DEVELOPMENT

Abdul Razak and his colleagues reacted swiftly to counter what appeared to them to be a serious threat both to racial harmony and to the supremacy of UMNO in Malayan politics; and on October 6th, 1959, Tunku Abdul Rahman announced that a new Ministry was to be set up specifically to improve the lot of the rural people, alleviate their grinding and perpetual poverty, and ensure that they received a fair share of the wealth that the country could expect to accrue in the near future due to improved technology. This department was to operate under Abdul Razak's direct and personal control, although in order to stress its importance in all future government policy it would, for a time, remain as part of the portfolio of the Prime Minister. This new Ministry, which was given the responsibility of coordinating the activities of all Federal and State government departments and statutory authorities concerned with economic development in the rural areas, was duly set up towards the end of December; and a few days later, on New Year's Eve, Abdul Razak made a Ministerial broadcast to the nation, during the course of which he outlined his general policy.

After explaining that although it was the intention, and indeed the duty, of the Alliance government to work for the prosperity and general well-being of all sections of the Malayan people no matter where they resided, he went on to say that it had been decided, however, that for a start top priority must be given to the task of improving conditions for those living in country districts, because they were so much worse off than anyone else.

> ... the aim of the newly created Ministry ..., [he declared,] will be to provide a sound economic foundation for peasant agriculture to ensure that the man on the land receives the full reward for his work and enjoys the amenities of Malayan life in the same measure as his brother in the town.
> ... This will be done by establishing through the agency of the Federal and State Land Development Authorities as many areas as possible where economic smallholdings and estates, with processing and

National and Rural Development

marketing facilities, may be developed intensively around modern villages offering the services and amenities appropriate for a settled, well organised and prosperous community.

This task, besides being complex, is an urgent one and calls for special methods of planning and execution. In order that this may be achieved in the shortest possible time, it is the intention of the government to marshal all available resources and to deploy them with such determination and energy as were used to free the country from the menace of Communist terrorism.[1]

On July 31st, 1960, the communist insurrection officially came to an end; and Abdul Razak then felt that while continuing to act as Minister of Defence, he could safely give up the added responsibility for internal security that he had borne since independence, thereby leaving himself free to devote far more time to rural development. He therefore took over complete control of this Ministry from his Prime Minister and so immersed himself in its problems that the attainment of its aims quickly became the pivot around which his whole political life revolved. His eventual achievements in this field won him a permanent place in the hearts of the rural Malays, who dubbed him 'Father (i.e. Architect) of Development', a title equal in honour to that given to Tunku Abdul Rahman — 'Father of Independence'. Unfortunately, however, it also earned him an entirely unwarranted reputation among large sections of the country's Chinese and Indian communities as a political hard-liner and a fanatical Malay nationalist.

THE TWELVE-YEAR PUTT

THE PROBLEM

By far the greatest problem that Abdul Razak had to face — and the one least easy in the circumstances to solve — had to do with the dualistic nature of the Malayan economy, the continuation of which helped to perpetuate, and even increase, the disparity in wealth and progress among the main racial divisions of the community. This was because basically the indigenous Malays were the 'have-nots' and the immigrant races and foreigners the 'haves'. There were, of course, as Lee Kuan Yew was later to point out, poor people of all communities, but with the Malays the situation was endemic, arising from the fact that 73 per cent. of those among them who were classed as 'gainfully employed' earned their living from peasant agriculture, or small-holding, while only 7 per cent. were engaged in commerce and industry[2]. The Chinese community, on the other hand, though it amounted to only about 39 per cent. of the total population, provided, according to the official 1957 census, 68 per cent. of all those then working in commerce, industry, mining and quarrying, that is in those parts of the private sector of the economy, for the Malays were fairly well represented in the higher ranks of the various government services, offering the greatest financial rewards.

This economic dichotomy, formed along racial lines, was made worse by a number of basic factors. The first among these was that from 1950 until 1957 the gross production of peasant agriculture and smallholdings had been in recession; and this at a time when the overall population of Malays living in the rural areas was rapidly increasing[3]. Second, that although industrialisation and the increasing scale of commercial ventures were, as planned, creating new job opportunities, comparatively few of these were going to Malays, so that the movement of young people to the towns, which might have helped ease the overpopulation of developed agricultural areas, was negligible. This meant, among other things, that the Malays who as a race lacked those entrepreneurs and business managers who might be expected to favour employing their own people, were also denied the opportunity to acquire the necessary commercial and industrial expertise to remedy this deficiency; while their want of income militated against the accumulation of business capital.

Although the huge sums of money that the Alliance government had injected into peasant agriculture had already, by 1959, begun to have some effect in raising production and per capita income[4], the plight of the Malays was still serious, for in real terms their general standard of living was falling still farther behind that of the other main racial groups. It therefore became obvious to Abdul Razak, as he reviewed the situation while planning his development campaign, that in addition to investing further large capital sums in the rural economy, it would be necessary also to change radically, perhaps even traumatically, the Malay peasant mentality, mode of living and traditional working practices.

IMPLEMENTATION

One other section of the community whose traditional attitudes Abdul Razak saw he would have to change before any real progress could be achieved, comprised those government servants who were to work directly on development projects. This was because, as he put it to them in his briefings:

> ... any government run under a former colonial system tends to be merely custodian and carry out little more than basic minimum administration with no sense of urgency and no dedication to development for the sake of the nation. Because the civil service after Independence is the same civil service which has served during the days of colonial dependence, the first thing which has to be done ... is to bring about a chance of attitude in the hearts and minds of all government employees; to instil a sense of urgency, a sense of dedication to development, a spirit of initiative and a feeling of belonging, not to an impersonal, bloodless, lifeless administrative government machine, but rather to a vital, lively and loyal group of human beings, dedicated not merely to their monthly pay packets, but rather to the development and service of their country.

In order to give a lead to his subordinates and to encourage his senior officers to get out of their office chairs and work actively in the field, Abdul Razak himself spent as much time as he could possibly spare from his numerous other duties touring the rural areas wherever development projects were being implemented, travelling by landrover, boat and helicopter to check even the most remote construction sites. Under his leadership middle-ranking government officers were encouraged to devote less time to paper work and instead personally supervise, inspire and lead the teams of experts and artisans for whom they were responsible; and to display initiative in solving problems on the spot instead of seeking to 'pass the buck' on to higher authority.

MILITARY STYLE OPERATIONS ROOMS

Some two months after he took over full responsibility for the rural development programme, Abdul Razak began to set up at Federal, State and District levels that complex system of military-style operations planning rooms, closely patterned upon those formerly utilized by the security forces to direct field operations against the communist terrorists, with which his name soon became nationally and even internationally identified. In each of these planning centres, whatever its level, was kept a large collection of visual aids, consisting mostly of maps and charts mounted upon sliding rollers. For every project in that particular area that remained uncompleted, there was a series of such maps and charts, one for each participating government department, clearly showing every relevant detail of the site location, progress to date, and precisely what remained to be done and when it was likely to be achieved, Whenever development teams met, these maps were brought out and used by the particular departmental officer responsible for that section to illustrate for the benefit of his colleagues, and any important visitors present, just what he was doing to keep things moving. The main object of this was to lay the scheme open to constructive suggestions and criticism that would help to remove any obstacles to successful completion of that sector of the overall plan; for it was Abdul Razak's contention that:

> ... the purpose of these operations rooms is not to keep one's finger on the pulse of progress when the pulse is beating, but rather to be able to put one's finger on the places where (it) ... has stopped ... so that an accurate diagnosis of difficulties and delays can be carried out, and the defects rectified with speed.[5]

These operations rooms, though they saved lots of time and duplication of effort by keeping everyone concerned in immediate touch with the current situation, were also surprisingly cheap to run; for the smaller units could often be worked by a single clerk. This was because each head of department, or other officer in charge of a project, had been made personally responsible for maintaining all of his own maps and for keeping them up-to-date; thus effectively pinning down responsibility on the person concerned, so that if later it was found that a map was wrongly marked, or a project incorrectly located, blame could not be passed on to a subordinate.

As soon as these command posts were activated, it became an established routine that whenever a Minister of the Federal Government or of a State toured development projects he would, before going into the field to inspect the actual work, first visit the area operations room in order to receive a comprehensive briefing on progress, so that what he saw later could be accurately related to the entire venture. Seldom, during such briefings, did the departmental officers concerned know which parts of any particular project were later to be visited; and so of necessity each person's information had to be accurate and truthful, because the Minister might thereafter drive straight out to check the progress of any individual aspect for himself.

An indispensable feature of each of these operations planning units was the series of 'Red Books' — king-size volumes each containing a number of maps, every one of which was concerned with some facet of an individual current project, such as access roads, system of drainage, the buildings already completed or planned, and other essential aspects requiring constant checking. These books were always prepared and maintained in triplicate, so that one copy could be kept in the District Office of the area actually administering and working the scheme, a second in the operations room of the State in which this was located, and the third in that Federal Operations Planning Room in Kuala Lumpur which, being adjacent to his office in the Prime Minister's Department, was under Abdul Razak's direct personal supervision. This meant that if the system was worked as it was meant to be, that every stage of every development project would at all times be observable by three levels of the administration, ranging from the Chief of Staff to the unit commander.

Although generally these operations rooms proved to be a great asset, so much so in fact that several developing countries adapted the format to their own needs, difficulties soon arose, as Abdul Razak had always feared that they would, in getting a certain number of the higher grade government servants to work them efficiently, accurately and above all continuously. These were men who were, as Abdul Razak was forcibly to remind them during sometimes stormy monthly briefings at the National Development Operations Room, far too prone to sit in their offices and wait for their subordinates to come to them with their problems and excuses, whereas if the operations rooms were used correctly, they should be in a position to anticipate such obstacles to progress and take action to deal with them before the situation became serious.

There was also, he reminded them, far too much of a *laissez faire* attitude left over from colonial days, which had finally and ruthlessly to be eradicated. As he went around the country checking progress, he was asked for extra money for all kinds of major and minor projects; requests which he tried hard to meet through increased Federal allocations. Naturally, once this extra expenditure had been authorised, he expected immediate action to be taken to put the money to good use. Yet in many cases he had found that months later absolutely nothing had been done with it, not because it was beyond the capacity of the District Development Committee to spend the money or of the Public Works Department to implement the scheme, but due mainly to the inability, or disinclination, of the officer-in-charge to get on with the job.[6]

This brought Abdul Razak to another cardinal sin of some development planners — wasting time; for this, he held, was not only a commodity as valuable and as scarce as money, but one which once lost was irrecoverable. At which point he usually rolled out his favourite Chinese proverb, the one that suggested that it was impossible to buy an inch of time with an inch of gold. The key factor in his development plans was, therefore, the amount of time that a present day union-orientated labour force would, within the set period, devote to it.

In the five years allocated to each plan, [he was wont to say,] there are 1,825 days, but if you deduct all non-working days such as Sundays, half Saturdays, public and religious holidays, and all those days given up to leave, sickness, bad weather, flooding, breakdowns and other causes — then a five year plan does not give one a full five years in which to implement development — one really has only 1000 full working days.

It was therefore the responsibility of the subordinate planners to see that these 1000 precious working days were put to the most profitable and constructive use.

THE SECOND FIVE-YEAR PLAN

Malaya's first five-year plan, which still had a year to run when Abdul Razak took over as Minister of National and Rural Development, had been formulated and launched in the year before Independence had been achieved. At the beginning of 1961, however, a much more ambitious plan was started, one which envisaged the expenditure of 2,150 million Malayan dollars* on government development — more than

THE REAL POWERHOUSE

*At present exchange rates M$2.50 is approximately equivelant to 1 US$ and M$5.25 to 1 £ sterling.

twice that of the first plan — of which 545 million was to be devoted to rural development, 80 per cent. of it going to improve peasant agriculture and small-holdings.[7]

By 1965, when the plan ended, sixty two land schemes each covering roughly 4000 acres, most of it newly recovered from the jungle, were in operation for the resettlement of peasant families moved from overpopulated developed agricultural areas. Abdul Razak described the basis and purpose of these projects to newsmen while he was touring Australia in April 1967.[8]

> Many of our rural people are either landless or land hungry. They are tenant farmers who don't always get a fair return for the work they put in, and being poor and ignorant, they often fall into the clutches of a vicious parasite — the money-lender ...
>
> To leave such a man to his own resources, to give him ten acres of jungle and tell him to start a new life, simply does not work. He starts off without the reserves of money, knowledge or sheer human spirit to undertake such a formidable task. He may burn down the jungle, plant a few crops and make a few dollars; but before long, the jungle, the moneylender, his own ignorance and despair come creeping up on him and drag him down again.
>
> Our method is different. First we send in the surveyors armed with a soil map to find a suitable patch of jungle where rubber or oil palm or some other crop can be grown successfully. Then the bulldozers move in to clear the jungle, and roads are laid on, with piped water and in some cases electricity as well. Good wooden houses are built according to a village plan, with a school, a community centre and a place of worship. Then the settlers move in together with a village administrator and they begin to cultivate high quality rubber or oil palm under the supervision of experts. While the rubber is growing they receive a small monthly allowance from the government which they supplement with earnings from their vegetable plots. After six years, when the rubber is ready for tapping, the village becomes a thriving community. The rubber is collected and processed under expert guidance and marketed for the settlers at the best possible price so that the middlemen and the moneylender will not be able to come in again and wreck the whole scheme.
>
> By this time the settler begins to earn about 400 dollars a month, and he can well afford to repay the government for his house, his land and the other expenses in developing the settlement. He pays the money back in small instalments over ten or fifteen years so that he does not feel the pinch ... Every settler has ten acres which he cannot sell or subdivide, and anyone who does not make the best use of his opportunity is kicked out, and his place given to someone more deserving.

In such a way some 12,000 families, amounting to about 70,000 persons in all, had, by 1965, been happily resettled on the 145,000 acres that had been reclaimed from the jungle by Federal agencies. This was in addition to the benefits that had been brought to so many of those who remained on their existing mini-farms or small-holdings, for with government aid three-quarters of a million acres of their land was planted, or re-planted, with special high yield rubber, which meant that at least half of all smallholder acreage had been made far more productive and profitable. Several irrigation and drainage schemes had also been completed, increasing the acreage of rice-fields capable of being double-cropped from 38,000 in 1960 to 193,000 by 1965.

Two further important steps sponsored by Abdul Razak in his bid to aid peasant farmers became viable during 1965, Bank Bumiputra and the Federal Agricultural Marketing Authority. The first, which was Malay owned and Malay run, although it had government financial backing, was intended primarily to provide loans on reasonable terms for agricultural projects and to inject capital into business ventures undertaken by indigenous entrepreneurs. The second to advance money for the planting of crops and then to market the end product at fair prices, thereby cutting out the squeeze by unscrupulous merchants and loan-sharks to which so many subsistence farmers and smallholders were still subject.

THE FIRST ALL-MALAYSIA PLAN

In 1963, after long negotiation with the participants and considerable agitation from neighbouring countries which opposed it, a Federation of Malaysia was inaugurated, comprising Malaya, Singapore, Sarawak and British North Borneo, which thereafter became known as Sabah. This widening of responsibilities greatly increased Abdul Razak's problems in the implementation of rural development, for both Sarawak and Sabah were backward and, though potentially rich in natural resources, almost totally lacking in such modern facilities as roads, bridges and other necessary adjuncts to communication and transportation. There, too, peasant agriculture was being carried on in even more uneconomical and inefficient ways than it had previously been in the Malay States.

The third five-year plan, to cover the years 1966-1970, was therefore named the First Malaysia Plan; and had as its first stated objective the promotion of the gradual integration of the peoples and States of Malaysia, which was to be achieved by embarking upon a development plan designed to advance the welfare of them all. This plan called for 4,550 million Malayan dollars of government spending, a 46 per cent. increase on the previous five years, of which just over 1000 million was to be allocated to agricultural and rural development. As neither Sarawak nor Sabah had the financial, technical and mechanical resources nor the skilled manpower necessary for their part of this reorganisation and expansion, it meant that Malaya, already hard-pressed to meet its own commitments, would have somehow to provide them. Fortunately in neither Sabah nor Sarawak was rural development a complete innovation, for the colonial governments of both territories had been allocating a substantial part of their total incomes to this end from early in the 1950's; and so their own existing four-year plans were successfully incorporated into the much more comprehensive all-Malaysia plan.

DIVERSIFICATION

One of the special problems that Abdul Razak had to face in improving conditions for the rural people, was the over-dependence of this sector of the economy on rubber at a time when the price of that commodity was steadily falling because of the release of large quantities of it from the American strategic stockpile on to a world market that was already overburdened with synthetic substitutes. Diversification therefore became important; and one of the main crops selected gradually to alleviate the situation was palm oil.

Between 1955 and 1967, the acreage under oil palm was raised from 100,000 to a quarter of a million; which once such estates were in full production, made Malaysia the largest exporter of palm oil in the world. A further world record for this product was expected to be attained on completion of Abdul Razak's most ambitious development scheme, the Jengka Triangle Project for the resettlement of 12,000 peasant families in the central part of his home state of Pahang, for then the Federal Land Development Authority, which was to run it, would become the world's largest single producer.

THE MAGSAYSAY AWARD

In 1967 Abdul Razak's efforts to raise the standard of living of the more impoverished of his fellow countrymen happily received international recognition when he was successfully nominated for the Magsaysay Award, on Asian equivalent of the Nobel Prize, as a reward for his outstanding contribution to Malaysia's national and rural development. The citation made public by the Foundation in August of that year declared that: 'by this election the Board of Trusteers recognizes a politician administering with quiet, efficient and innovating urgency the reshaping of his society for the benefit of all'.

Chapter Twelve
The Haj

There should come to every pious Muslim at least once during his lifetime a supreme moment of religious revelation when he feels the joyous urge to visit in Arabia the holy places of Islam and the birthplace of the Prophet Muhammad. Such a pilgrimage is one of the five main pillars of his faith and binding upon every member of the religion whose health and financial circumstances permit him to undertake the journey. For many this may well entail nearly a lifetime of self-denial in order to accumulate the necessary money.

Even for those to whom the cost is of no great moment, however, the decision to embark upon this pilgrimage should not be taken lightly; for its completion in purity and understanding is the equivalent of an absolution from sin and a spiritual rebirth on the road to paradise. Its timing should not be planned merely to suit personal convenience, but should rather depend upon a call from the heart when the pilgrim can proclaim with conviction: 'I come in Thy service, O Lord'. Abdul Razak felt such a call early in 1961 and immediately obtained permission from his Prime Minister to answer it.

He left Kuala Lumpur by air on Wednesday May 17th accompanied by another Minister, Muhammad Khir Johari; and, following a brief stop-over in Bangkok and a change of aircraft at Bombay, arrived early in the morning of Friday May 19th at Jeddah airport, where he was welcomed by the Malayan ambassador to Egypt, Muhammad Ghazali Jawi. As Deputy Prime Minister of a friendly Muslim country, Abdul Razak automatically became a guest of the Saudi Arabian government and was provided with an official car and driver for the duration of his stay. Everywhere he went a protocol officer accompanied him to smooth away the difficulties and to protect him from the attentions of the hordes of petty traders and souvenir vendors who batten upon the more susceptible pilgrims.

Although a town has existed in the Jeddah area from time immemorial, it was of little economic importance until after the death of the Prophet Muhammad, when it was chosen by one of his successors, the Caliph Othman, as a harbour to serve the holy city of Mecca. The present port, which is situated about half-way down the Red Sea coast of Saudi Arabia, some 70 kilometres to the west of Mecca, is the country's main centre for foreign trade and, because the movements of non-Muslims are restricted in certain areas of the country that are sacred to the Islamic religion, also the diplomatic capital where the various foreign embassies and legations are located.

A good Muslim is required to pray five times every day and on Fridays should attend a congregational service at the Mosque in lieu of the midday prayer. Abdul Razak, accompanied by his entourage, therefore visited the main Jeddah Mosque at noon that day; and on the way there was greatly impressed when he observed that for the brief period from the beginning of the call to prayer from the minaret until after the end of the service, all shops and places of business in the town closed down and that all cars, lorries and even taxis, were stopped at the side of the road while their drivers got out to pray.

MECCA

For the three days before the actual pilgrimage ceremonies began, the entire Malayan party was accommodated in an air-conditioned hotel close to the Jeddah airport; and when, on Saturday May 20th, they visited Mecca for the first time, returned to it in the evening. Before he left Jeddah for the holy city, Abdul Razak, like every other male pilgrim, had to exchange his usual clothing for two lengths of unsewn white cotton cloth; one of which he wore about his waist like an unstitched sarong, while the other covered his upper body. These simple garments, with the addition of a pair of sandals and a small cloth holdall to contain essential personal belongings, were all that he might wear or carry with him until after the main ceremonies of the pilgrimage had been completed; for they were an outward sign that he recognised and accepted that in Islam every man, no matter what his rank or wealth, must approach his God humbly and without ostentation.

Unfortunately for all concerned in it, the pilgrimage had this year fallen in the worst of the hot season; and so Abdul Razak's party, travelling the 70 odd kilometres to Mecca, was glad of the ice-box full of soft drinks that had been strapped to the back of the official car. They proceeded along a broad modern highway that followed an ancient caravan route across the coastal plain and through a series of desolate hills into the fertile valley of *Wadi Fatimah*. Then, about thirty miles from the coast, they passed between a pair of great pillars, each surmounted by three small domes, which marked the beginning of the forbidden area inside which no non-Muslim is knowingly permitted to pass. Soon they obtained their first sight of the holy city of Mecca standing in a shallow rocky depression surrounded on three sides by low barren hills. For a Muslim, arrival at the birthplace of the Prophet Muhammad and the place where the first verses of the Holy Quran were revealed to him by the Divinity through the agency of the Archangel Gabriel, is a profound emotional experience, for there he hopes to become, in the mystical sense, as one with God.

That evening Abdul Razak and the members of his suite were included among the five to six hundred privileged persons who were invited to attend a state banquet at the Royal Palace in Mecca. As the ranking guest, Abdul Razak sat on the right of King Saud, who had reigned since 1953 but was to lose his throne to his more dynamic brother Faisal in November 1964, and who presided not only as sovereign of his country, but also as Leader of the Muslim Congregation of the Pilgrimage. Because of the solemnity of the occasion, no entertainment other than dinner was provided; and after the King's speech, which by tradition dealt with the dignity and importance of the experience they were about to undergo, the guests dispersed and the Malayans returned to Jeddah.

THE HAJ

The following afternoon Abdul Razak and his party again made the journey to Mecca; and after attending sunset prayers at the Great Mosque, left the holy city for Mina where, following a tradition of the Prophet, they were to stay the night. On arrival they found their tents pitched close to the Royal Palace, outside which the King's own entourage was already encamped. They left again at sunrise the next morning and travelled by car, via Muzdalifa, to another tented encampment that had been prepared for them close to the Namirah Mosque. There, after taking breakfast, they slept until just before noon and then, having performed the necessary ritual ablutions, joined those among the great concourse of worshippers who intended to follow in every detail the Prophet Muhammad's method of performing the pilgrimage. They duly listened to the customary sermon preached on the objects and meaning of the ceremony they were undertaking, but because of the great numbers of believers gathered about them, found it next to impossible to perform properly the correct prostrations during the prayers that followed.

They then moved on to the plain of Arafat, where they remained until sunset, joining with the great multitude assembled there in communal prayers, readings from the Holy Quran and declarations of repentance of their past sins. This is, so Muslims aver, one of the most solemn moments of the pilgrimage, for it is in this place that the believer expects to feel God's presence and hopes to receive His mercy and forgiveness.

Immediately after sunset, the great crowd began the exodus to Muzdalifa, some five miles distant, where they camped for the night. As soon as the evening meal was finished, each pilgrim entered the surrounding wilderness to gather in the darkness the forty nine small pebbles that would later be required for a ceremony known as 'stoning the three devils'. The next morning, before daybreak, the pilgrims assembled on the ground surrounding the Muzdalifa Mosque for a brief period of silent prayer; and then as dawn broke, packed up and made their way back to Mina, each taking his forty nine pebbles with him.

Tradition has it that the Prophet Abraham dreamt that he was commanded by God to offer up his son Ismail as a blood sacrifice; and that the next day, while they were working together in the fields, the Prophet told his son what had been demanded of them. Ismail accepted his fate without argument and obediently accompanied his father to the place selected for his execution. During the time that it took to walk to the sacrificial site Ismail, who was following several paces behind his father, was three times exhorted by the Satan to run away and save his life. On each occasion he refused to be tempted and drove off the evil entity by throwing stones at it. Such outstanding piety was soon rewarded with clemency, for when Abraham attempted to make the kill, the sacrificial knife was deflected away from his son's body by supernatural means. To commemorate both Ismail's piety and his deliverance, a stone pillar has since been erected at each of the three places where the Satan appeared; and these are stoned by every pilgrim, a symbolic gesture indicating his desire to reject evil and submit to God's will.

Arriving at Mina on Tuesday, the 'Day of the Feast of the Sacrifice', Abdul Razak and his party went at once to the pillar, or 'devil', sited just below the place where it was intended that Ismail should be sacrificed; and there each of them cast at it the required seven stones. So dense was the crowd milling about this symbol, however, that it proved impossible for most people to push forward close enough to aim properly and several times the Malayans, who due to their official escort were able to attain a privileged position, were hit on the back by missiles thrown eagerly but inaccurately from the rear.

This duty completed, Abdul Razak and the others then returned to their camp to arrange for the animal sacrifice that every pilgrim who could afford it was expected to provide that day. These animals were not killed within the camp area, but in a special place set aside for the purpose; nor were they destroyed wantonly, for their carcasses were used to provide food for the poor.

The next morning Abdul Razak and his party travelled back to Mecca in order to undertake the required seven circumambulations of the Holy Ka'aba and the symbolical running between Safa and Marwah. Once in the Holy City, they performed their ritual ablutions and then entered the courtyard of the Great Mosque through Abraham's Gate. There they paused in veneration as they beheld in front of them the most revered monument in all Islam, a large cube-shaped building impressively draped in a huge black cloth embroidered in gold thread with verses from the Quran. This is the edifice toward which all Muslims, wherever in the world they live, turn their faces when they pray. To them it is the centre of their Universe.

The original Ka'aba is said to have been a replica of a temple in heaven around which the angels circled whilst worshipping God. It contained within it a single large rectangular stone which served as an altar; the surviving fragment of which is the Black Stone that, sheathed in silver and set in one of the walls of the present-day Ka'aba, is still revered and kissed by Muslim pilgrims.

To a non-Muslim, especially in these days when religion plays such a small part in the lives of the majority of the people in the West, the depth of feeling that the mere sight of the Ka'aba arouses in pilgrims is difficult adequately to appreciate. This emotion was well described a long time ago by one very literate pilgrim, who wrote:[1]

> The whole assembly stood there in the greatest reverence before this highest majesty and most powerful inspirer of awe before which the greatest soul becomes so little as to be almost nothing. And if we had not been witness of the movements of the body during the salat (prayer period) and the raising of the hands during the prayers, and the murmuring of the expressions of humility and if we had not heard the beating of the hearts before this immeasurable grandeur we would have thought ourselves transferred to another life. And truly we were at that hour in another world; we were in the House of God and in God's immediate presence, and with us were only the lowered head and the humble tongue and voices raised in prayer and weeping eyes and the fearful heart and pure thoughts of intercession.

As Abdul Razak and his companions pushed their way into the circling, prayer-chanting Muslims thronging the great courtyard they became incorporated into a huge Congress of the Faithful, drawn from every race and from every part of the world into which the Islamic religion had penetrated; a milling kaleidoscopic mass united in an ecstacy of shared emotion that for a few glorious days would transcend all thoughts of national politics, racial bigotry and class consciousness.

Every pilgrim was required to circle the Ka'aba seven times in an anti-clockwise direction — the first three at a quick pace and the remaining four more sedately — all the while praying and with his thoughts concentrated upon the greatness of the One God. Among those engaged in the circumambulation were the old and decrepit, the blind and the crippled, the beggar, the merchant, and even the prince, all intent on attaining personal salvation. Occasionally men and women performed the rite together, but more usually the women preferred to stay apart. All struggled for a chance to kiss the Black Stone, but as this was physically impossible due to the great number of pilgrims circling the building, most had to be content with merely saluting it in passing.

The next step in the ritual was for Abdul Razak and his party to pray at the Place of Abraham and then, after a brief halt near the door of the Ka'aba, to follow a further tradition of the Prophet of Islam and drink a little water from the Zamzam, or Well of Ismail. They found, however, that pilgrims could no longer directly approach the well, as it was at that time completely enclosed within a domed building that had been raised to stop those who believed that suicide by immersion in the holy waters would wash away their sins and ensure them of a place in Paradise, from jumping into it.[2]

When the Mecca rites had been completed, Abdul Razak and his companions returned to Mina, where they were required to spend a further two nights. On arrival there, they all underwent the ritual haircut, which in their case entailed merely the snipping off of a few token hairs; and then, the strict requirements of the pilgrimage being at an end, they were free to change out of their white pilgrims' garb and back into everyday costume. On each of the remaining two days that had to be spent at Mina there was one further duty to perform, although this was considered more as a meritorious action than an essential requirement of the ritual. It was to cast seven of those pebbles which they had collected at Muzdalifa at each of the three pillars, or 'devils', while they recited religious texts.

On the morning of Friday, May 26th, having successfully fulfilled the main purpose of their visit and now being entitled to be addressed as Haji, they returned to Mecca where, after the midday prayer, they performed their last seven circumambulations of the Holy Ka'aba, took a final cup of ZamZam water and then left the Great Mosque by the Farewell Gate. Their official car was waiting to take them to Jeddah, where they were to spend the night before setting out for Medina, a journey by road of some 480 kilometres.

THE CITY OF THE PROPHET

The city of Medina lies some two thousand feet above sea level and is situated in the middle of a fertile oasis, famous for its fruit and dates, that is partially surrounded by barren hills. Although non-Muslims may land at its airport in order to change planes, they are forbidden to enter the city or that part of the surrounding countryside in which the holy places are located. It was not strictly necessary for Abdul Razak and his companions to visit Medina as part of their pilgrimage, but they wished to do so, for this was the city that thirteen centuries earlier had given sanctuary to the Prophet Muhammad when he was forced to flee from Mecca; and it was there that much of the Holy Quran had been revealed to him.

Muhammad died in Medina and was buried under the house of his wife Aisha. His tomb now forms part of the Prophet's Mosque, the original building of which Muhammad himself helped to construct. It was a very simple structure made from locally available materials, with rough clay walls and a thatched roof supported upon pillars made from palm-trunks. At the time of Abdul Razak's visit, however, the Mosque was, by comparison, a magnificent edifice that had recently been completely renovated, enlarged, and beautified by the addition of two minarets. Within the Mosque the Prophet's tomb retained its simplicity, however, for this was in accordance with his own stated wish.

When Abdul Razak and his party reached this holy place, they joined a continuous procession of other pilgrims who filed slowly past the sarcophagus in order to pay their homage. As each member of the Malayan party arrived at the sacred tomb, he paused to repeat the words that had been used by the mourners at Muhammad's funeral. 'Peace be upon you O Prophet! We bear witness that you have justly conveyed the Message and that you have faithfully followed the Lord's path until He has glorified His religion bringing it to perfection.'[3]

Their duty at the Mosque finished, it remained only for the Malayans to visit Ahud, a place some five kilometres to the north of Medina that is celebrated in the annals of Islam for the battle that was fought there in the year 625. It was an engagement in which the Prophet's forces were defeated by the army of Mecca; Muhammad was himself wounded and his uncle, Hamzah Abdul Mutallib, killed. Every year, after he had completed the pilgrimage, Muhammad liked to visit the grave of his uncle and those of the other martyrs who died with him in the battle; and so it is considered meritorious for modern pilgrims to do likewise.

The next day, their religious obligations in the holy city being at an end, Abdul Razak and his companions returned to Jeddah and, after spending a last night there, flew back to Malaya by way of Cairo.

*****   *****   *****

Soon after he returned to Kuala Lumpur Abdul Razak, who was of course already a qualified Barrister-at-Law, learned that on June 10th, during its Convocation for 1961, the University of Malaya intended to confer on him an honorary doctorate degree.

DOCTOR OF LAWS

During the course of a ceremony that took place directly after the new graduates had been awarded their degrees, the University's Public Orator said of him in his citation:[4]

> ... he has played an illustrious part in the achievement of Merdeka (Independence), and a tremendously important role in the emergence and evolution of Modern Malaya.

The Razak Report on Education laid the foundation of educational policy in this country, fostered the spirit of unity in the nation, while recognising the richness of (its) diversity. He has spearheaded the rural development movement, designed to bring prosperity and well-being to the great mass of our people. The Deputy Prime Minister is a dedicated man with a sense of urgency ... He has upheld in many ways the three L's that Disraeli postulated as the basis of a good University — Light, Liberty and Learning.

To a man already laden with many honours and distinctions, and fresh from his pilgrimage to Mecca, the University is proud to offer its own tribute, in recognition to his many services to education, particularly to higher education ....

In his reply, Abdul Razak allowed something of the bitterness he still felt from the days of his youth, when he had first been deprived of a sound formal education by an imperialist war and later denied through red tape a place at the University of London to study for his LL.B., to show through.

.... Let me say from the depth of my heart, [he began] (that) I am indeed grateful to the University for conferring upon me the highest honour in its power to bestow. It is gratifying to me that having failed to obtain a degree from the University in the normal way I now have one conferred upon me. Although I have taken part in a ceremony which has some similarity to this colourful and august occasion once in my life before, and that was when I wore a gown to be admitted to the Bar as a Member of the Honourable Society of Lincoln's Inn, it appears that the learned gentlemen of Universities are not inclined to regard the Membership of an Inn as being quite the same as a degree.

Therefore .... I take great personal satisfaction in being honoured today with a degree in law — the first I have ever possessed. I shall treasure this honour all the more for the reason that it is bestowed upon me by the University of my own country.[5]

A NEW EDUCATION POLICY

As is usual in Malaya on such occasions, Abdul Razak then went on to make a major policy speech which, although delivered to a University gathering, was certain to reach a national audience through full press coverage. He began by reminding his listeners of the aims of the current education policy which had been formulated by him in 1956 when Minister of Education. This had been to provide every child with a primary education, either in a national or in a government-aided school; and to promote Malay as the national language of the country, and make it a compulsory subject in all schools, while still allowing other languages to be used, at least for an interim period, as the chief media of instruction whenever parents insisted upon it. Now, the government indended that from the beginning of 1962 subsidies to aided schools would be increased so that all primary education could be provided free of charge.

> Thus, [he continued,] not only will a place be found in primary schools for all children, not only will parents have the right to choose whether their children shall go to Malay, English, Chinese or Tamil primary schools maintained by the government, but also, and for the first time, no fees will be charged in any of these schools. At the same time .... common syllabuses and timetables have been promulgated for use in all schools so that whatever language is used, all pupils learn the same things in the same way, with the object of fostering a national Malayan outlook.

Beginning also in 1962, said Abdul Razak, the government intended that every pupil should be given three extra years of schooling. As this post-primary, or secondary education was to be paid for out of public funds, however, there was to be a stipulation that it must be taken mainly in one or other of the two official languages, Malay or English, with the reservation that as soon as practicable instruction would be given solely in the national language. He then went on to deal with a situation to which the government was at that time particularly sensitive, for the previous month an MCA candidate, standing on the Alliance ticket, had lost a by-election to a Chinese Independent who had formerly been not only a member of their party, but also an Assistant Minister in the Federal government. The latter had resigned his office, and from the party, in protest against that section of the education policy which laid down that Chinese secondary schools wishing to apply for financial aid from the government must use either the national language or English as their main teaching medium[6]. Not surprisingly, some politicians in opposition to the Alliance had made considerable capital out of this defection, to the embarrassment of the ruling party.

> There are some who allege falsely and in some cases I am afraid mischievously, [said Abdul Razak] that our education system denies to many of our citizens the opportunity of learning and studying their ancestral cultures. This allegation is completely untrue .... It is not surprising to us that political opportunists .... made these charges in order to get the support of the Chinese for their political ends. But it is strange that it could be believed in face of all the facts.
>
> What are the facts? Here in the Federation in institutions wholly maintained out of public funds, a Chinese child can have six years of primary education wholly in the medium of Chinese. What is more, ... after this free primary education, (he) can continue to study Chinese language and literature as a subject in a secondary school where, for this subject, the medium both of instruction and examination is Chinese. He can thereafter take an honours degree, if he so wishes, in the Department of Chinese Studies now set up in this University ....

This, argued Abdul Razak, was surely not the programme of a government set upon destroying Chinese language and culture — or for that matter the institutions of any other Malayan community — although it was vital that the country's education system should not for too much longer continue to operate in a number of separate communal compartments, each isolated from the others. Instead, the government's aim was to unify the system through the eventual use of one language, Malay, common to all the people; even though the attainment of this objective must lie still some five or six years in the future.

COMMUNAL REACTION

This speech did not go unchallenged by the country's mainly non-Malay opposition parties, however, a number of the leaders of which reacted violently. Speaking in his home territory of Malacca Mr Tan Kee Gak, leader of the Malayan Party, stated that in his opinion the current education policy was killing other cultures; while Mr D.R. Seenivasagam of the Peoples Progressive Party was even more critical. Addressing a political meeting in Ipoh on the day following Abdul Razak's speech, he said that despite what the Deputy Prime Minister had had to say, the Alliance government was deliberately following a policy of discrimination against Chinese and Indian education; and was prepared to go to any lengths to silence any member of the opposition who criticised their actions.

This controversy over whether or not Chinese language and culture should gradually be phased out in Malayan schools was particularly embarrassing to the Malayan Chinese Association, which was sometimes accused of supporting the aspirations of the Malays to the detriment of its own community. Despite such internal stresses and strains, the Alliance retained the electoral support of the great majority of the people of all races; a circumstance that encouraged the coalition government to take a calculated risk in still further diversifying the racial composition of the State, by inviting Singapore, Sarawak and North Borneo to join Malaya in an enlarged Federation to be called Malaysia.

Chapter Thirteen
Malaysia

From the time of the Japanese Occupation, when the idea of complete independence for the various colonial territories in Southeast Asia first became a serious possibility, the more extreme among Malay nationalists had tried to promote interest in a union of predominantly Muslim and nominally Malay countries, or segments of countries, to be known as Malaysia. This idea had never been really popular among their compatriots in the Peninsula, however, because to any thinking person it meant, no matter what the paper guarantees, inevitable domination by Indonesians, who outnumbered their Malay cousins by about 20 to 1. Nevertheless, when one was being mathematical, the point invariably arose that in Malaya, as it was then constituted, non-Malays made up nearly half of the population; so that if ever Singapore joined the Federation, as most people expected that some day, out of sheer economic and military necessity, it must, then the Malays would truly be a minority — and an increasingly underprivileged one at that — in their own country. As a matter of long-term planning, then, Tunku Abdul Rahman, Abdul Razak and the other UMNO leaders had to consider ways and means of preparing for this eventuality and neutralizing its destructive potential for their race, its culture and religion.

Federation with Singapore was a theme beloved of certain sections of the MCA, for the automatic increase in the Chinese electorate resulting from such an act, would present them with two possibilities for political advantage: either to continue as moderates supporting a multi-racial Alliance and, by becoming indispensable to UMNO if it was to remain in office, increase their bargaining power; or, with sufficient support from their own and the Indian communities, look forward to one day dominating a predominantly non-Malay coalition government. Abdul Razak and his colleagues realised that for UMNO there were three possible tactical answers to this: the first to integrate Malaya with Indonesia; the second to try to persuade Thailand to let them have the Patani Provinces, which would add over half a million Malays to the population; or three, the most practical, to unite with Brunei and the British Crown Colonies of Sarawak and North Borneo (Sabah). In this latter case the Malays would, of course, have to assume that the native peoples would be willing to join them in opposing any attempt by the immigrant communities, either there or in the Peninsula, to unite and impose their political will on the indigenous races.

The matter attained a certain urgency as the pressure upon colonial powers to divest themselves of their remaining dependencies mounted; for the Malayan government feared that as soon as the British finally withdrew from Singapore either the Communists, rising internally, or the Americans, invading from outside to forestall them, would attempt to fill the power vacuum left in that strategically situated island. As this fear was shared by both the British government and that of Mr Lee Kuan Yew in Singapore, a basis for mutual agreement seemed already to exist. It was a bold and perhaps reckless course to pursue; and so the UMNO leadership talked and hesitated.

At this point, however, Tunku Abdul Rahman unexpectedly, but with typical dash and enthusiasm, jumped the gun. On May 27th, 1961, he chose for his unscheduled public suggestion of a Malaysian Federation consisting of Malaya, Singapore and the three Borneo States a luncheon party given in his honour, in Singapore, by the Foreign Correspondents' Association of Southeast Asia. He could hardly have picked a better occasion, or venue, for getting his message across to all concerned; and so, for better or for worse, the project was launched. Abdul Razak and some of his more pragmatic colleagues had initial doubts about the wisdom of rushing headlong into new responsibilities before Malaya had fully recovered from the effects of the 12-year Communist insurrection, especially as both Indonesia and the Philippines were known to have territorial ambitions in the north of Borneo, but they loyally stood by their chief and prepared to try to make his proposals work.

SINGAPORE POLITICS

The reason for all these doubts and misgivings over the future of Singapore was not difficult to understand; for the island was plagued with labour and student unrest, often of an extremely violent and provocative nature, that was in many instances deliberately contrived and exacerbated by professional agitators and left-wing political adventurers. So prevalent had this trouble become, that in many people's view only the known presence of a strong British military force was preventing a complete break-down of law and order as a prelude to the establishment of a Communist-dominated dictatorship. For this reason, when the Colony had in 1958 been granted a large measure of self-government, certain safeguards against political subversion, civil disturbance and riot had been imposed from Westminster. The most effective of these being the enforced composition of the island's Internal Security Council; for of the seven members only three were Singaporeans, another three being nominated by the British, while the Chairman, who held the casting vote, was appointed by the government of Malaya.

This was adequate for the time being, but the trial period set for self-government was due to expire in 1963; and as that time approached, it would be difficult, if not impossible, for the British to refuse full independence to the Colony, even if they managed for a while to retain sovereign military bases there. If this should happen, then internal security would automatically become the sole responsibility of the elected Singapore government, a body which, after an overwhelming socialist victory in the 1959 elections, was already well left of centre and might, if the power struggle taking place within the ruling party went against Lee Kuan Yew, soon become even more radical and extreme. Tunku Abdul Rahman's suggestion came therefore at an opportune moment.

In a Colony where Chinese made up roughly three-quarters of the population, it was not difficult for an anti-colonialist chauvinistic party, the majority of whose candidates were Chinese presenting themselves as the sole champions of Chinese interests, language and culture, to get itself elected. This Lee Kuan Yew's People Action Party (PAP), an organisation that already controlled the greater part of the island's militant trade union movement, did ruthlessly and, as ever with anything that Lee supervised, efficiently. The PAP which, unlike the moderate centre parties opposing it, had gained a considerable following by openly defying and refusing to cooperate with the British administrators — who being themselves skilled in politics were not too alarmed by this legitimate manoeuvre — swept into power when it won forty three of the fifty one seats available in the Legislative Assembly.

This party's political membership ranged over a very broad spectrum, however, from staid social democrats to rabid Communist fellow-travellers; and soon after taking power the hard-liners of the left, who had accepted Lee Kuan Yew's leadership because of the high regard in which he was held by the masses and because of his undoubted personal charisma, honesty and intellectual ability, instigated a number of abortive attempts to replace him. They were not without some popular support, for Lee, once faced with the social and economic realities of government, swung sharply to the right and bulldozed the party executive along with him. He began to take a renewed interest in the possibilities of merger with the Federation of Malaya — a subject which had formed part of his party's election platform — not only in order to help stabilize his own position in Singapore, but also because he saw in it a chance to become political leader not just of an island State, but of a medium-sized nation, rich in natural resources, that could make of him an international figure.

On June 3rd, 1961, only a week after Tunku Abdul Rahman had delivered his Malaysia speech, Lee Kuan Yew took advantage of Singapore's National Day to acclaim the idea in principle in his official address, stressing particularly the economic advantages that would accrue from such a merger. His support for this scheme very nearly brought about his own downfall, however, for those Members on the extreme left-wing of his Parliamentary party, realising that with federation their activities would be seriously curtailed, if not proscribed altogether, deserted the PAP and founded instead their own political party, the *Barisan Socialis* or Socialist Front. When these radicals crossed the floor of the House to join the Opposition, Lew Kuan Yew found himself left with a bare working majority of three. He remained unshaken in both his resolve and his ambition, however, and planned and executed his moves and counter-attacks in the 'battle for merger', as he termed it, so brilliantly that he soon regained much of the public support that the Barisan Socialis defection had cost him.

THE RESPONSE IN BORNEO

The first reaction from the Borneo territories to the suggested Federation came on July 28th, 1961, when, at a meeting of the Commonwealth Parliamentary Association Regional Conference held in Singapore, the leaders of the Sabah and Sarawak delegations raised the matter with their counterparts from that island state and Malaya. The outcome of this was the formation of a Malaysia Solidarity Consultative Committee, the declared primary objectives of which were: to collect and collate views and opinions concerning the creation of, to disseminate information on the question of, to initiate and encourage discussions on, and to foster activities that would promote and expedite the realisation of, Malaysia.

It was unanimously decided that first Sabah and then Sarawak should provide the opening venues for this top-level Committee, so that it could set about dispelling the fears of many of the native leaders in those States that with merger their people, who were mostly backward and ill-educated, would be subject to exploitation and suppression by the Malays. Abdul Razak, still retained some doubts about the wisdom of the Malaysian venture, which he felt could easily be misconstrued by many people as a British trick to maintain economic influence in an area where their power to hang on to colonies was almost at an end. Nevertheless, he decided to give the full support of his considerable prestige to this Committee, which he joined in Jesselton, as the administrative capital of Sabah was then called, just before its first meeting was held there on August 21st.

His decision to take an active part in promoting the new Federation became justified, he felt, when on August 23rd, during the course of a meeting between Tunku Abdul Rahman and Lee Kuan Yew, the latter had readily agreed, as part of a general settlement of the terms of merger that would leave him with control over his State's education and labour policies, to accept an allocation for Singapore of only fifteen seats in the future Malaysian Federal Parliament. As the island State then had a population only a little less than one fourth that of Malaya, which was to have 104 seats, he might with reason have claimed far more. This willingness temporarily to sacrifice his own political ambitions in order to calm Malay fears seemed to show that he and the Peoples Action Party had no intention, at least for some years, of seriously challenging the political supremacy of the Alliance, or at least that of UMNO, which augured well for future Sino-Malay relations within Malaysia.

While working with the Solidarity Consultative Committee, first in Sabah during August and then in Sarawak in December, Abdul Razak found to his regret that although the idea of merger was welcomed by the bulk of the local Malays, it was by no means so popular with either the Chinese or the various races native to the area, who of course constituted the majority of the population. This reluctance was, in the case of the latter at least, mainly due to folk memories of earlier times when their lands had formed part of the Brunei Malay Empire and the people subjected to corrupt and oppressive rule. Additionally they feared that their privileged and protected position, established under British rule, would be usurped by the local Malays once they passed under the control of Kuala Lumpur; while their leaders, though keen on independence as a means of increasing their own personal power and prestige, feared that with their lack of formal education and political expertise they would fall ready victims to the more sophisticated and experienced practitioners of Malaya and Singapore.

Many of the more progressive leaders were eventually won over, however, when Abdul Razak revealed to them the generous terms of entry that Kuala Lumpur was prepared to offer. The most notable among these, next to the financial and practical help to be given for economic development, being the allocation of 40 seats in the proposed Federal Parliament, 24 for Sarawak and 16 for Sabah, although the combined population of these two States numbered nearly half a million less than that of Singapore Island alone. This was not of course entirely altruistic, as it was also designed to strengthen the political position of the indigenous people generally vis-a-vis the Chinese and Indians.

Large sections of the Borneo Chinese posed a separate problem which was beyond Abdul Razak's powers of diplomacy to solve, for these insular and economically viable communities felt themselves far better able to manipulate for their own benefit a purely local government than a Federal one based in Kuala Lumpur. This concept was particularly prevalent among the traditionally anti-Malay, Chinese-educated, element in the population, which openly opposed the whole idea of Malaysia; and whose leaders even went so far as to ally themselves with some of the small extremist political Indonesian-Malay organisations in Sarawak and with the Brunei opposition party of A.M. Azahari, all of whom advocated eventual independence through a federation of Sarawak, Sabah and Brunei into some form of Commonwealth.

The greatest headache of all, however, came when Abdul Razak was given the thankless task of persuading the tiny oil-rich state of Brunei to give up its nominal independence in order to join Malaysia. He got this unsought chore because it was felt in high places that he enjoyed a considerable advantage over the other members of the Committee in having been a school companion, at the Malay College, Kuala Kangsar, of the country's autocratic feudal Ruler. As a personal friend of the Sultan he was, of course, quartered in the royal palace and treated with the utmost consideration and courtesy, although it soon became obvious to him that the Ruler and his immediate advisers were determined, both for personal reasons and in order to retain the very considerable oil revenues, to resist his blandishments.

This was because the Sultan, who until he had recently been pressured into granting a Constitution under which nearly half of the seats in the new Legislative Assembly were decided on a people's vote, had ruled as an absolute monarch; and still hoped to be able himself to continue controlling Brunei's internal policies through a personally nominated majority, and to maintain his State's independence from outside aggression and interference with the aid of the British. He therefore declined to commit his Sultanate to become part of a Parliamentary democracy, yet at the same time sensibly left the door ajar so that further future negotiations were not precluded.

THE LONDON TALKS

Naturally the British had not been left out of these negotiations, for the ultimate success of the plan depended largely upon their cooperation; which, in the event, was willingly given. Lord Selkirk, the British Commissioner-General in Southeast Asia, had, on instructions from Westminster, started things moving through the colonial Governors of Sarawak and Sabah and the British High Commissioner in Brunei[1]; and had himself liased between London and Kuala Lumpur, an effort that culminated, towards the end of 1961, in a series of exploratory talks held in the British capital.

With these necessary preliminaries out of the way the main conference, at which Abdul Razak acted as adviser to his Prime Minister on matters connected with economic development and defence, began. This was largely concerned with protecting the future well-being of the peoples of Sarawak and Sabah; and in furtherance of this it was decided that a top-level Anglo-Malayan Commission, headed by Lord Cobbold a former Governor of the Bank of England should tour those two territories to find out more about the attitude to Malaysia of the ordinary people. It was also authorised to try once more to persuade the Sultan of Brunei to participate in the proposed new Federation.

In mid-1962 the Report of this Commission was presented for the consideration of both the Malayan and the British governments; and on the strength of its findings, that a clear majority of the people concerned wished to attain independence through merger, it was decided, at a second London Conference, that plans for the formation of Malaysia could go ahead, with the provisional date of August 31st, 1963, set for its inauguration. Brunei, for the reasons already given, had still not agreed to participate.

Abdul Razak, acting in his capacity as Minister of Defence, then took the opportunity to reach preliminary agreement with the British for an extension of the current Anglo-Malayan Defence Treaty to cover the whole of Malaysia; and, with the permission of Lee Kuan Yew's government, negotiated at the same time the retention by the United Kingdom of its important military, air and naval bases in Singapore. He was then appointed as Deputy Chairman[2] of an intergovernmental committee, headed by Lord Lansdowne and consisting of nominees from all four interested territories, charged with working out details of the necessary constitutional arrangements needing to be made, and formulating a series of specific safeguards for the indigenous peoples of Borneo, that would nevertheless be acceptable to all parties. With this in hand, Abdul Razak, Tunku Abdul Rahman, Lee Kuan Yew and Malayan Finance Minister Tan Siew Sin returned in triumph to Kuala Lumpur where, on August 9th, 1962, they were garlanded and cheered by enthusiastic crowds.

FISHING IN TROUBLED WATERS

This Lansdowne Commission, of which Abdul Razak was Deputy Chairman, finished its investigations toward the end of 1962 and early in the new year submitted for the consideration of the two Borneo State Legislatures its recommendations on safeguards for their various peoples. Long before this happened, however, the Malaysia plan had already run into trouble internationally; the first blow against it being struck in mid-1962 when, following a campaign in the Manila press, President Macapagal of the Philippines laid claim to a large slice of Sabah, demanding its return as an integral part of the Republic's own national territory.

This claim was based upon the contention that certain very substantial areas of that State had, during the course of the eighteenth century and long before the British had started to exploit it, been ceded by the Sultan of Brunei to his then vassal the Sultan of Sulu; the sovereign rights and territorial possessions of whose successors had, when independence was granted by America, passed to the Philippines Republic.

The British, on the other hand, while admitting that the disputed area had, a long time before, belonged to the Sultan of Sulu, claimed that it had been sold outright by him to a Baron Overbeck, in his capacity as agent for the firm of Dent Brothers, and that company's successors the British North Borneo Company, for a fixed annual payment; so that when, at the end of the Second World War, the United Kingdom acquired all the assets, debts and responsibilities of the former Chartered Company, sovereign right to the whole of Sabah had automatically passed to the British Crown. The real point at issue was, of course, whether the former Sulu territories had been leased or sold, for if the former were the case, Sabah, in its present form, obviously could not be incorporated into the Federation of Malaysia without Filipino consent, which in the circumstances was hardly likely to be forthcoming. In the event, however, the British refused even to discuss the case with the Philippines government, and the plan for the formation of Malaysia proceeded as scheduled.

In December of that same year a further set-back to Malaysia occurred, not so much from the actual event itself, as from the fact that it marked the beginning of 'Confrontation' between Malaysia — supported by Britain, Australia and New Zealand — on the one hand, and Indonesia on the other. This *Confrontasi*, an invention of President Sukarno, covered every kind of provocation and harassment short of actual war: including raids by armed Indonesia-based guerillas, the encouragement and support of local subversives, arson, piracy and, of course, vituperative propaganda.

REVOLUTION IN BRUNEI

The prelude to this inconclusive and wasteful contest was played out not by Indonesians, however, but by the followers of an anti-Malaysia Brunei politician of Arabic ancestry, Sheikh A.M. Azahari, who mismanaged an abortive revolution aimed at forcing the Sultan of Brunei to lay claim to Sabah and Sarawak, both of which had in bygone times been part of the Brunei Empire, and to declare, as a *fait accompli*, the establishment of an independent State comprising all three territories. Azahari, whose Brunei Peoples Party had won all the elected seats in an earlier Legislative Assembly election, had lived in Indonesia during the Japanese Occupation; and had later served in the Republican Army there that had fought for independence from the Dutch[3]. It is not surprising, therefore, that when he began to organise a clandestine army to achieve his aims, which by then included eventual union with Indonesia, President Sukarno should have supported him financially and with arms and training facilities.

At the time that the actual revolt broke out, that is during the night of the 7/8th December, 1962, Azahari was in the Philippines, ostensibly seeking further financial support for his imperialistic venture. This uncoordinated and poorly led insurrection was anyway doomed to failure even before it started, because regardless of what happened locally, Britain was bound by Treaty to put it down sooner or later. For many weeks before Azahari's guerillas made their move, the fact that they existed and the object of their training was known to British military intelligence, which naturally passed this information on to the local police. Despite this prior warning, no useful effort was made to prevent the revolt from taking place; and the only extra precautions taken seem to have been to send out a few armed policemen to act as bodyguards for the Sultan and some of his more important advisers.

Early in the morning of December 8th, parties of rebels mounted a number of mainly abortive attacks on key installations within the capital. They successfully took over the power station, which anyway was unguarded, but were easily driven off when they attempted to kidnap the Sultan. His Highness than took refuge in the police barracks [4]; and when later the full force of rebels attacked this strong-point, they suffered heavy casualties and after a short while surrendered unconditionally. Thereafter, the Sultan requested military assistance from the British base in Singapore; and later that same day two companies of Ghurkas arrived by air, to be followed after a brief delay by Marine Commandos and British infantry.

In the meantime other rebels had captured the two important Brunei oil centres of Seria and Kuala Belait; and had also seized the town of Limbang, which was in an area of Sarawak that had long been claimed by Brunei, and indeed is still so claimed today, as part of its national territory. Their success was short-lived, however, for the military support they were expecting from Indonesia did not materialise and they received little help or encouragement from any of the indigenous people other than from a small extremist faction of Brunei Malays. Within five days the oil installations and the two Brunei towns had been retaken by troops and police; while Marine Commandos had landed from the sea and, after a brief but bloody battle, re-occupied Limbang. Those rebels remaining alive and uncaptured fled deep into the jungle with the avowed intention of waging guerilla warfare.

CONFRONTATION

In mid-1961 relations between Malaya and the Philippines had been cordial enough for them to have sought mutual economic cooperation through membership of the Association of Southeast Asia (ASA). This friendliness continued until soured by President Macapagal's territorial claim against Sabah; but disappeared altogether when the Philippines tacitly supported Azahari's anti-Malaysia Brunei revolt and granted him temporary asylum in Manila when it failed. For a time after the Brunei fiasco Indonesia stayed uncharacteristically quiescent, until on February 13th President Sukarno, in his opening address to a 'Joint Conference of the Central and Regional National Front', held in Jakarta, declared that Malaysia was a neocolonialist creation designed to encircle Indonesia, and that it would have to be crushed.[5]

In an attempt to ease tension before the situation should escalate beyond control, Vice-President Pelaez of the Philippines, taking advantage of the presence in Manila for an ECAFE conference of Abdul Razak and the Foreign Minister of Indonesia, Dr Subandrio, arranged a series of high-level discussions with himself in the chair. Any good that might have come from these unscheduled talks was nullified, however, when, on April 12th, about 30 armed and uniformed men who, it was later claimed, were members of the Brunei guerilla army who had escaped after the revolt, invaded Sarawak from Indonesia[6]. A few days later a second expedition crossed the border in the same area; and British troops were sent to repulse them. Immediately the whole Colony was put on a full security alert and a limited curfew imposed. Malaysia, it became clear, was under armed attack even before it had begun to exist.

In the following month a return to sanity seemed to have occurred, when President Sukarno unexpectedly invited Tunku Abdul Rahman to meet him in neutral Tokyo; and this apparent olive branch was accepted. The meeting went well, for on May 31st the two leaders issued a joint communique stating their intention immediately to return to the spirit of the Treaty of Friendship that Abdul Razak had been instrumental in negotiating back in 1959. Furthermore, they declared, following a preliminary meeting of Foreign Ministers, there would be a summit conference of Heads of Government held in Manila, in which President Macapagal of the Philippines would also participate, so that outstanding points of controversy among the three neighbouring nations could all be settled amicably.

Abdul Razak represented Malaya at the meeting of Foreign Ministers that took place in Manila from the 7th to the 11th of June. Despite some later argument over exactly what had been agreed upon, the Conference bore all the outward appearances of having been a success, for the delegates had decided that a Commission of neutral investigators should be invited to tour Sabah, Sarawak and Brunei to find out what the real feelings of the people there were towards Malaysia, before any further steps were taken to inaugurate it. Having apparently already achieved a significant breakthrough, the participating ministers, in a burst of misplaced optimism, then went on to agree to set up an organisation, Maphilindo, to promote political and economic co-operation among their three nations, all of which, they claimed, were of common Malay origin[7]. These proposals were to be ratified at the meeting of Heads of Government that was scheduled to take place sometime in July.

Early in June Sarawak had held its first ever general election. These had been to decide the composition of the twenty four District Councils from among the members of which the new State Legislative Assemblymen were later to be chosen[8]. The main significance of the election results, from the point of view of the Malayan and British governments, was that they were thought to show that more than two-thirds of the seats contested had been won by pro-Malaysian candidates, thus proving that a substantial majority of the electorate was in favour of the proposed union.

Meanwhile, although the discussions held in Kuala Lumpur to agree the financial terms for the entry into the Federation of Singapore and Brunei had ended in failure, the disputants had been prevailed upon to re-open their talks in London. There, Abdul Razak headed the Malayan delegation which, after much hard bargaining, finally worked out a compromise solution with Lee Kuan Yew's government. Brunei, however, because the Sultan remained adamant over the control of his oil revenues, finally decided to stay out of the association. It was only then, with the terms of merger with Singapore already settled, that Abdul Razak telegraphed Prime Minister Tunku Abdul Rahman to fly to London[9], where, on July 8th he, and representatives of Britain, Singapore, Sarawak and Sabah, signed an Agreement which meant that on August 31st, 1963, Malaysia would at last become a reality.

This announcement, although it was hailed by the United States and most member nations of the Commonwealth as a significant step towards freeing the area from colonialism, provoked a fresh outburst of vituperation from Indonesia, where President Sukarno accused Malaya and Britain of conspiring together to rob the peoples of northern Borneo of their right to determine their own future. It was therefore his intention, he declared, to destroy Malaysia, no matter what the cost; and he immediately gave weight to this bombastic threat by provocatively ordering the mobilization and enlargement of the Indonesian armed forces and the formation of specialist commando assault and sabotage units to be held ready to attack anywhere within the proposed Malaysian territories.[10]

For a time it seemed that such immoderate actions, which practically amounted to a declaration of war, would wreck the Heads of Government meeting that was scheduled to take place in Manila. Fortunately, however, commonsense prevailed in time and the Conference, which lasted from July 31st until August 5th[11], ended by confirming both the agreement reached earlier by Abdul Razak and the other Acting Foreign Ministers to accept the findings of one last organised survey of the feelings of the people of the Borneo States towards Malaysia and the proposals for setting up Malphilindo. When the session closed, Tunku Abdul Rahman and the Presidents of Indonesia and the Philippines joined together in issuing an appeal to the Secretary-General of the United Nations, U Thant, to send a neutral team of international observers to Sarawak and Sabah to settle once and for all whether or not those States wanted the federation to take place. U Thant was quick to respond to this request, for a United Nations team arrived in Borneo on August 16th.

In the meantime, however, an acrimonious argument had broken out between Britain on the one hand, and Indonesia and the Philippines on the other, over how many Asian observers were to be admitted to the two colonial territories under investigation, and who they should be. This was a carefully engineered dispute that provided President Sukarno with both the opportunity he had been seeking to withdraw from the whole affair and an excuse to refuse to accept the United Nations team's findings should they not coincide with his own views, which it was by then fairly obvious that they would not.

Troubles, which are said never to come singly, also arose in Singapore, where Lee Kuan Yew's Chinese-orientated government had not been amused either by the suggestion that Malaysia was to be a Malay State, or that it was to enter a new confederation of Malay nations, no matter how loose, called Malphilindo. This seemed to the PAP leaders to be a political move aimed directly against the interests of the Chinese; and so they made it clear that if the findings of the commission of enquiry then operating in Borneo led to a postponement of Malaysia, or anything else should happen to change the original concept of the federation, Singapore would demand, and if necessary take, its independence on August 31st, even if this meant standing alone.

This choleric outburst alarmed both Britain and Malaya, for it seemed to be playing directly into communist hands; a possibility which provoked the two governments into making the impetuous joint declaration that whatever the Commission's recommendations, Malaysia would be inaugurated on September 16th. In the event, the Report, which was published just two days before the set date, justified their decision, for the United Nations team was unanimous in its opinion that Malaysia was the people's choice as their way to attain independence.

Despite a theatrical and somewhat questionable unilateral declaration of independence by Lee Kuan Yew on August 31st while there were still more than sufficient British troops on the island to have made this abortive had the Governor been so instructed, Malaysia, comprising the Federation of Malaya, Singapore, Sabah and Sarawak came into being on September 16th. As expected, both Indonesia and the Philippines refused diplomatic recognition to the new State and both countries broke off relations with Malaya. Thereafter, Indonesia stepped up its armed aggression and political blackmail, not hestitating to employ its own military personnel, thinly disguised as Azahari's guerillas, not only in Sarawak, but also against parts of the Malay Peninsula.

Chapter Fourteen
The 1964 Elections

If Malaysia's period of gestation and birth had been fraught with dangerous complications, its infancy was certainly no more tranquil, for in addition to continual harassment and occasional outright military aggression resulting from Confrontation by Indonesia, internal stresses began almost immediately to appear. These latter were caused not only by the uncompromising opposition to the whole concept of the Federation by organisations so different in ideology and political ambition as the Pan-Malayan Islamic Party, the Sarawak United Peoples Party and the Socialist Fronts of Singapore and Malaya, but also by internecine warfare within the ranks of parties pledged to defend Malaysia, and personality clashes among their leaders.

This trouble stemmed largely from the fact that in neither the Federal Parliament nor in any of the State Legislatures, with the sole exception of the PMIP-dominated State of Kelantan, was the government formed from a single integrated and disciplined party, the administrations instead consisting of various combinations which often represented widely divergent racial, cultural and political interests. These were too often held together either by political expediency, or the ambitions of certain of their leaders to attain and hold high office. In such circumstances Abdul Razak, when visiting the Borneo member States in his capacity as Minister for National and Rural Development, sometimes found himself with the thankless task of acting as mediator or referee.

THE SARAWAK POLITICAL SCENE

When, in 1511, Malacca fell to the Portuguese, its position as a centre of Islamic learning, together with a certain amount of its non-European controlled trade, passed to Brunei; whose Sultans eventually ruled an empire that included the areas of northern Borneo now known as Sarawak and Sabah. As with all empires, that of Brunei enjoyed its century of glory and then began to fade into slow decline and disintegration. By the beginning of the fourth decade of the nineteenth century its territory of Sarawak; which had long been plagued by pirate fleets, was in near chaos following an insurrection organised by personally ambitious members of the Malay aristocracy. The Sultan there-

The 1964 Elections

fore gladly accepted an offer of assistance from a British merchant-adventurer, James Brooke, who, with the modern armament of his ship was able to rout the pirates and blockade the dissidents. For his services Brooke first became Governor of Sarawak and then obtained sovereign right over the territory which he, and two successors, ruled from 1841 as 'White Rajahs' until the Japanese invasion during World War Two.

Within their dominions, for from 1888 Britain controlled external policy and defence, the Brookes were absolute monarchs, although in later years the Rajah voluntarily decided to be guided in his decisions by an Executive and a Legislative Council. In 1941, not long before the Japanese invaded, a Constitution was granted that promised sweeping improvements. After the Japanese had surrendered, however, Sarawak was governed by a British Military Administration; and in 1946, on return to civilian rule, the State became a Crown Colony. Gradually, social services were introduced and rural development started; and the native peoples began slowly to emerge from the dark ages and their leaders to consider how best to protect them from future exploitation or even extinction, for with countries all around them becoming independent, it seemed that their British protectors must soon also depart from Borneo.

Nevertheless, emancipation from concern with purely parochial issues was long in coming, and so the first national political organisation, the Sarawak United Peoples Party (SUPP), was not formed until 1959. This organisation, although it presented itself to the people as a non-communal, multi-racial party, was patently very largely Chinese in support and sympathy; a circumstance that, in reaction, brought about the birth of several other parties, designed primarily to protect the interests of other particular groups or communities. The Dyaks, for example, founded Parti Pesaka Sarawak (Pesaka) and the Sarawak National Party (Snap), which could claim to represent up to 40 per cent. of the people; while the Malays and Muslim Melanaus, who in combination made up nearly 24 per cent of the population, came out with Parti Negara Sarawak (Panas) and Barisan Raayat Jati Sarawak (Barjasa) which, in 1964, amalgamated to form the Party of Indigenous Peoples (Parti Bumiputra).

Even before Malaysia had been formed, SUPP, which had wanted independence for Sarawak through federation with Sabah and Brunei, had been heavily infiltrated by the local clandestine — for the party was illegal — communist organisation; and this had led many moderate, and particularly middle-class, Chinese to prefer the Sarawak Chinese Association (SCA), the local equivalent of the MCA. Following the inauguration of Malaysia in late 1963, Snap, Barjasa, Panas, Pesaka and the SCA, had formed a coalition government as the Sarawak Alliance; with the Secretary-General of Snap, Datuk Stephen Kalong

Ningkan, as Chief Minister. SUPP went into opposition. Soon, however, the first of the inter-party conflicts that were destined to become a major feature of Sarawak politics occurred between members of the coalition government. In addition, there were occasional estrangements between elements of the Sarawak Alliance and the Federal Government in Kuala Lumpur which, after one such clash in 1966, did not hesitate forcibly to remove Datuk Stephen Kalong Ningkan from the Chief Minister's post, thereby putting Snap into opposition.

POLITICS IN SABAH

Sabah, too, had formed part of the Brunei Empire; but in the eighteenth century was ceded to the Sultan of Sulu as payment for reinstating by force of arms his feudal lord, the Sultan of Brunei, who had been deposed by an insurrection led by his own Chief Minister. This land was, in the second half of the nineteenth century, purchased by a group of European merchants, and in 1881 acquired from them by the British North Borneo Company. Sabah was occupied by the Japanese from 1942 until 1945; placed under British Military Administration from the end of the war until July 1946; after which it was a Crown Colony until independence was achieved in 1963 through entry into Malaysia.

Until 1961 there were no real political organisations in the State; but five parties were formed in time to contest the first-ever elections, that were held in December 1962. There were two non-Muslim Kadazan parties, which in 1964 amalgamated to become the United Pasokmomogun Kadazan Organisation (UPKO) and the United Sabah National Organisation (USNO) made up mainly of Brunei and Sulu Malays and converts to Islam among the native peoples. Then there were two Chinese Associations — for this community accounted for about 23 per cent. of the population — which, before the 1962 elections, combined to form the Borneo Utara National Party (Bunap). After the inauguration of Malaysia this last organisation changed its name to the Sabah National Party (Sanap) and eventually merged with, and became assimilated by, the Sabah Chinese Association (SCA).

The 1962-63 elections decided only the composition of District Councils and Town Boards; the members of which, in turn, chose from among their number nominees for the State Assembly and, after entry into Malaysia, for the Federal Parliament. In the year preceding Malaysia, all of the main parties joined a Sabah Alliance which did not, however, fight the elections as a unit. Donald Stevens* the leader of UPKO became the State's first Chief Minister; while Datuk Mustapha bin Datuk Harun, leader of USNO, took over as its first Head of State. This tenuous alliance soon ran into trouble when its Muslim and non-Muslim

---

*now Tun Haji Muhammad Fuad Stephens; a former Sabah Head of State.

elements fell out over certain provisions that had been incorporated into the original Malaysia Agreement to safeguard the rights of the native peoples. The main points of controversy were over actions designed to strengthen the position of the Muslims at the expense of other religious factions and pagans; for USNO wished to rescind those clauses that prevented the immigration into the State of large numbers of Malays from Malaya and the Southern Philippines, the recognition of Islam as the State religion, and the elevation of Malay to be the sole official language. Thereafter, these two parties moved farther and farther apart and there were frequent irate and emotive exchanges between their leaders Donald Stephens and Datuk Mustapha.

THE 1963 SINGAPORE ELECTIONS

Singapore, too, had its political divisions, both on racial and ideological lines. The former was, as usual, between the Malays and the Chinese; while the main ideological dispute involved two Chinese factions, at times almost equal in electoral strength, the Peoples Action Party and the Socialist Front (*Barisan Socialis*), the former vigorously supporting Malaysia and the latter urging withdrawal from it. The Malay community was bitter against the Chinese not only because it was economically weak, but also because, as it accounted for only about one sixth of the island's total population, it wielded little political power, even after entry into Malaysia. It was in fact itself split on this last issue, for many of its members were Indonesian immigrants whose families had arrived on the island less than a generation before, and who were therefore still prone to be sympathetic towards President Sukarno and to heed his propaganda.

Lee Kuan Yew had promised the people of Singapore that new State elections would be held as soon as practicable after entry into Malaysia. He wasted no time in honouring this pledge, for three days after his unilateral declaration of independence, while in fact the whole future of Malaysia was still in the balance, finding himself without a working majority in the House and therefore sometimes dependent upon the support or abstention of the Singapore Alliance to rule, he dissolved Parliament and nominated September 21st as Polling Day. Through this action Malaysia could easily have collapsed less than a week after it was inaugurated, for not only was the radical opposition, consisting of the Socialist Front and Ong Eng Guan's United Peoples Party — who whether they wanted it or not would also have the support of the local underground Communist organisation — expected to give the PAP a tough fight at the polls, but the Kuala Lumpur controlled Singapore Alliance showed every intention of opposing it too, regardless of the danger of anti-Malaysia candidates being elected in a number of vital constituencies by their doing so.

This local version of the Malayan Alliance consisted of the Singapore branches of UMNO, the MCA and the MIC together with a combination of small liberal-conservative parties jointly known as the Singapore Peoples Alliance. Its decision to contest the elections in opposition to the PAP as well as against other left-wing parties was thought by Lee Kuan Yew and his colleagues to show that certain leaders of the MCA, notably its President Tun Tan Siew Sin, were prepared to go to any lengths to ensure their defeat. This, suggested Lee, was because they feared that the PAP might one day replace the MCA as the Chinese element in the main Alliance. He expanded this theory in an Eve of Poll broadcast, in which he charged that the Singapore Alliance, as it had no chance at all of winning the election, was hoping to bring about a Socialist Front-UPP victory, so that the Federal Government would be provided with an excuse to take over Singapore by force and rule it by decree in the interests of national security [1]. In the event the Singapore Alliance, which had held seven seats at the dissolution, lost the lot. It therefore achieved nothing more than to antagonise Lee and cause him to decide to ignore the tentative bargain that he had made with UMNO leaders not to enter Malayan politics for several years.

The PAP, on the other hand, exceeded even its own expectations, by winning no less than thirty seven constituencies out of a possible fifty one. Of the remaining fourteen seats, thirteen were taken by the Socialist Front and the last by its electoral ally the United Peoples Party. This victory for the PAP, apart from securing its power base in Singapore, meant that under the terms of merger the party executive now had the right to nominate twelve of the fifteen members who eventually would sit for Singapore in the Malaysian Federal Parliament, while the Socialist Front would select the other three. Lee Kuan Yew was therefore in a strong position to retaliate for the encroachment by the Alliance on his special preserve, ineffective though that had turned out to be, and in April of the following year, when the Malay Peninsula held its Federal and State elections, seized the opportunity to repay this aggression by intervening in selected constituencies in direct opposition to MCA candidates.

MALAY STATES ELECTIONS

The Malayan Alliance, which was of course the incumbent administration, once again placed Abdul Razak in overall control of the direction of its combined election strategy; and in April 1964 went to the polls with complete confidence in victory, for Indonesian Confrontation had united the bulk of the nation behind it and provided it with a simple but effective platform to fight from — patriotism in the face of foreign aggression. This placed most of the opposition parties in an invidious position, for to continue to advocate the dissolution of the Federation while their country was being attacked and invaded by Indonesia in order to achieve that same purpose, was to risk being branded by the voters as traitors, or at best as puppets of Sukarno. Alternatively, to support Malaysia, as many socialist Chinese and Indians did out of fear of Indonesian domination through Malphilindo, was to appear to be a mere shadow of the Alliance.

One section of the opposition that Abdul Razak saw might conceivably cause the Alliance some electoral embarrassment, if not actual danger, was made up of two parties, fighting independently, that had originally been formed from splinter groups of two of its own communal components. The first of these, the National Convention Party (NCP), was an offshoot of UMNO; and the other, the United Democratic Party (UDP), from the MCA. The NCP had joined the anti-Malaysia Socialist Front, which until then had comprised only the Malay-orientated Parti Rakyat (Peoples Party) and the basically non-Malay Labour Party. The UDP, however, after initially opposing the Malaysian Federation, had later come to accept it, with some reservations, as a *fait accompli,* but nevertheless, in its election campaign, laid the blame for Confrontation, with all its attendant dangers, squarely on the Alliance government, which it claimed had mishandled the situation through a combination of arrogance and incompetence.

The National Convention Party had been started by some former members of a small socialist wing of UMNO who had advocated a far more radical policy of land reform and nationalisation of resources than the conservative majority was prepared to support. They had also criticized the party executive for forming political alliances with non-Malay organisations and lining up internationally with the West instead of joining the neutralist Third World of emerging Afro-Asia. The leader and most charismatic personality of this group was Abdul Aziz Ishak who, following the 1955 elections had been appointed Minister of Agriculture and Co-operatives. During his period in this office, he had gained a personal following among rural Malays, which he felt was larger than it in fact turned out to be. His popularity, such as it was, was due to the efforts he had made to raise the peasants' standard of living mainly through State financed co-operatives designed to eliminate non-Malay middlemen and moneylenders. Personal political ambitions and unorthodox methods of working rather than these praise-worthy objectives eventually brought him into head-on collision with his Cabinet colleagues — particularly Abdul Razak who was in overall control of rural development — and in 1962 Tunku Abdul Rahman decided to move him from Agriculture to the Ministry of Health.

By using threats of resignation Abdul Aziz succeeded temporarily in maintaining his position; but some time later was asked to resign from the Cabinet; and eventually was expelled from the party altogether. A sufficient number of his adherents followed him out of UMNO to make possible the formation of his own political vehicle, the National Convention Party; but his support at the polls, even in the Selangor constituency that had previously elected him, was very limited. In the 1964 elections neither he nor any other member of his party succeeded in winning either a Parliamentary or a State Legislature seat. His defection from and opposition to UMNO did produce one very important side effect, however, for in order to rally their supporters and defeat him in Selangor, the UMNO party executive, which over-estimated his backing as much as he had done, brought on to the political scene a dynamic lawyer, Datuk Harun bin Haji Idris, who was soon to emerge as an indefatigable champion of Malay rights and was later to play a most important, although often controversial part in UMNO and national affairs.

The United Democratic Party, which initially was based on an MCA splinter group, was led by that Dr Lim Chong Eu who, in 1958, had defeated the veteran Tan Cheng Lock for the party's Presidency. When, in the following year, UMNO had routed MCA dissidents protesting the allocation of seats for that year's general elections, Dr Lim had resigned his Presidency and temporarily gone into retirement. In 1962, however, he re-emerged to found a basically Chinese, though as usual in Malaya nominally non-communal organisation to oppose the Alliance. The UDP leadership, realising that in order to win elections it needed greater voting strength than the already split Chinese community alone could provide, actively sought members of other racial origins; and even went so far as to elect a Malay as titular President. With the advent of Malaysia, the party had visions of attracting Chinese and some other non-Malay support from the Borneo States; but failed to make any real headway, even in Malaya, either in the Federal or the State elections. Dr Lim won its only seat in Parliament and the party secured but four seats in the State Legislatures, all of them in Penang.

When the election campaign first opened, an attempt was made to form a united opposition capable of putting a sufficient number of all-community backed candidates into the field to offer the voters a viable alternative to the Alliance as the next government. Differences in ideology and communal interest proved too great to be overcome, however, and in the end only the anti-Malaysia Labour Party, Parti Rakyat and the National Convention Party combined together to fight as a unit, the Socialist Front. The Pan-Malayan Islamic Party, which once again seemed likely to provide the most effective challenge to the Alliance, at least in those northern States where Muslims were in the majority, ignored Malaysia as a main issue and instead concentrated upon the appeal to the rural people of a theocratic Islamic State and promises to amend the Constitution to increase the privileges and safeguards already enjoyed by the Malays and other indigenous Muslim peoples. The Peoples Progressive Party, although as a Chinese-orientated socialist organisation it was at variance with the Alliance on many issues, warmly supported Malaysia. Its field of influence was limited, however, for its votes were picked up mainly in Perak, from those Chinese who were dissatisfied with the showing of the MCA, but could not accept the pro-Sukarno policies of the Socialist Front.

For the reasons already given, the PAP decided to throw down the gauntlet in a few selected Chinese-majority areas in order to demonstrate to UMNO its potential electoral strength in the Peninsula when compared with that of the MCA and the Socialist Front. The party, although it made a great display of being multi-racial, clearly aimed its main appeal at the Chinese-educated workers, by offering them continued representation within the Alliance that would fight to ensure them equal rights with the Malays. At the same time, it ostentatiously avoided trying to win Malays away from UMNO; and in fact its speakers went out of their way to proclaim that the party wanted the Alliance, under the leadership of moderates like Tunku Abdul Rahman and Abdul Razak, to win the election. This attempt to drive a wedge into the existing coalition neither frightened the MCA nor won over UMNO; for Abdul Razak, Syed Jaafar Albar and other Malay leaders not only called upon their own race to vote against the PAP, but pointedly warned the Chinese as a whole that to support its chauvinistic policies could only lead to serious trouble in the future.

As soon as electioneering properly got under way, Abdul Razak became the victim of a sustained and vicious personal underground whispering campaign that, to the one community sought to brand him as an ultra Malay nationalist who was fanatically anti-Chinese; and to another as a bad Muslim who was not above using the Islamic religion for his own political advantage. To the Chinese it was further suggested that if he ever took over the Premiership, which, if they voted in the Alliance, might well take place within the next year or so as Tunku Abdul Rahman was reputed to have a serious heart condition, their community would suffer severe racial discrimination and economic and cultural oppression. Unpleasant as this persistent smear campaign was for him personally, it had little real effect upon the outcome of the election, for the main considerations before the electorate were clearly matters of national, and for the Chinese should Sukarno be victorious, communal survival.

Stressing this telling point in one Perak constituency where non-Malays formed a clear majority of the registered voters, Abdul Razak told a giant rally that the only real alternative to the Alliance as the next government would be either the Socialist Front or the Pan-Malayan Islamic Party.[2]

But both of these parties, with their anti-Malaysia policies, [he said] have shown clearly that they will bring our country under the domination of Sukarno and the Indonesian Communist leader D.N. Aidit if they ever get into power .... Therefore the supreme issue before you when you cast your vote on April 25th is clear. Either you want to continue as an independent nation, or to be an Indonesian colony. The Indonesian threat is real .... It is a question of 10 million people in Malaysia being dominated by 100 million in Indonesia.

This theme of collaboration with Sukarno proved to be a powerful weapon in the hands of the Alliance, for several of the leaders of these two opposition parties, which posed the only positive threat to UMNO, were well known for their earlier lobbying for a total union of Malaya with Indonesia. In fact, the leader of Parti Rakyat, Ahmad Boestamam, had at the time that he was arrested in February 1963 under the provisions of the Internal Security Act, been accused of supporting the anti-Malaysia Brunei revolt of the previous December that had sparked off Sukarno's Confrontation[3]. Alliance spokesmen also condemned the Socialist Front and the PMIP for accepting money from Indonesia to help with their election expenses; and added that both parties were also being aided by the Indonesian State Radio, which was beaming broadcasts to the Peninsula calling on Malayans to vote for them.[4]

When arms and ammunition were discovered on the beach at Bachok in Kelantan, a PMIP stronghold, Abdul Razak went on record as saying:[5]

... The ammunition and the ship came from our enemy, Indonesia. It is now clear that the PMIP leaders have connections in this matter. The PMIP leaders have often been the champions of President Sukarno and his colleagues in our country. Now we have found deadly weapons in Kelantan — probably for their plans to resort to violence.

PMIP leaders were quick to refute this charge and to deny categorically that they had any intention of resorting to violence to achieve their aims. Instead, they were quite prepared, they said, to accept the verdict of the ballot box. In the event, this went against them, for they lost heavily in both the Federal and the State elections.

Polling Day was on April 25th and despite the acrimony with which the election had been fought, the accusations and counter-charges that were levelled, the sensitive inter-communal issues raised, and the element of religious fanaticism deliberately whipped up in the East Coast States, there had been no rioting nor any other form of civil commotion. Nearly four-fifths of the electorate voted and the result, as widely forecast, was a decisive victory for the Alliance which, in the elections for the Federal Parliament, won 15 constituencies that had pre-

The 1964 Elections

viously been held by members of the opposition, or by independents, and ended up with 89 out of a possible 104.

Abdul Razak once again successfully contested the Pekan constituency in Pahang, defeating his Pan-Malayan Islamic Party opponent by more than 10,000 votes, a majority that was close to 4,000 higher than in 1959 in a similar two-party contest. The declared result was:

Tun Haji Abdul Razak bin Hussein	11,858
Abdul Hamid bin Hitam (PMIP)	1,711
majority	10,147

Of the 104 seats fought for in the Parliamentary elections the Alliance won 89 and were given 58 per cent. of the valid votes cast, against the 74 seats and 52 per cent. obtained in 1959. The opposition, on the other hand, did badly; with the PMIP securing 9 seats against the 13 it had won in 1959, the Socialist Front 2 against 8, the PPP 2 against 4, and the United Democratic Party and the Peoples Action Party, both offering themselves for the first time in Peninsular Malaysia, 1 seat each. Party Negara failed to win a seat and no independents were elected. The number of candidates who lost their deposits through obtaining less than one-eighth of the valid votes cast was 49, of whom 14 were from the United Democratic Party, 11 from the PMIP, 9 the Socialist Front, 6 the PAP, 3 Party Negara, 2 PPP and 4 independents. None was from the Alliance.

When the representatives of Singapore, Sabah and Sarawak, who had, on this occasion, been nominated by their respective State Assemblies, were counted together with those elected in Malaya, the numbers of seats held in the Federal Parliament held by individual organisations or coalitions of parties were: Malayan Alliance 89, Sarawak Alliance 18, Sabah Alliance 16, PAP 13, PMIP 9, Parti Negara Sarawak 3, Sarawak United Peoples Party 3, Barisan Socialis Singapore 3, Malayan Socialist Front 2, PPP 2, and UDP 1. This meant that the combined Alliance, which formed the Central Government, disposed of 123 seats, against 36 held by a divided opposition.

In the Malay States elections, the Alliance won every seat in the Kedah, Pahang, Negri Sembilan and Johore Legislative Assemblies; and obtained majorities in all the other Peninsula States except Kelantan, where the PMIP took 21 of the available 30 seats. In all, the Alliance won 240 out of a total of 282 seats, 33 more than in 1959. Here too the opposition parties did badly. The PMIP securing only 25 against the 42 seats they had held in 1959; the Socialist Front 8 against 16; the PPP 5 against 8; and the United Democratic Party, which had not contested in 1959, got 4. Party Negara which had won 4 seats and independents who had held 5 in the previous elections, failed, as did the PAP, to win a single seat. In this political battle 156 candidates lost their deposits: 37 of them from the PMIP, 35 the United Democratic Party, 32 the Malayan Socialist Front, 25 independents, 13 from Party Negara, 8 from the PAP, 5 the PPP and only 1 from the Alliance.

CONFRONTATION CONTINUES

Throughout 1964 the main preoccupation of the Alliance leaders, especially Abdul Razak in his capacity as Minister of Defence, was, however, with the continuing Confrontation by Indonesia and, to a lesser degree, the more passive hostility toward Malaysia displayed by the Philippines. In January, in an effort to east tension between the principal protagonists, the United States Attorney-General, Mr Robert Kennedy, held two meetings with President Sukarno, the first in neutral Tokyo and the other on his home ground in Jakarta. The outcome of these talks, at which the United States representative was believed to have exerted considerable financial pressure, was that the Indonesian President reluctantly agreed to a temporary truce in Borneo. However, no sooner had Mr Kennedy left the country in order to obtain the Malaysian government's agreement to this, then Sukarno began making further provocative speeches about Confrontation, declaring that it would soon be resumed in other, more potent, forms.

Nevertheless, the cease-fire duly went into operation; and early in February was followed by a meeting of Foreign Ministers in Bangkok at which Malaysia was represented by Abdul Razak, Indonesia by Dr Subandrio, and the Philippines by Mr Salvador Lopez. At the end of almost a week of fruitless discussions, the talks finally broke down when the Indonesians refused point-blank to withdraw their guerillas from Sabah and Sarawak until after a political settlement of the entire Malaysian dispute had been reached. At the same time, Dr Subandrio demanded a total withdrawal of all British military, air and naval forces from the area; but this Abdul Razak declained even to consider, declaring that the British were there for the sole purpose of defending Malaysia against outside aggression and that they would remain as long as Indonesia made their presence necessary.

Further talks between representatives of the three governments took place in Bangkok at the beginning of March; but again broke down over the refusal of Indonesia to withdraw its troops and guerillas from Malaysia's Borneo territories. Thereafter, relations with Indonesia worsened, for spasmodic fighting had continued throughout the period of the cease-fire; and on March 10th Abdul Razak, as Minister of Defence, announced that as heavier and more widespread attacks must be anticipated, all citizens between the ages of 21 and 28 would, very shortly, be liable to be called up for National Service in either the armed forces or the civil defence. This caused new inter-racial tensions within Malaysia itself, provoked by vociferous opposition to conscription by certain non-Malay elements, which erupted mainly in Singapore. Furthermore, rumours soon began to circulate among the Malays that large numbers of Chinese and Indian youths were leaving the country in order to avoid the call-up. Internationally, things came to a head on April 8th, when the Malaysian government officially announced that as its intelligence services had learned that weapons and explosives intended for the use of Indonesia-supporting subversives and saboteurs had recently been smuggled into both the Malay States and Singapore, the cease-fire was over.

At the end of May the situation temporarily improved, for the Philippines government made a genuine and praiseworthy effort to find a formula for peace. First of all diplomatic relations between Kuala Lumpur and Manila were resumed; and this victory for commonsense was soon followed by the news that due to secret negotiations successfully carried out by Special Envoy Salvador Lopez, there would be a summit meeting in Tokyo in June, in which Tunku Abdul Rahman, Abdul Razak and the Presidents and Foreign Ministers of the Philippines and Indonesia would all participate.

When the preliminary meeting of Foreign Ministers that preceded by two days the Heads of Government summit of June 20th took place, Abdul Razak stated Malaysia's position unequivocally: 'there are troops in our country which have no right to be there. So, if these troops are removed ... it will be easy to resolve our dispute [6].' Dr Subandrio then indulged in a little dissimulation by declaring that this was not as simple as Abdul Razak seemed to think, because these troops and guerillas were not there by order of the Indonesian government alone, but because of deep individual personal convictions. Their objective, he said, was to win for the peoples of Borneo true independence [7]. At a final session of this round of talks Abdul Razak, disappointed by the lack of real progress, told the Indonesian delegates bluntly: 'There are two ways open to us: peace or war. You cannot have it both ways ,.,,[8]'. But Dr Subandrio's position, which remained unaltered throughout, was that Indonesia could not be the aggressor against Malaysia, since no such State existed.

Following the inevitable breakdown of these Tokyo talks, the scale of Indonesian military intervention was stepped up; regular troops, armed and trained for the purpose, replacing many of the para-military volunteers fighting in Borneo. The situation became even worse in mid-July, when it was reported that President Sukarno had ordered his navy to sink any Malaysian boats found using the Malacca Straits. Piracy was certainly practiced against some fishing boats; and those captured were later used to land parties of saboteurs at various places around the coast of the Peninsula. This dangerous escalation towards war reached its zenith on August 17th, when a raiding force of more than 100 armed and uniformed guerillas, of whom 27 were Malaysian Chinese, landed at three separate places on the west coast of Johore.

This landing was more intended to provide reinforcements for, and stiffen the calibre of, local guerillas already active in that area than as a serious invasion, for Sukarno remained convinced, despite intelligence reports to the contrary, that revolution was imminent in the Malay Peninsula. Even before the first thoughts of Malaysia had been mooted by Tunku Abdul Rahman, the Indonesian equivalent of the CIA, intent on promoting Sukarno's plan for a 'Greater Indonesia', had begun employing dissident elements in both Malaya and Singapore for fifth column activities. Later, these clandestine groups were strengthened by volunteers who had been recruited, or so the local authorities were led to believe, to fight for the 'liberation' of West Irian, the last remaining Dutch colony in the Archipelago.

When Malaysia was at last inaugurated, this fifth column was further reinforced by local opponents of such a union; and it is said to have played a leading part in fermenting the racial disturbances, between Malays and Chinese, that broke out in Singapore on July 21st and again in the first week of September. These clashes had as one of their primary objectives the further widening of that rift between the PAP and the Alliance that was already threatening once more to bring about the premature demise of Malaysia.

Chapter Fifteen
Singapore Leaves Malaysia

When, before the formation of Malaysia, Lee Kuan Yew had agreed to accept as few as fifteen seats as Singapore's allocation in the Federal Parliament he had naturally exacted a price for his forebearance. This was that Singapore should retain complete control over its own policies for labour and education. Without these concessions he would probably never have won the 1963 election; for the Singapore trade unions were as suspicious of the motives of the ruling Alliance as its ultra-conservative wing was of their's. In addition, the majority of Singapore parents disagreed with the pre-eminent position given to the Malay language in the Malayan system of education.

Necessary as these concessions were at the time, they were resented by the members of a powerful ultra-nationalistic lobby in UMNO, who held the view that the unions and the Chinese Middle and High Schools in Singapore were the main breeding grounds for Communism; and that failure of the central government to control them could put the whole Federation in danger from spreading subversion or even from a new insurrection. They therefore opposed the proposed merger; and only the personal intervention of Abdul Razak, acting as usual as the Tunku's trouble-shooter, saved the situation and Malaysia. At an emergency meeting with these extreme right-wing UMNO leaders held at his home, *Sri Taman,* he patiently worked on them until at last they grudgingly agreed not to obstruct the Malaysia plan. Nevertheless, these influential Malays retained their suspicion of Lee Kuan Yew, and their belief that his party was a hot-bed of Communism, for as long as Singapore remained a part of the Federation. Such right-wing fears, when taken in conjunction with the latent anti-Malay feelings held by a substantial proportion of the Chinese majority in the Singapore population, made for a potentially explosive situation.

SINGAPORE RIOTS

Following Singapore's entry into Malaysia and the total defeat of the Alliance candidates in the State elections a few days later, the UMNO executive despatched to the island the party's Secretary-General, Syed Jaafar Albar, with instructions to reorganize their local branches and prepare them for a new trial of strength in the future. He tried to instil a more rabid nationalism into the branch leaders and this eventually led to demands on behalf of the local Malay community for privileges and safeguards equal to those enjoyed by the indigenous Muslim peoples of the Malay States. Although the PAP government was prepared to make concessions, it felt unable to meet the full demands; and so racial tension, deliberately exacerbated by members of a strong anti-Malaysia underground movement, bubbled dangerously just below the surface.

On July 19th, 1964, the Malays mounted a protest demonstration, which unfortunately turned out to be the catalyst needed to spark the dormant antipathy into bloody violence. In the riot that followed two people were killed and many more injured. The worst was yet to come, however, for two days later, on the occasion of the birthday of the Prophet Muhammad, fighting broke out along the route of the traditional Malay procession when ardent Muslims, whose religious zeal had been taken advantage of by pro-Indonesia agitators, battled with hordes of left-wing Chinese hooligans. Before peace was finally restored some twenty more persons had lost their lives and about a further 200 had been injured. The police made many hundreds of arrests.

An uneasy truce was observed by both parties until the beginning of September, when a further riot occurred, which was, however, firmly put down by the Singapore government. Although it was generally agreed that anti-Malaysia subversives had gone out of their way to promote these clashes, Lee Kuan Yew and other members of his party decided to lay part of the blame on those UMNO leaders from Kuala Lumpur who had, they claimed, stirred up partisan and anti-Chinese feeling among the local Malays. In support of this contention they quoted a leaflet said to have been circulated in some Malay areas on the day before the July riots. Among other statements, this warned that Chinese gangsters were planning to attack the Prophet's birthday parade; and had ended with the suggestion that: 'before Malay blood flows in Singapore, it is best to flood the State with Chinese blood'.[1]

Whatever the truth of these charges and counter-accusations, the central government realised the danger of inter-communal rioting spreading to the Malay States, and so did its best to cool tempers. Abdul Razak, speaking officially in Kuala Lumpur, accused pro-Indonesian agitators and fifth columnists from both communities of fermenting the disturbances; and called upon all Malays and Chinese to save their hatred for the common enemy who was attacking their country. Some sections of the Malay press, which were totally opposed to co-existence or cooperation with the PAP, continued however to print articles blaming that party, and particularly the Singapore Work Brigade[2], a militant PAP youth organization, for the violence.

LEADING IN OPPOSITION

The extent of this inter-communal conflict and the bitter reaction it brought forth from opposing political leaders, was a clear warning to both the Alliance and the PAP of the dire consequences that could follow if this antipathy was allowed to escalate. So both sides informally agreed temporarily to avoid raising sensitive issues, or to encroach on each other's political preserves, until peace had been fully restored. Unfortunately, this truce did not last very long, for the more militant elements in both camps found it impossible to resist indulging in barely concealed moves one against the other. In addition, there were conflicts of interest between the PAP and the Alliance over the collection and re-spending of Federal taxes; and a steady rise in PAP political blood-pressure as it became obvious that UMNO was still intent on reorganizing and strengthening the Singapore Alliance so that it could more effectively oppose Lee Kuan Yew's party in the forthcoming 1967 State elections.

The end result of all this was that the PAP began openly to oppose not only the MCA, but also UMNO, which it accused of beggaring the other communities within Malaysia in order to divert a disproportionately large share of public funds to providing benefits for its own community. Lee Kuan Yew, during the course of one of his many speeches overseas said,

> One of the most dangerous myths in Malaysia, is that only the Malays are poor; but in actual fact, a number of Malaysian Indians and Chinese are equally impoverished. So there should be in Malaysia two sharp economic divisions; the haves and the have-nots — after all a person's admission into the have-club or the have-not-club is not dependent on his culture, race or religion, but on an accident of birth. Therefore, the have-nots should, in their collective interest, band together to raise their economic status, and to fight for better amenities.[3]

Thereafter, Lee left the Alliance in no doubt that he saw himself as the champion of the have-nots of all communities and intended to try to rally them, under his personal banner, to fight the forces of reaction as represented by the conservative Alliance. His opportunity to forge a powerful, united opposition seemed to have arrived when, between January 27th and 29th, 1965, Special Branch officers of the national police arrested the Chairman of the NCP, the President and Vice-President of the PMIP, and several prominent members of the Socialist Front[4], all of whom were accused of being associated with a pro-Indonesia plot to overthrow the legally elected government of Malaysia by force. Two weeks later the Socialist Front organized a protest rally in Kuala Lumpur, which quickly degenerated into a riot. Many people were arrested, including several more leading left-wing politicians.[5]

This left much of the opposition leaderless and demoralised; forming a political vacuum into which Lee projected himself with considerable enthusiasm and skill. In May he succeeded in uniting the PAP, SUPP, UDP, PPP and Machinda — a predominantly Chinese party formed in Sarawak in 1964 — in a Malaysia Solidarity Convention that was pledged to build a Malaysian, as against a Malay, Malaysia. All of the parties in this organization were largely Chinese in membership and sympathy, and all but the PAP had, at some time or another, been against the formation of Malaysia. Despite this; it was widely rumoured that Lee saw it as a vehicle through which he would eventually attain his ambition to become Prime Minister of Malaysia; for he was probably the only Chinese at that time who could possibly have had any hope of so doing.

TOWARDS SECESSION

By this time many members of the UMNO executive had become doubtful whether the union with Singapore could last much longer; for they recognised that if Lee could succeed in combining the main Chinese and Indian vote with that of a substantial proportion of the indigenous peoples of Sabah and Sarawak, he might in time conceivably win sufficient seats to head a non-Malay government. In addition, there were persistent rumours circulating that he was planning, purely as an alternative, to form a new combination of states consisting of Singapore, Sarawak, Sabah and, because of its large non-Malay population, Penang.

As the seriousness of the challenge to their political hegemony filtered down through the ranks of UMNO members, the party leadership found itself inundated with demands that the Singapore State Legislative Assembly should be dissolved and the island administered directly from the Federal capital. Though obviously aware of this Malay backlash occasioned by his open campaign of communal denigration, Lee continued inexorably on his suicidal collision course with central authority.

The Malaysia Solidarity Convention gradually stepped up its campaign against UMNO, both inside the various Legislative Assemblies and at public rallies, by making a catch-phrase out of the slogan 'a Malaysian Malaysia'. This, in itself might not have infuriated the Malays too much, had it not been coupled with insinuations that the Alliance government, because it was dominated by UMNO, was so determined that this multi-racial concept should never become a reality that it had already prepared plans to alter the Constitution so as to prevent it. The dangers of such intemperate handling of sensitive issues was so apparent, that it eventually provoked even such a normally undemonstrative man as Abdul Razak to declare bitterly that if Singapore really wished to remain as part of Malaysia, it should find a more stable and cooperative leader. Lee responded to this by claiming to believe that it meant that he was in imminent danger of detention without trial under the Emergency Regulations and that some of his party colleagues might soon have to flee the country.

Overcoming his well-advertised fear of such an eventuality, Lee Kuan Yew chose May 27th, 1965, to throw down his main challenge to UMNO when, in the Federal Parliament, he moved an Amendment to the Royal Address, the official statement of future government policy, regretting that it contained no assurance that the country was soon to become a genuinely Malaysian Malaysia. The debate that followed was so emotionally charged and acrimonious that on June 3rd the gentlemanly but, when provoked, volatile Tunku Abdul Rahman wisely decided to leave it to his tough, unflappable Deputy, Abdul Razak, to make the closing speech for the government.

The real point at issue had, of course, very little to do with whether or not Malaysia was going to be truly Malaysian, for this was merely a legitimate Parliamentary excuse to enable Lee to introduce into a debate a variation on his theme that the central government was trying to condition the general public to accept that his party was subversive and should be proscribed. His argument was that the key to this intention was contained in that part of the Royal Address that dealt with the threat to the security of Malaysia that came 'from within'. This, he gave his listeners to understand, was clearly levelled at the PAP in general and himself in particular.

Dismissing this notion as 'sheer conceit', Abdul Razak replied by saying that as the Prime Minister of Singapore was, in his official capacity, given copies of all security service briefings, and further as he had his own representative sitting on the National Defence Council, he was well informed as to the identity of those posing the 'threat from within'. He knew, for example, that some 1500 persons from Sarawak and at least 150 Communists from Singapore and the Malay States were actively working for Indonesia[6]. There were also others who were not Communists but who, because they had chosen to support Indonesia against their own country, had been placed in preventative detention. If the government had thought that Lee was numbered among these, he would already be in prison; for they would not hesitate to act against anyone who was a security risk, no matter what his position.

Lee, Abdul Razak continued, had tried unsuccessfully to get the MCA thrown out of the Alliance and the PAP brought in to take its place. It was only after this ploy had failed that he had suddenly produced his bogy of a Malaysian Malaysia and discovered what he alleged to be a Malay plot to dominate the other communities within the country. In order to achieve his personal ambitions he was even prepared to instigate a break-up of the Federation.[7]

> He has also said that probably the peoples of Penang, Sabah, Sarawak, Singapore and Malacca could come together. In short he has suggested that Malaysia must be broken into two .... Malay Malaysia and Mr Lee Kuan Yew's Malaysia, or as he calls it Straits Settlements Malaysia. Hence the reason for bringing this Amendment to the Royal Address and alleging that we in the central government consider him a threat to the security of the country ....
> The Prime Minister of Singapore .... is like a bride who was madly in love with a man and having married him, finds the new home unsuitable and would like to go back to mother .... Having married into this new family, the bride is not content with being just a member of the family, or having the right to inherit the family property, she wants to dominate and rule the family at the same time ....
> The Malaysia which he (Mr Lee) once supported is no longer the Malaysia that he wanted .... If he were part of the central government, as he had wanted to be, then everything would be all right .... The truth of the matter is .... the PAP have found that they cannot adapt themselves to the new situation. They cannot accept the fact that they are only one of the fourteen States of Malaysia; and that the Prime Minister of Singapore is the leader of the government of only one of those States. Mr Lee Kuan Yew has found himself like a frog in a big lake .... He has to croak in order to show his presence and to be heard.

Abdul Razak then went on to criticise Lee's attempts to further his political ambitions, no matter what the cost to others.

> He decided to try to drive a wedge between different races. At first, in order to make friends with UMNO and the Malays, he attempted to discredit the MCA, stating that it did not represent the Chinese or stand up for their rights. When he found that this would not work and that UMNO was determined to stand firm with the MCA, he switched tactics and attacked UMNO and the Malays. By doing this he hoped that he would get the non-Malays to support him. This is a dangerous way of attempting to gain political support in a multi-racial country. This method must surely lead to racial strife and tension and ultimately to trouble and chaos. I do not believe the Prime Minister of Singapore cares very much about this as long as he has a chance of getting additional support for himself.

Although at the conclusion of this speech Lee's Amendment was defeated by a massive 108 votes to 14, it had become clear that unless something drastic was done to placate Malay opinion, there would soon be a new spate of inter-racial trouble to contend with. By June 11th, when Tunku Abdul Rahman was due to leave for London to attend the

1965 Commonwealth Prime Ministers' Conference, most of his Ministers were agreed that the government had been left with only two alternatives; either Lee Kuan Yew must be replaced as Prime Minister of Singapore, or that State should withdraw or be expelled from Malaysia. The amiable Tunku was reluctant to force either issue and instead called on his Deputy, Abdul Razak, to step once more into the breach to see if there was, perhaps, still some chance of a reconciliation.

On the day that Tunku Abdul Rahman departed for Britain, Abdul Razak temporarily took over as Acting Prime Minister. Loyally, he acceded to his friend's request and towards the end of the month arranged a private meeting with Lee in the hope that at an informal discussion, where both were freed from the necessity of maintaining an attitude in front of their supporters, a formula could be worked out that would save everybody's face. This they failed to achieve, however, and so Abdul Razak had reluctantly to advise an ailing Tunku, who had stayed on in London to convalesce from an illness that had overcome him during the Conference, that there remained little chance of Lee modifying the position that he had adopted. The Kedah Prince implored him not to give up as long as the slightest chance of a reasonable compromise existed; and so against his better judgement, Abdul Razak agreed to continue to fight for what he already felt to be a lost cause.

Throughout the greater part of July further negotiations were carried on, this time between Abdul Razak and Dr Goh Keng Swee, the former economist who was Singapore's Minister of Finance. Despite long hours of work and the great determination with which Abdul Razak tried to preserve Malaysia intact, the attitude of the Singapore ministers with whom he treated remained unaccommodating. By the end of the month, therefore, he had to concede that further negotiation had become pointless and that there was no alternative to Malaysia and Singapore going their separate ways. Once this conclusion had been reached, Abdul Razak decided that it would be better for all concerned if the break were made as quickly as possible. He so informed the Tunku, whose sole responsibility it was to make the ultimate decision, and was eventually told to go ahead and make arrangements for Singapore's expulsion. Abdul Razak therefore recalled Dr Goh, told him what was to happen, and requested him to head the Singapore delegation that would have to help work out the terms of separation.

MALAYSIA MINUS SINGAPORE

When Lee Kuan Yew heard the bad news he rushed down from the Cameron Highlands holiday resort, where he had been sitting in spendid isolation on the sidelines, to confer with his Deputy. The next day,

August 7th, the Singapore Prime Minister met with the recently returned Tunku and with Abdul Razak in a desperate last minute attempt to avert the inevitable. It was pointless; and as the document specifying the terms of separation had already been prepared, it remained only for the two sides to ratify it. The PAP Ministers then left for Singapore which, on August 9th, 1965, was to become an independent Republic.

Despite the many conflicts of interest that had brought about the enforced separation of the two States, Abdul Razak and Goh Keng Swee had managed to arrange for a wide measure of continued cooperation, particularly in the fields of defence and commerce. The former was of course necessitated by Indonesia's continued Confrontation, to which both countries were still subject. The provisions included: the setting up of a Joint Defence Council; mutual assistance in the face of outside aggression; the continued use of military bases and logistical facilities in Singapore by the Malaysian armed forces; and agreement not to conclude Treaties with any third party that would be detrimental to the interests of either of the signatories.

In the Federal Parliament the PMIP suggested that since Malaysia had been partly dismembered, that it would be a good idea to break it up altogether and so put an end to Confrontation. There was a different, though predictable, reaction from the Borneo territories, where there was widespread fear that the departure of Singapore would give complete political power in the Federation to the Malays. There were renewed rumours of negotiations for the setting up of a new Association of States, to comprise Singapore, Sarawak and Sabah; and so persistent were these, that first Tunku Abdul Rahman and then Abdul Razak undertook goodwill tours of the East Malaysian States in order to reassure their political leaders. These two tours were successful, for eventually talk of further secession faded into the background.

With the return to Singapore of that island's members of the Federal Parliament, the Malaysian government ruled that the PAP, as a foreign-based political organisation, was illegal. So Mr Devan Nair, the sole remaining elected Federal representative of the party, changed its name, but not its objectives. He called the new organisation the Democratic Action Party (DAP) and confirmed that it still stood for a Malaysian Malaysia. Despite such skirmishes, relations between Singapore and Malaysia improved; and military cooperation proved successful. This prompted Abdul Razak to announce that the two States were jointly to seek a new defence pact with Britain that, if possible, would also include Australia and New Zealand.

The partial break-up of Malaysia was hailed by Sukarno as a sure sign that total victory would not long be denied him; but before he could begin properly to exploit the situation, he became the victim of a Communist-inspired and airforce and navy backed coup. Early in the morning of October 1st, a supposedly auspicious day for the Communists, six of his leading generals were assassinated; and a Revolutionary Council set up. Before the instigators of this *coup d'etat* had time to consolidate their position, however, they were overthrown by the army; but because the Communists showed every intention of fighting a long-drawn-out battle, a compromise settlement was worked out that left Sukarno as President, albeit with greatly reduced powers. When this game of political musical chairs ended, Malaysian leaders found to their disappointment that they were very little better off than before, for at Sukarno's behest the new regime confirmed that Confrontation would continue unabated.

***** ***** *****

AFRICAN INTERLUDE

On November 11th, 1965, Mr Ian Smith, head of a colonial government representing the European settlers who were a minority in Rhodesia, unilaterally declared the independence of that country from Britain. He did so in an attempt to prevent the eventual introduction of a universal suffrage that would inevitably have led to negro political domination. His action generated much violent criticism — most of it directed against Britain — but little action, in the United Nations, the Commonwealth, and within the Afro-Asian community. The British Labour Government of Mr Harold Wilson, at which Smith aimed his defiance, applied rather ineffective economic sanctions; but, despite widespread pressure to do so from outside the United Kingdom, resolutely refused to resort to military force in order to regain control of this former self-governing colony. The measures taken failed to satisfy some of the more aggressive, newly independent African States, however, and so at the beginning of January, 1966, Sir Abubakar Tafawa Balewa, the Prime Minister of Nigeria, hoping perhaps to force Wilson's hand and certainly to halt a threatened break-up of the Commonwealth — for Ghana and Tanzania had already broken off diplomatic relations with the United Kingdom — invited member countries to a summit meeting of Heads of Government, or their deputies, in Lagos.

Malaysia willingly accepted this invitation; and Abdul Razak, in his capacity as Deputy Prime Minister, was appointed to head a 14-man delegation that also included Datuk Ghazali Shafie, Permanent Secretary to the Ministry of External Affairs and Dr Lim Swee Aun, the Minister of Commerce and Industry. Addressing a press conference on January 8th, the day that his delegation was due to leave for Lagos, Abdul Razak, after stating unequivocally that Malaysia could never accept the imposition of military-backed minority communal rule in Rhodesia, nevertheless went on to counsel moderation in criticising the method by which Britain had chosen to handle the situation. It was better, he said, to go to Lagos and listen carefully to Harold Wilson's side of the story before taking a positive stand.

The Deputy Prime Minister and the members of his delegation reached Lagos in the evening of Sunday January 9th. It was not the first time that Abdul Razak had been in Nigeria, for in 1960, on his initial visit to Africa, he had officially attended the country's independence celebrations. The scenes that greeted him on this occasion, while being driven from the airport to his hotel, were far different and less open to optimism, for many of the shops and houses were heavily shuttered and squads of steel-helmeted and armed police were patrolling streets that were cluttered with the remains of cars and other vehicles that had been burnt during a bloody riot that had earlier cost the lives of several people.

The next morning Abdul Razak paid a courtesy call on the Nigerian Premier for the purpose of handing him a letter from Tunku Abdul Rahman, apologising for his inability personally to attend the Conference. It was not pleasant to be abroad in the streets, even on the Marina in the select suburb of Ikoyi where Sir Abubakar had his official home, for the riot police were again out in force; and it was common knowledge that in one of the outer suburbs they had already had to use teargas, and later firearms, to disperse demonstrators and arsonists blocking one of the two main roads leading into the centre of the capital. Troops and sailors in full battle equipment, or armed police in riot formation, stood guard at every important interesection; while armoured cars patrolled the main roads in the vicinity of the Conference Hall. It was feared that unruly mobs might deliberately provoke violence in the presence of the delegates and foreign newspaper correspondents in order to draw international attention to the political oppression then rampant in the Western Region of Nigeria; a quarter of the country that was widely believed to be on the brink of civil war.

On Tuesday and Wednesday, the 11th and 12th of January, the delegates to the Conference met in the Federal Hotel under the chairmanship of Sir Abubakar Tafawa Balewa. During the course of these talks Abdul Razak, speaking for Malaysia, began by associating himself with the others in welcoming Singapore to the Conference for the first time as an independent State. It was an added pleasure for him to do so, he told them, because it was Malaysia that had sponsored Singapore for membership of the Commonwealth.

After outlining the measures that Malaysia had so far taken against Rhodesia, including banning such trade as had previously been carried on between the two countries, Abdul Razak suggested that the British government should plan alternative measures in case the sanctions already imposed should fail to work; and that these should not preclude the possible use of military force. At the same time, there should be preparation for what was to follow after the illegal regime had been made to surrender.

Obviously, he went on, the British government would, for a period, have to impose direct rule; but this should not be a mere return to colonialism, but a period of apprenticeship to enable nationalist Africans to be taught the business of government so that later they could gradually take over the administration under supervision, as a prelude to complete independence. He appealed to all member States of the Commonwealth to make immediate arrangements to train African Rhodesians, so that they might more quickly be able to run their own country without too great a reliance on expatriates. Finally, he asked that the economic and technical assistance being considered for Zambia in order to offset the effects that sactions against its neighbour Rhodesia would have on its economy, should, if necessary, be extended to cover Malawi or any other African Commonwealth country similarly affected.

It was a trying time for Britain's Prime Minister, Harold Wilson, but he came out of the battle practically unscathed; for despite the generation of heat and acrimony, at the conclusion of the Conference the delegates, after unanimously agreeing to reconsider the whole matter after the lapse of another six months, joined together in issuing a communique backing Wilson's policy of sanctions. The Commonwealth had been saved, and if anything strengthened, by this meeting which, from Sir Abubakar's point of view, had been a brilliant international success. It was not to prove enough, however, to starve off the internal insurrection that blatant corruption, widespread nepotism and vicious oppression had made almost inevitable within his own country.

When, on January 14th, Abdul Razak and his party left their hotel at 11 pm to drive to the airport, rumours were rife that as soon as all the foreign delegates had left the country, martial law was to be proclaimed and the main opposition political parties proscribed. They reached the airport just before midnight and were amazed to find that no one from the Nigerian government was there to see them off. The Nigerians had other things to worry about, however, for at that very moment a meeting of junior service officers was taking place in the capital at which individual commanders of task forces were being told of the part that they were to play in the imminent military coup.

Abdul Razak's plane left Ikeja airport at 1 am; and when it landed at Cairo, he was informed that the armed forces had already overthrown the Nigerian civilian government and that Sir Abubakar Tafawa Balewa and Chief Festus Okotie-Eboh, the Finance Minister, had been abducted and were feared to be dead. A conjecture that some days later proved to have been correct.

The aircraft bearing the Malaysian party had cleared Lagos little more than an hour before the first violence had erupted.

***** ***** *****

THE END OF CONFRONTATION

About three weeks after Abdul Razak had returned from Lagos, President Sukarno, who had in the meantime regained most of the power which had been stripped from him following the 1965 revolt, reinstated the anti-Malaysia Dr Subandrio to the position of his deputy and increased Communist participation in his administration. Indonesia was in such a state of turmoil, however, that a flare up in Confrontation seemed to offer the best opportunity for diverting the attention of the ordinary people from the corruption and runaway inflation that stemmed largely from Sukarno's incompetent interference in the management of the economy.

Early in March, long before his scheme of self-preservation at the expense of Malaysia could have any chance of success, student riots broke out in Jakarta. Predictably, Sukarno over-reacted and the guard regiment from his palace, arbitrarily despatched to end this defiance, killed a number of young demonstrators. This had the opposite effect to what was intended, for it merely increased the violence of the protest; and so on March 12th the army took over once again and Sukarno, although he still retained all the outward trappings of power, in reality was little better off than a prisoner. Real power then passed to a triumvirate consisting of General Suharto, Foreign Minister Dr Adam Malik and an economist, the Sultan of Jogjakarta. In the belief of the majority of the Indonesia people, however, Sukarno was still the country's dictator; and so, in order not to present any opportunity for an insurrection to reinstate him, the plan gradually to phase him out of State affairs had to be carried out slowly and with circumspection.

Although the new rulers' official position was, therefore, that Confrontation would continue, they let it be known in Kuala Lumpur that they were anxious to put an end to this pointless enmity. Acting upon this knowledge, Abdul Razak, with the full backing of his Premier and the Cabinet, instigated the opening moves designed to lead to a final settlement. He chose as his agent Des Alwi, the adopted son of former Indonesian Prime Minister Shahrir and a close personal friend since their student days together in London.

Because of the personal enmity of President Sukarno and Dr Subandrio toward his family, Des Alwi had sought and been granted political asylum in Malaysia. Despite this defection, he still had many acquaintances in Indonesian political and diplomatic circles, former friends and supporters of his father, whom he was able to contact from Kuala Lumpur by radio. In April it had been announced from Jakarta that diplomatic relations were soon to be re-established with Singapore, a move which initially led to fears that the Indonesians might be hoping to use that island as a base for further attacks upon the Malay States. But when, on April 30th, Foreign Minister Adam Malik went out of his way categorically to deny any such intention, conciliation seemed to be in the air and the way open for direct negotiation if the two parties could be brought together.

Secret unofficial negotiations were begun using Des Alwi as a go-between; and these were followed, early in the morning of May 25th, by an even more secret flight into Kuala Lumpur of an Indonesian military aircraft containing a goodwill mission of army officers. These emissaries were met at the airport by Ghazali Shafie, who brought them in a small convoy of closed cars to *Sri Taman* for a working breakfast with Abdul Razak. Later that morning, the military mission flew to Alor Star, capital of the State of Kedah, for a series of meetings with Tunku Abdul Rahman. They returned to Indonesia on May 27th; and two days later Abdul Razak and Adam Malik met at the home of the Thai Foreign Minister in neutral Bangkok. By the end of the month comprehensive measures for the ending of Confrontation had been worked out and agreed upon; and on June 1st the two negotiators left for home to report their success to their respective governments.

All of the main points of this negotiated peace were approved in separate secret sessions by the two governments, but due to the petulant opposition of the reluctant puppet, Sukarno, whose signature as titular President was still necessary on the Indonesian side, the formal ratification was postponed, although all warlike exchanges between the two States were totally at an end. On June 3rd, in anticipation of the official end of Confrontation, full diplomatic, trade and cultural relations were re-established between Malaysia and the Philippines, with both countries agreeing that the question of Sabah, while it was to remain an issue in dispute, should eventually be settled by negotiation or arbitration. Finally, on July 5th, Sukarno was publicly stripped of most of his remaining ceremonial functions and titles, although as a courtesy he was still left as puppet President; and with the impediment of his opposition out of the way, the Indonesian government formally announced that Confrontation was at an end.

A month later, Abdul Razak led a top-level delegation to Jakarta to sign the Peace Treaty. The Malaysians received an enthusiastic welcome from a huge crowd that had gathered at the airport to greet them; but because Sukarno, who while still President could not be completely silenced, continued openly to oppose the peace, there had been rumours that some fanatic who still supported him might attempt to assassinate Abdul Razak, or even the whole delegation. The drive through streets lined by tens of thousands of cheering, flag-waving people, while making their way to the house of the Foreign Minister, where they were to be accommodated, was therefore a nerve-wracking experience; and throughout the whole of their stay, the Malaysians were never entirely at ease.

All went well, however, and Abdul Razak even had an unexpectedly amicable meeting with President Sukarno; although all the actual negotiations were worked out with Adam Malik and General Suharto These culminated, on August 11th, 1966, in the signing of an Agreement which ended hostilities and re-established diplomatic relations. As a face-saver for the Indonesians, however, it was at the same time announced that the peoples of Sabah and Sarawak were, as soon as practicable, to be given a chance to reaffirm, through the ballot box, their willingness or not to continue as citizens of Malaysia.

SHADES OF MAY 13th

Neither the end of Confrontation, nor the secession of Singapore, meant that Abdul Razak was free to relax; for new troubles almost immediately appeared over the horizon to replace those that had been dealt with. Foremost among these was a resurgence of Communist activity, which became even more serious than would normally have been the case, because it coincided with a new wave of racial and religious ill-feeling that manifested itself in many forms of inter-communal bickering and the raising of sensitive issues. It was a combination of these factors, culminating in the bloody violence of May 13th, 1969, that made Abdul Razak probably the only man in modern times first to become virtually the dictator of his country, then voluntarily to relinquish that position in order to become Prime Minster of its elected government, and finally to be democratically re-elected to that office three years later with an overwhelming Parliamentary majority.

Part Three
Dictator and Democrat

Chapter Sixteen
Prelude to Tragedy

'May 13, 1969, will go down in our history as a day of national tragedy,' wrote[1] Abdul Razak in the preface to an official report on the race riots that followed closely upon the declaration of the greater part of the results of the 1969 general elections. 'On that day the very foundation of this Nation was shaken by racial disturbances whose violence surpassed any we had known. It was only the firm and prompt action of the government, together with the loyal support of the Armed Forces and the Police, which quickly brought the situation under control. Had it not been for the immediate preventative measures, there is no doubt that the whole country would have been plunged into a holocaust.'

He then went on to admit that these excesses had jolted people of all communities and walks of life out of their former complacency into the realization that the measures so far taken to bring about racial harmony and social justice had been grossly inadequate. This had led to a situation in which political agitators and other opportunists had been able, almost at will, to play upon the miseries and frustrations of large sections of the population with results that might well have led to a national disaster, perhaps even to civil war.

This then was the unfortunate vehicle that, in mid-1969, was to bring Abdul Razak to the pinnacle of political power in Malaysia; pledged to correct these social ills and promote inter-racial harmony, mutual tolerance and national unity. Aims that were to be the driving force behind his political career over the next few years; the ultimate implementation of which would require no less than the complete restructuring of the country's non-egalitarian society and of its racially unbalanced economy. The other great upheaval carried out during this same period was to be in the field of international relations; involving a spectacular re-alignment of foreign policy, which would face up to the realities of the redistribution of military and economic power in the world and take Malaysia firmly into the Afro-Asian camp, particularly the Pan-Islamic part of it.

This was still all in the future, however, and before any of it could happen, it was destined that certain Malaysians of all communities, protected by the democratic processes they so often flouted and blinded to the dangers they courted by the magnitude of their own ambitions, would walk recklessly along the road that led towards national and communal self-destruction.

***** ***** *****

When Confrontation with Indonesia finally ended, it might have been expected that the peoples of Malaysia and Singapore could look forward to a period of peace and tranquility. This was not to be, however, for with the main external threat removed, new internal dissensions began quickly to appear. First of all a wave of apprehension was stirred up throughout the Chinese and Indian communities of both these territories when politicians began once more to talk of those countries in Southeast Asia having large Malay populations joining together in a new Maphilindo. There were rumours too that trouble was to be deliberately fermented in Singapore so as to force the Malay nations, in the interests of their own security, to take it over. These vague fears were given some measure of substance, and agitators provided with welcome political capital, when in the same month, August 1966, that the Peace Treaty between Malaysia and Indonesia was ratified, a number of Malays were arrested and held in preventative detention on charges of plotting to overthrow the government of Singapore.[2]

A RESURGENCE OF ARMED COMMUNISM

The ubiquitous Communists had, of course, been active in both the Malay Peninsula and the Borneo states throughout Confrontation, although their deeds had often, for reasons of political expediency, been included among the exploits attributed to a pro-Indonesia fifth column. They were, at the time that Confrontation ended, operating as two entirely separate commands: one in Sarawak, which had its main links with the Indonesian Communist Party; and the other, in north Malaya, formed from the remnants of the Communist guerilla army that had been driven into the jungles of southern Thailand during the late 1950's. Both began to step up their direct attacks on constituted authority by ambushing parties of Malaysian soldiers and police, assassinating Chinese detectives or immobilizing them by intimidating their families, and by indulging in minor acts of arson and sabotage more effective for the publicity they generated than for the actual damage caused.

Soon, however, Abdul Razak, who as Minister of Defence had been directly concerned with combating these attacks upon the armed forces, and Dr Ismail who, until Abdul Razak took over from him in June 1967 when he resigned for reasons of ill health, was responsible for internal security, came to the conclusion that these overt acts of aggression were

Prelude to Tragedy 191

mere camouflage designed to cover far more insidious moves against the government. These turned out to be concerned with the large-scale infiltration of certain quite legitimate socialist organisations in the Borneo states and the Malay Peninsula for the purpose of using them for a new political offensive aimed at weakening the country's power to resist a future armed insurrection.

FURTHER TROUBLE IN BORNEO

Although strenuous efforts at the highest level had been made to prevent Sabah and Sarawak from following Singapore out of Malaysia, there was at least one Minister who might well have welcomed it. This was the Minister of Finance, Tan Siew Sin [3], who had the difficult task of finding the money to implement the plans for the Borneo states' economic advancement. One of the main factors in persuading Sabah and Sarawak to join Malaysia in the first place, had been the very great benefits that had been promised them from participation in Abdul Razak's schemes for rural and national development. This expenditure had always been dependent upon financial assistance from Singapore, however, and in fact arrangements for a loan of M$150 million for this purpose had been included in annex J of the Malaysia Agreement that had been signed in July 1963 [4].

Despite this, the Singapore government had later sought to make this loan conditional on the immediate formation of a Malaysian common market, designed largely to provide a hinterland take-off for its industrial production; and so by the time of separation, no part of this money had found its way into the coffers of the Federal government [5]. This meant that funds had to be diverted from long-term projects in the Peninsula in order to make good the short-fall; and so, to placate the Malays who were the ultimate losers, the Federal government was forced to make demands upon the Borneo states that stirred up further trouble in that area.

One of the many points of controversy centred around the Malayanisation, in contradistinction to Borneanisation, of the civil services in those two States; for the central government wished to replace the expatriate officers serving there with their own personnel, mainly Malays, from the Peninsula. The Borneo leaders, while in some ways sympathetic to the Federal government's efforts to provide employment for its supporters, wanted instead to retain these Europeans until such times as their own people were able to take over from them. They felt that to surrender most of the top and medium-grade civil service positions to nominees from Kuala Lumpur would be to invite a virtual, if concealed, take over of their States' affairs.

The most important clashes between the Alliance Federal government and various Bornean political interests came, however, with the enforced replacement of the Chief Ministers of both Sabah and Sarawak. The first of these political crises occurred in Sabah in the second half of 1964 as part of the power struggle between USNO and UPKO and the personality clashes between their respective leaders Datu Mustapha, the Head of State who was by special agreement still permitted to engage in politics, and Donald Stephens the Chief Minister. Towards the end of June representatives of these organisations and the Chinese party Sanap, which together formed the Sabah Alliance and so between them held all of the State Ministerial posts, held talks in Kuala Lumpur, with the Prime Minister as arbitrator, to agree on the composition of a new Cabinet. The outcome was that due to Federal pressure UPKO lost ground to USNO, which gained, among other things, the newly created post of Deputy Chief Minister.[6]

The second crisis, that in Sarawak, was brought about by the machinations of a powerful group within the State Assembly attempting to unseat the Chief Minister, Datu Stephen Kalong Ningkan, leader of the predominantly Dyak Sarawak National Party. This was due partly to the belief held by many of the Malays and native peoples in the Alliance that, because of the existence in Snap of a financially important minority of Chinese, the Chief Minister was inclined to favour that race at the expense of his own people; and partly to personality clashes with one of his own Ministers, Taib Mahmud of Barjasa, a Muslim Melanau at whose instigation, a new Native Alliance was eventually formed. With this achieved Barjasa, Pesaka and Party Negara Sarawak (Panas) withdrew from the Sarawak Alliance and demanded that Datu Ningkan resign.

The Chief Minister counter-attacked, however, and succeeded in getting on to his side the leader of Pesaka, Temenggong Jugah. The Temenggong then publicly accused Taib Mahmud of trying for his own ends to split the Dyak vote[7] and on May 15th led Pesaka back into the Sarawak Alliance. The next day Chief Minister Datu Ningkan officially accepted the withdrawal of Barjasa from the government and with it the automatic resignation of its two State Minsiters, one of whom was Taib Mahmud[8]. Due to the timely intervention of the central government, however, this dispute ended in a compromise; for the Chief Minister reinstated the two Barjasa members as Ministers. In a speech in the Federal Parliament on June 3rd[9], the leader of the Sarawak United Peoples Party (SUPP) placed the whole blame for this uproar, at the door of UMNO; a charge which Abdul Razak categorically denied.

The second and more serious Sarawak State Assembly crisis took place in mid-1966 and was occasioned by Taib Mahmud trying once again to form a Native Alliance from which Snap was to be omitted. Ostensibly, however, its cause was a difference of opinion between

UMNO and its supporters in Sarawak who wanted a speed-up of Malaysianisation and the acceptance of Malay as the sole official language, and the wish to Datu Ningkan to move more slowly and cautiously. On this occasion, however, Temenggong Jugah failed to support his fellow Dyak [10] and in fact even urged him to resign. On June 12th Datu Ningkan countered by dismissing Taib Mahmud from the Cabinet on the grounds that he was trying to undermine the authority of the government. The remaining Barjasa and Pesaka Ministers resigned the next day.

Then, as Abdul Razak was later to explain to the Federal Parliament [11], on June 14th twenty-one, or exactly half of the members of the State Assembly signed a letter to the Governor declaring their lack of confidence in the Chief Minister. Two days later the Governor called on Datu Ningkan to resign; and on the following day, after he had declined to do so, dismissed him. He then proceeded to appoint a nominee of the Federal Prime Minister, Pengulu Tawi Sli of Pesaka, in his place. Datu Ningkan held, however, that his dismissal was unconstitutional and invited the Sarawak High Court to agree with him. This it did on September 7th when it declared the dismissal null and void. Although Datu Ningkan then automatically once more became the Chief Minister, twenty-five of the forty-two Members of the House signed a petition for his removal. When the Chief Minister refused either to resign or to summon the House to take a Vote of Confidence, the central government decided to act. On September 19th Abdul Razak successfully moved a Bill [12] to Amend the Constitution so that the Governor could place a Vote of Confidence before the State Assembly and, should the Chief Minister lose it, dismiss him. Datu Ningkan was duly voted out of office on September 23rd, 1966, and Pengulu Tawi Sli once again appointed in his place. The Sarawak National Party went into opposition.

After a little consideration many of the Dyaks, including those that still remained within the Alliance, became less enthusiastic about this replacement, for they thought they saw in Datu Ningkan's humiliation an UMNO plot to strengthen the position of the Muslims, and especially the Malays, in Sarawak. That the former Chief Minister might well soon have a chance of winning back many of his previous adherents became painfully clear to Abdul Razak when, while attending an Alliance political rally in the State Capital he heard his colleague Temenggong Jugah, the Federal Minister for Sarawak Affairs, state bluntly that the interests of the Dyaks were being subordinated to those of the Malays. 'If this is the way it is going to be,' said the Minister, 'then this is not the Malaysia we wanted'. [13]

This outburst at a time when he was known to be present, was a clear indication to Abdul Razak that the local Alliance could well be on the point of breaking up still further; and was instrumental in causing him to convene a Party Convention in Kuching for the purpose of bringing irritations out into the open, cooling tempers and restoring inter-party and inter-governmental confidence and cooperation. At the close of this meeting a communique was issued that declared that, 'all the races that make up the Malaysian people are guaranteed by our Constitution and our laws to be equal'. Abdul Razak had succeeded in plugging the cracks in the local Alliance, at least temporarily.

This was by no means the end of his troubles, however, for a new Communist threat was developing to an extent that had caused the Federal government to declare on September 14th, 1966, that a State of Emergency existed in Sarawak. As Abdul Razak announced in the Federal Parliament on September 19th [14], over a thousand hard-core Communists, of whom about seven hundred had received guerilla training in Indonesia during Confrontation, were ready at any time to start a new insurrection. They were backed, it was believed, by several thousand active supporters and sympathisers who were prepared to help them with money, food and information. At the same time, he as the Minister responsible for internal security, knew that serious political and inter-racial troubles were also brewing in many parts of the Malay Peninsula.

VIOLENCE IN PENANG

During the course of 1967 the Labour Party, which included many Communist sympathisers and fellow-travellers among its membership, had been subject to a power struggle in which extreme radical elements plotted the overthrow of moderate leaders like Dr Tan Chee Khoon, so that they could be replaced by a more aggressive faction. Gradually, as these elements gained control, demonstrations against Alliance government policies, particularly after the announcement that from September 1st, 1967, Malay would be the sole official language in Peninsular Malaysia, had become a regular feature of the party's *modus operandi*. These demonstrations became more and more violent until, on Abdul Razak's instructions, the Special Branch of the national police began to crack down on them. Despite arrests and detentions under the Emergency Regulations, which put many of the better known activists out of circulation, in November 1967 various left-wing political associations, including some sections of the Labour Party, organised large-scale demonstrations and an attempted hartal in Penang to protest against the devaluation of the old currency. This led to an outbreak of serious rioting between Chinese and Indians on one side and Malays and other Muslims on the other.

The background to this inter-communal uproar between supporters and enemies of the Alliance government was a decision made in August 1966 that Malaysia, Singapore and Brunei, all of which had previously used a common form of money issued by the Malayan and North Borneo Currency Board, should, in the following year, each issue its own coins and notes which would, however, be interchangeable at par in all three territories. For convenience, it was also agreed that for the time being the money issued by the former Currency Board, which was backed by sterling, should be legal tender and be exchanged at parity with the State Bank issues of each of the three countries, although it would gradually be withdrawn and replaced with new currency as circumstances permitted. On November 18th, 1967, however, sterling was devalued against the Malaysian, Singapore and Brunei dollars, and so this old currency, of which a very large sum was still in the possession of the general public, was thereafter redeemable only at the devalued rate of about 85 cents in the dollar. The Penang branch of the Labour Party immediately took the lead in calling for pretest demonstrations and a general strike against the government.

On November 23rd, and again on November 24th, mobs of hooligans, stiffened by Chinese secret society gangsters, used strong-arm tactics to enforce the strike industrially and through the closing of shops and offices. This deliberate provocation led to counter-action by the supporters of UMNO; and eventually to large-scale inter-communal running battles in the streets. Despite curfews, censorship of news and other attempts to contain it, fighting soon spread to the neighbouring state of Kedah and even into parts of Perak. By the time that the police, backed by troops and armoured cars, had brought the situation under control, more than two dozen people had been killed and many hundreds more injured.

FORMATION OF THE GERAKAN RAKYAT

In 1968 the power struggle within the Labour Party intensified to the point where Dr Tan Chee Khoon, a man whose honesty and integrity was admired by people of all shades of political opinion, decided to quit. This came about when the Party's executive embarked upon a new policy of non-cooperation with the government that included the withdrawing of its representatives from the Federal Parliament and the various State Assemblies. Dr Tan Chee Khoon, a fervent supporter of the democratic process, refused to have any part of this, retained his Parliamentary seat and resigned from the Labour Party. Next, Dr Tan, together with Dr Lim Chong Eu, who had become disenchanted with and resigned from his own United Democratic Party, joined with a number of other moderate and mainly intellectual socialists to found a new opposition party the *Gerakan Rakyat Malaysia,* or Malaysian Peoples Movement. Unfortunately, as this organisation expanded its scale of operations, it picked up a large number of immoderate and less tolerant socialists.

THE FINAL BUILD-UP OF TENSIONS

An extremely dangerous new cause of inter-racial tension and antipathy arose in June 1968 over the impending execution of thirteen Malaysians, eleven Chinese and two Malays, who had earlier been sentenced to death, the former in Johore and the latter in Perak, for allegedly assisting Indonesian saboteurs who had landed in those Peninsular States during Confrontation. A storm of protest was whipped up, internationally as well as within the country — for even His Holiness the Pope interceded on their behalf [15] — culminating in the appearance in the streets of large and menacing demonstrations, especially in Kuala Lumpur in the vicinity of Pudu Jail where the executions where scheduled to take place [16]. Cars were stoned and overturned and attacks made on the police. A noticeable feature of the Kuala Lumpur demonstrations was that they seem to have been staged only in support of the eleven Chinese and not the two Malays.

Previously the Sultans of Johore and Perak, within whose States the alleged subversives had been sentenced, had refused appeals for mercy; but when Tunku Abdul Rahman told them of his fears that the executions could well be the signal for a further outbreak of bloody inter-communal violence, both Rulers agreed to commute the death penalties to life imprisonment. Certain elements were quick to see in this desire for peace a weakness that they felt could be exploited to their advantage in the coming general elections. Six weeks later the Labour Party announced that it would enter no candidates for election and called on all of its supporters to observe, and try to bring about, a total boycott.

THE ELECTION CAMPAIGN

When, early in 1969, Abdul Razak once again assumed responsibility for his party's tactics in the forthcoming elections, he was well aware that the Alliance was about to face far stiffer opposition than it had experienced in any previous electoral battle. It is almost certain, however, that until very much closer to Polling Day he did not realise quite the extent to which inter-racial hatreds and jealousies were to dominate the interests of the electorate, almost to the exclusion of all outside matters. In the previous general election the platform of patriotism against Indonesian aggression had served the Alliance well; and so early in this new campaign Abdul Razak directed his main efforts to exploiting the Philippines threat to Sabah. He had been closely associated with moves to settle this dispute amicably and therefore tended to project his own interest in the subject on to the electorate at large.

In August of 1967, during the first meeting of the Association of Southeast Asian Nations (ASEAN) in Jakarta, Abdul Razak and the Foreign Minister of the Philippines had made considerable progress towards a detente; but this was nullified in September of that year when the Philippines Congress passed a Bill purporting to incorporate Sabah into the Republic. Malaysia, in retaliation, once again broke off diplomatic relations. By January 1968, however, reconciliation had progressed sufficiently to permit a State visit to Malaysia by President Ferdinand Marcos and his wife; and this helped to re-promote friendship to such an extent that on February 6th Abdul Razak was able to inform the Federal Parliament that new talks were soon to be held at Foreign Minister level. Unfortunately, before these could even begin, a well publicised mutiny of Muslim Filipino recruits on the island of Corregidor in April revealed the existence of a para-military guerilla force intended, so dissident members of the organisation claimed in press interviews, for the invasion and occupation of Sabah. Soon afterwards a number of armed men were arrested on an island off the coast of Sabah; and when questioned by the police some of these admitted to having received military training in the Philippines.

To concentrate upon this subject in the election campaign was a minor tactical error, however, for the opposition, no section of which had ever supported the Philippines claim, were able to shrug it off as mere jingoism. As police and other security forces briefs showing the dangerous extent to which the Malays and non-Malays were drawing apart and being incited to hatred by political agitators became frequent, Abdul Razak and other Alliance leaders handling the election campaign began to realise the inroads, on two separate fronts, that were being made into their electoral support. With this re-appraisal of their situation came new, more direct tactics in attacking the PMIP on the one hand and the DAP, Gerakan Rakyat and the Peoples Progressive Party on the other.

As usual the PMIP played upon the theme of religion and tried to make capital out of UMNO's coalition with the MCA and the MIC; and on this occasion was unwittingly helped in the latter by the Alliance government's handling of the Penang riots of 1967, or rather the interpretation that was put upon it, after a little political prompting, by the Malays of the northern States. This was because many of them felt that part of the UMNO leadership, being over-anxious to preserve the multi-racial coalition, had failed adequately to protect them from the strong-arm tactics of the other communities. Here was a situation that the PMIP was quick to exploit for its own advantage.

The focus upon which this attack centred was Tunku Abdul Rahman, whose liberal approach to racial questions was deliberately distorted. According to what he has written [17] some PMIP supporters spread rumours that he was Siamese — probably of somewhat doubtful value as it was well known that his father was the late Sultan of Kedah — and therefore not really a true Muslim; and that this accounted for his lack of Malay nationalistic feeling. In support of this they circulated a picture that purported to show him at a Chinese dinner with a suckling-pig, anathema to Muslims, upon the table just in front of him. Later investigation showed that this latter item had been deliberately superimposed upon the original picture [18]. Meanwhile, in the Kedah constituency of Muhammad Khir Johari, they circulated copies of a different picture, showing the Federal Minister and his wife wearing traditional Chinese dress [19] of the Ch'ing Dynasty period which, it was claimed to susceptible peasants, showed that he too was a good friend of the Chinese.

The PMIP which, because of its racialist policies and religious fanaticism, could hardly expect to win many votes from non-Muslim Indians and Chinese, nevertheless did not hestitate to stand against MCA candidates in some northern constituencies where a large proportion of the voters were non-Malays. This laid them open to the charge, made tellingly by UMNO speakers, that they were cynically helping pro-Chinese opposition parties like the DAP by attempting to split the minority Malay vote, the greater part of which might otherwise have been expected to go to an MCA Alliance candidate if he were backed by UMNO.

Abdul Razak and the other Alliance leaders when speaking in the constituencies counter-attacked the PMIP onslaught by accusing it of accepting financial support from the Communists, who saw in its disruptive policies a chance to ferment trouble and so weaken the hold of the central government on the people. This ploy was aided by the anti-royalist comments of some PMIP campaigners, who pronounced themselves in favour of totally integrating the Peninsular Malay States into an Islamic Federal Republic. More constructively, Alliance leaders drew attention to the lack of economic progress made in Kelantan since the time that the PMIP had formed its last State government; and suggested that other areas would suffer similar stagnation if they voted this party into power.

One of the main reasons why the Alliance had been able to control the central government and every State Legislature, with the exception of that of Kelantan, for so long, had been because the opposition parties had failed to present a united front. Obviously the PMIP had so little in common with the non-Malay parties that such an alliance was most unlikely; but some attempt was made to put together a counter-coalition consisting of the DAP, PPP and the Gerakan Rakyat, although this would, of course, have lacked the Malay element that gave the Alliance its main strength. Negotiations failed, however, and the best that could be arranged was to make a loose electoral agreement, usually only on an individual constituency basis, not to enter or campaign against each other and so split the anti-Alliance vote. None of these parties, or even a combination of them, had the slightest hope of obtaining a majority of seats in Parliament; but they did aspire to two main objectives: firstly, to prevent the Alliance from obtaining the two-thirds majority in Parliament which was necessary in order to pass any new Amendment to the Constitution; and secondly to obtain among them a majority of seats in those State Legislatures, like Perak, Penang and Selangor, where a large part of the electorate was non-Malay.

Each of these non-Malay opposition parties arrogated to itself the championship of the rights of the Chinese and Indian communities, especially the protection of their languages, cultures and economic wellbeing. Unfortunately, in trying to outdo each other in this, some speakers lost touch with reality and incautiously went on to demand the deletion of certain Articles from the Constitution, especially Article 153 that safeguarded the special rights and privileges of the Malays, and to call for an end to preference for Malays in government employment. Others publicly and provocatively proclaimed that the Malays were no more indigenous to the country than any of the other peoples living there.

There were, then, several contending factions each recklessly raising fear and resentment among the supporters of the others; while in the background lurked the Communists and other subversive elements ready to fan into flame the underlying anger and hatred. This they were soon to do, first by the murder of one of UMNO's election workers and then with a direct challenge to the government's authority that fortunately stayed just short of bloody riot.

PRE-POLLING VIOLENCE

As Polling Day approached, it became obvious to those like Abdul Razak who were responsible for internal security that certain political groups were deliberately trying to provoke incidents that could, if not contained immediately, lead to savage outbreaks of inter-racial violence. It was one thing to know that this was likely to happen — and that the best way to beat it was by assembling an overwhelming show of force before the trouble could really get started — and quite another to know just where and when it would erupt. In the event this turned out to be the Jelutong area of Penang where, at about 8.30 in the evening of April 24th, 1969, an UMNO election worker was attacked and killed by a gang of thugs, said to have been undercover Communist agents [20], whom he had tried to stop from painting on the walls of buildings slogans calling for a complete boycott of the elections.

It was a vicious and quite deliberate murder, to which racial insult was added by smearing the corpse with red paint. Indiscriminate Malay retaliation could well have followed; but this was avoided when, at the request of the police, backed by UMNO leaders, the murdered man's family and the Penang Malay community generally, played down the political and racial aspects of the killing and buried the victim quietly.[21]

The next danger point was much farther south, being at Kepong, a small town a few miles from Kuala Lumpur, where on May 4th three policemen on patrol surprised a gang of youths who, in this instance, were busy painting 'boycott the elections' slogans on the public highway. When challenged, the youthful painters allegedly attacked the police with iron bars and other weapons with such violence that the constables who, as is customary in Malaysia, were armed, were forced to open fire in self defence. One of the attackers, a Chinese, subsequently died of his wounds in the Kuala Lumpur General Hospital. His corpse, which reputedly[22] was taken over by Communists, was thereafter used as a means of exciting anti-police and anti-government feeling among large sections of the Chinese community, to whom the youth was presented as a murdered martyr. Instead of being sent back to his home in Kepong, the body was kept in a Chinese death house in the centre of the teeming tenements of the old Kuala Lumpur Chinatown, while permission was sought to form a funeral procession.

The object of the organisers was, of course, to hold this as close to the election as possible; and in fact the application, when this was duly lodged with the Kuala Lumpur police, gave the date of the funeral as May 10th, or Polling Day for both the Federal and the State elections. This the police rejected, for they felt that it would provide a great opportunity for anyone wishing to do so to disrupt, or even prevent altogether, polling from taking place in the Federal Capital[23]; which would be a great tactical victory for the Communists and their supporters. Instead, a permit was granted for the funeral to take place one day earlier, on May 9th. This was issued on the clear understanding, however, that a route specified by the police would be followed and that the number of mourners would be restricted to less than one thousand[24]; which by Chinese custom is not necessarily an outstandingly large number.

Almost from the time that it left the death house, this procession took a route contrary to the one agreed upon; and one that was deliberately selected for the disruption it would cause to the business life of the city. Throughout the day agitators among the 'mourners' attempted to provoke the police to violence with insults, the open singing of Communist songs, and by making speeches to the milling spectators and distributing illegal pamphlets among them[25]. As soon as the organisers of this procession realised that the police had been ordered not to disperse them if it could possibly be avoided, they quickly increased their provocation. For their rowdiest demonstrations they chose particular Malay targets like the Mara building and the nearby headquarters of UMNO.

At both these places the police had great difficulty in holding back large numbers of angry Malays who wished to retaliate.

After about seven hours of this riotous behaviour the procession, which by then was estimated by official sources to number some ten thousand persons, finally reached Kepong, where it was expected that an attack would be launched on the police station. Several specially equipped riot units had been assembled there, however, which was probably why the demonstrators, after parading noisily and menacingly through the streets of that small town, filed in an unexpectedly orderly manner through the cemetary and then gradually dispersed without causing further trouble. The hard core of secret society gangsters who had held this demonstration together had been gathered from many parts of the country, however, which meant that on the eve of Polling Day there were in the Kuala Lumpur area large numbers of armed thugs and young agitators ready for any mischief, but whose main job as laid down by their paymasters was believed to be to 'persuade' people not to vote.

Chapter Seventeen
Black Tuesday — May 13th, 1969

In Peninsular Malaysia Polling Day for both the Parliamentary and State elections was on Saturday, May 10th. It was a worrying time for the caretaker Minister for Home Affairs, for with the lesson of the Kepong funeral in mind, Abdul Razak and those responsible to him for the policing of the country and the maintainance of its internal security, were fearful of more demonstrations and possible attempts to disrupt voting, especially in the vicinity of the Federal Capital. The police and other security forces were therefore maintained on full alert; but by the time the ballot boxes had been sealed at 8 pm, no disturbances, intimidation, or violence of any kind had been reported.

In Sabah and Sarawak too, polling commenced on May 10th; but because of inadequate internal communications and a general shortage of trained supervisory staff, the Election Commission had to arrange to oversee the voting district by district, which meant that polling would have to be staggered over a long period. In Sabah this was scheduled to take sixteen days and in Sarawak twenty nine days, with the proviso that all the results in each State should be announced on the same day; on May 25th and June 7th respectively [1]. There were to be no State elections in Sabah, however, as these had been held only two years before; while in the Parliamentary election ten Alliance candidates had been returned unopposed on Nomination Day, so that in only six constituencies were contests due to be fought.

SABAH ELECTIONS 1967 AND 1969

The first election in which Members were directly elected to the State Assembly were held in Sabah in 1967. At the time that the House was dissolved, all three political parties in the State were members of the Sabah Alliance; but after a series of disagreements over the allocation of seats, they split up and the election became a struggle between Tun Mustapha's USNO, together with its ally, the Sabah Chinese Association, and Datu Donald Stephens' UPKO, which was aided by a few Chinese independents.

When the results were declared, USNO and the SCA had won 19 seats between them, UPKO had taken 12, and an idependent Chinese — gaining a surprise victory over the former Chinese Chief Minister —

the one remaining. At first UPKO and the sole independent went into opposition, but after desertions from the party had weakened its position, UPKO suddenly dissolved itself and its leaders called on all of their members and supporters to join USNO. This left the Sabah Alliance with no real opposition to challenge it. At the time of the 1969 Parliamentary election still no effective opposition had emerged, so that as far as the political parties were concerned, preparation for it amounted to little more than the usual internal wrangle over the allocation of seats.

ELECTION PREPARATIONS IN SARAWAK

At the beginning of 1969 the various political organisations in Sarawak began to prepare for the first ever direct elections for the State Assembly as well as for the Federal Parliament. There were at the time three participants in the Sarawak Alliance: Party Pesaka, mainly Dyak in membership; Parti Bumiputra — which had been formed through a merger of Panas and Barjasa — the Muslim party; and the Sarawak Chinese Association. In opposition were Datu Stephen Kalong Ningkan's Sarawak National Party, the second Dyak party; and the socialist Sarawak United Peoples Party, the membership of which was very largely Chinese.

There was, as usual, disagreement within the Alliance over the allocation of constituencies; and because it was felt by the other participants that there was every chance that if Pesaka was not given what it demanded, it might leave the coalition and instead ally itself with Snap, with which it shared many communal interests, Abdul Razak was called in to arbitrate. During the course of a meeting with the leaders of these three parties, he worked out what he hoped would prove to be a satisfactory compromise allocation of the forty eight State constituencies. This would have given Party Pesaka twenty two seats to fight for, Parti Bumiputera fifteen and the SCA eleven [2]. Some time after he had returned to the Federal Capital, however, the Pesaka leaders rejected this offer and eventually, after further uncompromising argument, the Dyak party decided to go its own way and leave the other two to fight as the Alliance.

ELECTION SHOCKS IN THE PENINSULA

Abdul Razak naturally spent Polling Day in his constituency of Pekan, in his home state of Pahang, where he waited, not in any great trepidation, for the result of his electoral contest with Yazid bin Jaffar of the PMIP to be declared. When this was done, he found that although he had won by a very comfortable margin, his majority was down by 1,222.

He had in fact increased his vote by 783, but the PMIP candidate had increased his party's share by just over 2,000.

The official record showed:

Tun Haji Abdul Razak bin Datuk Hussein	12,641
Yazid bin Jaffar (PMIP)	3,716
majority	8,925

Early in the morning of May 11th the first election results began to come in; and from the very beginning it was clear to Abdul Razak that the Alliance was doing badly. The first real shock came as seat after seat was lost in Penang; and this was soon followed by the fear that the State Assemblies of Selangor and Perak might fall to the opposition. At the same time Parliamentary seats were also being lost and the chances lessening of maintaining the two-thirds majority in the House necessary if the party should feel it required to make future amendments to the Constitution as it had done to remove the recalcitrant Chief Minister of Sarawak. One, at least, of the opposition's main objectives seemed likely therefore to be achieved.

When all of the results for Peninsular Malaysia had been declared, Abdul Razak and the other Alliance leaders found to their chagrin that they had lost 23 seats in Parliament and a further 79 in the State Assemblies. Worse still, they had lost Penang to the Gerakan Rakyat, failed to dislodge the PMIP in Kelantan, had secured only 19 of the 40 seats in the State of Perak, and exactly half of the 28 seats in the State Assembly of Selangor. In all of the other States they had managed to obtain clear majorities; although the opposition parties had made substantial inroads in Malacca and Negri Sembilan, where there were large non-Malay populations.

In Parliament, having won 66 constituencies in the Peninsula and being sure of the 10 uncontested USNO seats from Sabah, the Alliance was at least assured of forming the next government in the 144 seat House, whatever the outcome of the contests still remaining to be fought in the Borneo States. The opposition line-up at that time consisted of DAP 13, a gain of 12 seats; PMIP 12, 3 more than in 1964; Gerakan Rakyat 8, a gain of 6; and the Peoples Progressive Party 4, exactly double what they had had when the House had been dissolved. This made a total of only 37 even if, which seemed extremely unlikely, they could agree upon a common programme. One seat, due to the death of a candidate between Nomination and Polling Days, remained vacant.

Immediately the full story of the Alliance losses was known, certain powerful interests in UMNO, alarmed by the possibility that non-Malay governments might soon be set up in three of the Federation's semi-autonomous States, looked around for scapegoats. Inevitably, the first selected was the MCA, which had suffered the heaviest proportional losses and which, declared this vociferous faction, was also partly responsible for many Malays turning away from UMNO to the PMIP.

In the Parliamentary elections, while UMNO had lost only 8 of the 59 seats it had held at dissolution, the MCA had lost 13 out of 27. Additionally, the MCA had failed to hold any of its seats in the Penang State Assembly, had lost all but one of its 12 seats in Perak and 7 of its 8 seats in Selangor. In these two latter States — for UMNO too had done badly in Penang — the Malay party had lost only 4 out of its 22 seats in Perak and only one of 13 in Selangor [3]. There were impractical demands that UMNO should form a new coalition — presumably with the PMIP, although this was not specified — that would exclude all future Chinese representation. This demand eventually became so embarrassing to the MCA leaders that, on the afternoon of May 13th, they informed the caretaker Prime Minister that as their party had obviously lost the backing of the Chinese community, they felt that it should no longer be represented in the Cabinet, although all its members would continue to support the Alliance government in Parliament.

MOVES IN PERAK AND SELANGOR

As soon as he knew the full results of the elections for the State Assemblies of Perak and Selangor and was officially informed of the tension that was building up there among the Malays, Abdul Razak, who as caretaker Minister for Home Affairs was still responsible for maintaining law and order until a new government was sworn in, flew back to Kuala Lumpur from his constituency in Pahang. On arrival, he felt that he could safely disregard Penang for a while, as its loss was not likely to arouse the same amount of racial and nationalistic feeling, as due to its long association with colonialism it was not regarded as a true 'Malay State'. Instead, he concentrated the whole of his efforts on sorting out the explosive situation that had arisen in Perak and Selangor.

First of all, he consulted with the various police chiefs and military garrison commanders and instructed them that while remaining alert to meet any eventuality, they were to make every conciliatory effort commensurate with public safety to cool tempers and de-escalate racial hatreds. He then turned his attention to Perak where the Alliance, although it had emerged as the largest single political organisation in the State Assembly, was still in the minority and therefore had to await the outcome of the attempts of the next largest party, the PPP, to form a coalition government. This effort depended ultimately upon its obtaining the cooperation of the lone PMIP Member, either actively or as the non-voting Speaker. In the event, the PMIP representative refused to join in any association with non-Malays and so aborted the whole operation, as with him supporting the Alliance — purely in order to keep the opposition out of power — the two sides were split 20-20. A similar situation obtained in Selangor, where the two sides found themselves equal in strength, and equally impotent, at 14-14.

In the meantime, however, Abdul Razak had not been idle, for he clearly saw that the one hope of avoiding inter-racial confrontation lay in the moderate leadership of the Gerakan Raayat. He therefore held talks with former MCA Chairman Dr Lim Chong Eu, who had already been nominated by the Gerakan Raayat to be Chief Minister of Penang and who was, therefore, anxious to cooperate with the central government in maintaining law and order, and succeeded in persuading him to agree that the party would not support any anti-Alliance coalition in either Perak or Selangor. Unfortunately, this decision to remain neutral was not publicised by the Secretary-General of the Gerakan Raayat until early in the evening of May 13th, by which time events had already been set in motion that made the havoc of Black Tuesday almost inevitable.

'VICTORY' CELEBRATIONS

During the two days immediately following Polling Day both the DAP and the Gerakan Raayat held 'victory' celebrations through the streets of Kuala Lumpur that were distinguished by the intensity of their anti-Malay bias and immoderate jubilation. These illegal processions — for no police permit had been issued or even applied for — were rowdy in the extreme; with participants, many of them believed to be secret society gangsters who had infiltrated the parades in order to stir up trouble, deliberately disrupting traffic, openly displaying insulting placards and banners and threatening and jeering at Malay members of the security forces and civilians whenever they were encountered. From the Malay point of view the depths of this hooliganism occurred when an unruly mob of youths riding on motor-cycles and scooters invaded the grounds of the official residence of the caretaker Chief Minister of Selangor, Datuk Harun bin Haji Idris and demanded that, as UMNO no longer ruled the State, he vacate the house immediately, or they would throw him out. They were with difficulty dispersed by the police.

Incensed by this and other unprovoked attacks on their race and political organisations, the Malays decided to hold their own victory procession; and scheduled it for the evening of May 13th. This counter-demonstration was to be on a huge scale and was to be organised and protected by members of a specially trained division of the UMNO youth movement, the Corps of Rugged Youths*[4], a militant faction that

―――――――――
*Pemuda-Pemuda Tahan Lasak.

had repeatedly been accused by the PMIP, both before and during the elections, of using strong-arm tactics in order to intimidate voters who were not supporters of the Alliance. Unknown to Abdul Razak and other moderate Malay leaders, agitators were already at work deliberately inflaming tempers that were near to breaking point; and at the same time suppressing, or discounting, the news that the Gerakan Raayat, which held the balance of power in both Perak and Selangor, had already been persuaded by Abdul Razak not to join any anti-Alliance coalition.

The elections had taken place during the Muslim month of Safar, which in Islamic tradition is an ominous time redolent of misfortune and evil. This psychically dangerous period is said to end on the last Wednesday of the Arabic month, however, and on that day many of the more conservative among Muslims like to take a ritual bath* in the sea, river, or at the village well, in order to cleanse themselves of lingering evil influences. In Malaysia, in modern times, this custom, which is not part of orthodox religious observance, has generally now become a time for communal celebration often in the form of picnics at various popular beaches. One such resort is situated at Morib in Selangor, not far from Kuala Lumpur, and forms part of the State constituency contested and won by Harun bin Haji Idris. These celebrants from Morib, many of whom, it has been suggested, were members of the Corps of Rugged Youths who had been deliberately assembled there from all over the country, were transported to Kuala Lumpur on May 13th in order to reinforce local marchers in the 'victory' procession that was scheduled to start from Harun's residence at 7.30 that evening. They were in a state of great excitement and racial and religious fervour.

A little after seven in the evening of May 13th, while Abdul Razak was at his home *Sri Taman*, he was called to the telephone to speak to Harun, who told him that the UMNO procession in the process of forming up at his house was rapidly getting out of hand and asking him to come there right away to try to pacify the demonstrators. Before he could leave the house, however, he received another call, this time from police headquarters, which informed him that sporadic fighting had broken out between Malays and Chinese in the Kuala Lumpur district of Setapak, one of the constituencies in which a DAP member had been elected to the Federal Parliament.

Abdul Razak then telephoned to tell Tunku Abdul Rahman, who had of course already been similarly informed by the police, that he intended to go at once to Setapak to take charge of the situation, but the Prime Minister, despite his Deputy's pleas to remember his age and

Mandi Safar.

failing health, insisted upon himself going to the troubled area. Eventually, however, he agreed to wait until Abdul Razak arrived to join him; and the Deputy Prime Minister, accompanied by Abdul Ghaffar Baba, the former Chief Minister of Malacca, who had been visiting *Sri Taman* at the time, hurried off to dissuade him from putting himself in danger. He knew what the genial Tunku would not admit to anyone at the time, perhaps not even to himself, that his popularity with the bulk of the Malays was then at its lowest ebb. While Abdul Razak was still arguing with the Tunku, the Officer Commanding the Kuala Lumpur Police District arrived, this time to advise them not to go either to Setapak or to Harun's house, as the disturbances had developed into a full-scale riot and the situation was such that their personal safety could not be fully guaranteed.

Despite this warning and the evidence they saw in the streets of large scale violence, the three Ministers went by car to the High Street police station, where they were briefed on the extent and location of the trouble. From police reports it appeared that news of the fighting in Setapak, the extent of which had, either deliberately or inadvertently through panic, been grossly exaggerated to the point where it appeared that the Chinese there, led by armed secret society gangsters, had launched an all-out attack on the Malays. This news, it was claimed, had so infuriated the demonstrators at Harun's house, many of whom were in possession of, or had quickly acquired, weapons of various kinds, that they had run amuk, attacking innocent passers-by, most of them Chinese, killing or maiming men, women or children without distinction.

This fighting had soon spread to other parts of the town, where it was conducted with such ferocity and hatred that no quarter was given, or apparently expected, by either side. As he looked over the lists of incidents and casualties, Abdul Razak realised that if the police alone were expected to handle the situation, violence might well soon engulf the whole country and so, in order to show his utter determination to stop the killing, he immediately ordered the military garrison within the city to clear the streets; and followed this by placing the whole area of the Federal capital under a strict curfew.

In spite of these precautions, fighting and the destruction of property continued spasmodically throughout the night; necessitating the declaration, on May 14th, of a State of Emergency. By this time the worst of the young trouble-makers, together with a mass of frightened and bewildered ordinary UMNO supporters who had been brought in from many parts of the country to take part in the 'victory' procession, had been confined to an area around the Kampong Bahru Mosque, which they had turned into a strong point, and from which they defied the police to eject them. Many were armed with machetes and other makeshift weapons, while it was known that the shop of a local arms dealer had been looted and all of the guns and ammunition passed to the people camping in the Mosque compound.

Any attempt to dislodge or disarm these refugees would, Abdul Razak realised, only lead to more bloodshed and hatred, for many of them had been worked up by fanatical agitators to believe that they were engaged in a kind of holy war* and that to die gloriously on holy ground would ensure for them entry into paradise. He therefore hastened to withdraw all non-Muslim police and soldiers from the Kampung Bahru area and to replace them with men from the 5th and 7th battalions of the Royal Malay Regiment; and when this was done sent in food and other necessities to the beleaguered refugees through the agency of moderate local religious leaders, who had also been charged with the task of calming everybody down.

RESCUE AT THE MOSQUE

At the time of this outbreak of rioting a group of South Indian Muslims were giving a series of religious lectures in the Kampong Bahru Mosque in order to raise funds for the building of their own mosque in India. When Haji Ali bin Munawar, one of the local religious leaders bent on restoring peace, visited the Kampong Bahru Mosque on the 14th to supervise the feeding and welfare of the people who had taken refuge in the compound, one of these South Indians, who spoke good Malay, handed him a key and told him that a non-Muslim Chinese was hidden in a locked room there, but that if the mob came to know of this they would surely kill him. The next day, when Haji Ali visited the Mosque once again, he handed over the key to the senior caretaker, who had accepted the dangerous task of feeding and protecting this refugee, and told him that arrangements would be made to smuggle the man out as soon as possible.

On the morning of the 16th Harun Haji Idris and Ghazali Shafie arrived at the Mosque and, working to a preconceived plan, distracted the attention of the people in the compound while the young Chinese, who had innocently been caught up in the first day's rioting while passing the Mosque, was hidden in the boot of their car. Soon afterward, they managed to drive away with the man still undiscovered, and take him to the safety of a police station. Later that same day Abdul Razak arrived at the Mosque in a police patrol car and, after assuring the Malays camping there that they were in no further danger from either the Chinese or the security forces, promised them that they would all be sent home in transport provided by the government.

*Jihad.

The most immediate task to be undertaken in order to restore law and order was obviously to disperse the bulk of the rioters back to their villages before any further inter-communal clashes could be engineered by the trouble-makers; and, because of the large numbers involved, the only practical way open to the government of doing this was through the use of military transport. This led to an unfortunate misinterpretation of the situation by some of the members of the foreign press who were at that time confined by the curfew to the inside of the Merlin Hotel.

Because the bulk of the refugees at the Mosque were still frightened of reprisals, they refused to leave what they considered to be the safety of holy ground unless they were allowed to keep their weapons while in transit and were provided with an armed escort of Malay soldiers. Regrettably, though understandably, the members of the international press who saw the convoys passing by, each truck with Malay soldiers in its cab and the back filled with armed civilians, reported that the army was actively engaged in helping Malay rioters to attack the Chinese and Indian communities; statements which exacerbated an already explosive situation and which decided Abdul Razak to impose even more stringent government censorship.

CHINESE SECRET SOCIETIES

The promptness with which Abdul Razak had called in the military, clapped on a curfew and then dispersed the mass of rioters back to their village homes, quickly brought the situation under control; but the damage that had been done to race relations would, inevitably, last over the years. Communist terrorists seem to have taken no part in the fighting; although indirect support for them among the Chinese community undoubtedly increased immediately following the riots. One normally submerged section of society did, however, play and important part in defending Chinese areas against attack, and in consequence gained considerable prestige in quarters where it had previously been denigrated.

The great majority of police and soldiers in Malaysia are Malays; and so when the Chinese found themselves under attack by Muslims they felt, rightly or wrongly, that they could not depend upon the normal guardians of law and order to go against their own people, or religion, to defend them. They therefore turned back the clock and put their trust in the secret society bravos who had done most of the serious fighting on the Chinese side. These thugs therefore gained a dangerous prestige and popularity that probably put back the government's chances of totally suppressing them by a generation. Respectable people, who all their lives had feared and hated these bullies and extortioners, found that they needed them badly. The gangster suddenly became respectable, a modern-day folk hero.

In China militant secret societies are as old as history; for they were the traditional means by which the common people might, when driven beyond endurance, oppose the feudal, or even Imperial, tyrant. When, during the nineteenth century, Chinese from the Southern Provinces poured into the Malay Peninsula, they brought their societies with them. These were branches of the Triad Society, or Hung League, an organisation formed in the late seventeenth century ostensibly to overthrow the alien Manchu, or Ch'ing dynasty and to restore an indigenous, or Chinese dynasty. Such organisations, beside being political, also fulfilled many of the functions of trade unions or benevolent societies; and it was in that guise that they flourished in Malaya, for workmen in a particular trade had little choice but to support them.

They had always arrogated to themselves the sole right to rule and police their own members; and so were often in conflict with the Malay or Colonial authorities, or even in insurrection against them. In the Malay States in the nineteenth century they did not hesitate to enter with considerable armed force conflicts of royal succession; while in the Straits Settlements they controlled the opium farms and vice generally. When registered and later suppressed by the British, they went underground and gradually degenerated into mere criminal gangs, engaged largely in smuggling and the protection racket. Their strength, as always, came from the solemnity of the oaths taken during initiation and their reputation for violence, often amounting to the sadistic murder, or execution, of those who reneged or turned traitor. In modern times they have sold their strong-arm potential to local politicians, or to anyone else, including in a few cases the Communist terrorists, willing to meet their terms.

These then were the forces loose in the Federal Capital and its environs, with every chance that, unless the most stringent precautions were taken, the violence and bloodshed would spread to envelope large areas of the country — wherever, in fact, there was a mixture of races in the population. So, on May 16th, the State of Emergency was extended to cover the whole country; and on that same day the Paramount Ruler, on the advice of the Prime Minister, suspended Parliament and all State Assemblies for an indefinite period and enacted that the nation should be governed by an Operations Council, headed and controlled by Abdul Razak, who would thereafter rule Malaysia by decree.

Chapter Eighteen
From Director of Operations to Prime Minister

Abdul Razak officially took up his appointment as Director of Operations on Sunday May 18th, less than five days after the riots had first erupted. It was a position which gave him almost unlimited executive powers; so that although a new Cabinet was sworn in two days later with Tunku Abdul Rahman once more as Prime Minister, it was he, in fact, who from that date was the chief decision-maker of the country. He was advised by, but not responsible to, a National Operations Council. This was headed by Tun Dr Ismail bin Datuk Abdul Rahman who, although a sick man, had voluntarily returned to public life as Minister for Home Affairs, in order to relieve Abdul Razak of the responsibilities of that position; and consisted also of the President of the Malayan Chinese Association, the President of the Malayan Indian Congress, the Minister for Information and Broadcasting, the Chief of Armed Forces Staff, the Inspector-General of Police and two senior civil servants, one of whom was Tan Sri Ghazali Shafie. Although the original intention had been that this body should concern itself primarily with matters connected with internal security — the reason for including members from the armed forces and police — the unusually wide powers conferred upon its Director by Royal Proclamation meant that in reality it superseded, instead of complemented, the Cabinet.

There were many important outstanding problems demanding Abdul Razak's immediate attention when he accepted this position, for in addition to the paramount one of safeguarding people's lives, property and economic wellbeing, there was also the urgent necessity to provide alternative methods of governing the various member States of the Federation, all of which had had their Legislative Assemblies suspended indefinitely. This latter problem he solved by nominating members to serve on similar, but subordinate, Operations Councils that he ordered set up in each individual State; and by delegating to them the authority to form regional councils, each under the leadership of the local District Officer, to assist them in the day to day running of their areas of the country. In this way he established an army-type chain of command that was able quickly and decisively to implement, without the need for the time-wasting discussion and argument seemingly inseparable from the normal democratic process, the instructions that he passed down to them.

THE SECURITY SITUATION

Upon examining the police reports on internal security, Abdul Razak found that there had been no actual outbreaks of violence in the country anywhere other than in Selangor and Malacca; and very little inter-racial tension of any kind in the East Coast or Northern States — not even in opposition-controlled Penang. The one possible additional sensitive area, although the Alliance — even the MCA — had done unexpectedly well there in the elections, was Johore. This was because soon after the May 13th riots, inter-racial violence had broken out in neighbouring Singapore, where it was believed that the attacks on local Malays, which had left four persons dead and at least another thirty injured, had been instigated by Chinese secret society fighters who had entered the Republic from across the Causeway[1], as retaliation for the Kuala Lumpur killings. Abdul Razak therefore ordered the police not only to step up raids within the state, but also to double-check everyone leaving Johore for Singapore in order to make sure that none were armed or known trouble-makers. This move was apparently effective, for no further outbreaks of violence were reported from the island.

Necessary as they had been at the time of imposition, the curfews still in force in various parts of the country had had a serious adverse effect on the economy; and so Abdul Razak considered it essential that they should be reduced as quickly as possible to the absolute minimum consistent with public safety. In parts of Selangor, too, there were shortages of some basic foodstuffs to overcome; and in the Federal Capital emergency distribution centres, which Abdul Razak had himself set up and organised before he became Director of Operations, were still being worked by volunteers. Progressively, however, the curfew was shortened and everyday affairs began once more to return to normal; although it was noticeable that in Kuala Lumpur night-life remained almost at a stand-still, with few people who had not got to do so venturing out after dark.

By mid-June the curfew, everywhere except in an area of Kedah close to the Thai border where armed Communist guerillas were still active, had been reduced to a few hours daily, specifically from 1 am to 4 am. Tensions, too, had almost disappeared. Then, on June 28th, there was a new outbreak of violence in the Kuala Lumpur area. This time the fighting was mainly between Malays and Indians; and in it five persons were killed, many more injured, and a row of houses set on fire[2]. Despite the natural fear and panic that this engendered throughout a large area of the capital, the police rapidly brought the situation under control; and the trouble fizzled out as quickly as it had begun. Thereafter, however, secret society gangsters, who were already making a good thing out of selling personalised physical protection, enforced an economic boycott against Malay traders, stall-holders and even taxi-drivers, that for a brief period caused renewed uneasiness and considerable financial hardship to some sections of the community. Abdul Razak declined to be drawn by this provocation into instituting counter-measures, however, and before long the boycott quietly faded away.

MORE TROUBLE FROM THE COMMUNISTS

On the very same day that he had taken over as Director of Opertions, Abdul Razak, speaking over the national television and radio networks, had warned that various subversive elements within the country, which he identified as Communist guerillas and their sympathisers, were planning to take advantage of the ill-feeling that inevitably remained after the inter-communal rioting. Some had already been discovered and taken into custody, but many more were believed to be standing by awaiting their opportunity. 'On Friday (May 16th),' he had said, 'the government arrested ninety hardcore Communists and their supporters in hiding; and last night another sixty were detained. They were fully equipped with dangerous weapons and were ready to do battle with the police and army .....'

Despite such alarming manifestations, it was not until almost the end of July that the hard-line Communists made any effective anti-Malay move; and when this came, it was not in the Kuala Lumpur area, but in Kedah, just south of the border with Thailand. There, on July 27th, a gang of armed and uniformed guerillas made a daylight incursion into a village in order to murder a female police informer. This 'execution' was carried out primarily for the purpose of baiting a trap, however, for when a squad of Malay soldiers from a battalion that had been part of the Kuala Lumpur garrison during the May riots was sent to investigate, the guerillas ambushed them on the outskirts of this village.

After those soldiers still able to do so had retreated, the terrorists affixed explosive booby-traps to the bodies of the slain; so that when reinforcements arrived to remove the cadavers for burial, there were more casualties. In all six members of the Malay Regiment were killed and a further eight wounded. Follow-up operations were immediately mounted; but this and other threats to internal security in the same area caused Abdul Razak also to re-introduce methods of control, the like of which he had not used against recalcitrant communities since the end of the 1948-1960 Emergency. This was forcibly to resettle two entire villages, against the inhabitants of which there was evidence of assisting the terrorists, albeit often under duress, well away from the dangers of the border region.

CLASHES OF PERSONALITY

Little more than a month after he assumed executive control of the country, Abdul Razak had to divert his attention temporarily from national matters in order to settle what could easily have escalated into a dangerous schism within his own party, UMNO. This clash of personalities occurred when a future Cabinet Minister, Dr Mahathir*, one of the newly emerged intellectual leaders in UMNO, already a member of its Executive Council and, until he was narrowly defeated by a PMIP candidate in the elections, a Member of Parliament, launched a vigorous personal attack on the party's President, Tunku Abdul Rahman. On June 18th, two days after the Prime Minister came out of hospital, he received a letter from Dr Mahathir, blaming him for the desertion from UMNO to the PMIP of large numbers of Malays and demanding on behalf of the party, the bulk of which this radical young man did not then in fact represent, his resignation of the Premiership and withdrawal altogether from politics[3]. This letter was later cyclostyled and widely distributed, which took it out of the realms of personal vendetta and made it a matter for party discipline and indirectly of national concern.

Tunku Abdul Rahman, who because of his personal involvement barred himself from dealing with the matter, sent a copy of the letter to Abdul Razak who, acting in his capacity as Deputy Chairman of UMNO, called a meeting of the party's Executive Council to adjudicate upon it. This meeting, from which everyone who was not a member of the Executive Council of UMNO was excluded, was held at *Sri Taman* on July 12th; and although Tunku Abdul Rahman did not attend, Dr Mahathir was present personally to conduct his own case. If he was expecting that the Deputy Chairman would be pleased by this attempt to oust the incumbent which, had it been successful, would inevitably have given him the leadership of the party and also the Premiership, he was to be disappointed; for one facet of Abdul Razak's political life that never varied, was his outstanding loyalty to Tunku Abdul Rahman, the man who so many years before he had persuaded, against his then inclinations, to enter active politics.

After several hours of heated discussion it was at last decided that due to the delicacy of the internal security situation such a disagreement, now that it had been made public, might lead to a fresh outbreak of trouble by setting Malay against Malay. Dr Mahathir was therefore asked to resign from the party's Executive Council. This he did and with

*Dr. Mahathir Mohammed, now Deputy Prime Minister of Malaysia.

it retired temporarily into the political wilderness, only to emerge some years later, without malice, to serve under Abdul Razak as a Cabinet Minister.

THE NATIONAL CONSULTATIVE COUNCIL

Although he was currently wielding more power than any Prime Minister, and doing it with both circumspection and humanity, Abdul Razak proved to be a reluctant Dictator, for he believed that,

> if you want to serve the people, too much power is no good. Because even if you don't intend to misuse it, you may do so inadvertently .... especially through delegation. You can't check everything yourself. You may be sincere, but can you be sure that all your officers who act in your name are sincere? Now with a democratic system you've first of all got Parliament and the State Assemblies to put a brake on you; then you've got the opposition parties, who will make a public outcry if things start to go wrong; but most important of all you know that every few years you've got to face the electorate, who will hold you accountable for all that has been done.

With these sentiments in mind, Abdul Razak began voluntarily to seek ways whereby the country might return to Constitutional rule by an elected Administration without the attendant risk of incurring another 'May 13th'. As an opening move in this direction, he decided, in January 1970, to set up a National Consultative Council 'with the serious intention of initiating a dialogue among the various segments of the population with the objective of discussing ways and means of strengthening racial harmony and providing a secure and permanent base for the restoration of Parliamentary democracy[4]' and to 'establish positive and practical guidelines for inter-racial cooperation and social integration for the growth of a Malaysian identity[5]'.

When it first met, this 66-member Council represented a wide variety of interests and opinions and disposed of many different talents and forms of expertise, for it was made up of politicians from both the Alliance and the opposition parties, religious leaders of all denominations, industrial managers, trade union leaders and people from the professions. Among all this eagerness to cooperate one sour note was struck, however, when the Democratic Action Party refused to participate after its candidate Lim Kit Siang, one of the party's leaders and an elected Member of Parliament, was rejected on the grounds that, as he was at the time being detained under the Emergency Regulations, his nomination was not serious, but intended only as an act of defiance against the authority of the Director of Operations.

RESUMPTION OF ELECTIONS

As the first anniversary of the May 13th, 1969, race riots approached, Abdul Razak ordered the entire security forces of the country to be put on a full alert. This was so that any trouble that broke out could quickly be isolated and then eliminated by overwhelming force before it had a chance to spread. On the night of May 12th such a clash between Malays and Chinese did occur in the Perak town of Ipoh; and although it was successfully confined to that one area, at least eight people were injured before peace was fully restored[6]. Generally, however, all was quiet; and the situation deemed to have improved to such an extent that Abdul Razak, acquiescing to the wishes of the local people stated through their political leaders, decided that the time had come to complete the suspended elections in Sabah and Sarawak.

There had been no inter-racial violence whatsoever in the Borneo States and comparatively little trouble from Communist saboteurs, but the delay in renewing elections there had been occasioned mainly by Abdul Razak's fear that if contentious issues were raised, and particularly if the vote went even further against the Alliance, more ill-feeling might be generated in the Peninsula. This was because Abdul Razak and the other UMNO leaders all felt that there was little chance of attaining lasting peace until the Constitution had been amended to entrench Malay rights and privileges, the target of many previous attacks by the opposition, beyond the bounds of further dispute. In order to do this, the Alliance would need a two-thirds majority in the Federal Parliament, which meant that it had to win a minimum of twenty of the thirty seats still to be contested. In the circumstances, the chances of accomplishing this seemed extremely poor. Additionally, there was a strong possibility that a non-Alliance, perhaps even anti-Malay, State government would be elected in Sarawak, leading to still more strained relations within the Federation.

On May 12th, 1970, after very careful consideration of all aspects of the matter, Abdul Razak decided that he had to take the risk if there was ever to be any real progress toward an early return to Parliamentary democracy. He therefore authorised the resumption of polling within those two States, but as a precaution imposed a number of restrictions on the form that electioneering might take. Active soliciting for votes, the holding of public meetings and the dissemination of party propaganda were all banned. Candidates were allowed only to display posters bearing the exhortation 'vote for' below either a personal picture or an authorised party symbol — nothing more. These regulations were eased slightly in the case of those two Parliamentary constituencies where new nominations had been accepted where each person standing was, in addition, permitted to make a single issue of a political manifesto containing his picture and setting out the aims and objectives of his party. In all the other constituencies those candidates who had contested in 1969 continued where they had left off. There was, however, the strict proviso that this manifesto should contain nothing considered by the authority to which it must be submitted as either seditious or likely in any way to stir up inter-racial hatreds [7].

In Sabah polling took place from June 21st to the 27th. Before the elections had been suspended in 1969, ten USNO candidates had already been elected; and on resumption, another USNO candidate was returned unopposed for Tuaran. Of the five Parliamentary seats then remaining to be contested, three were won by the Sabah Chinese Association and the other two by USNO. Although this was welcome news to Abdul Razak and the other Alliance leaders, it still left them needing 14 further seats before they could consider themselves secure.

In Sarawak, where voting started on June 6th but the results were not declared until July 4th, matters were more complicated, for of the 24 Parliamentary seats, Parti Bumiputra won 5, the SCA 2, Party Pesaka 2, an Independent 1, SUPP 5 and Snap 9. Even when the Independent subsequently joined Pesaka, this gave the full Malaysian Alliance a grand total of only 92 seats, or just 4 short of the two-thirds majority needed. Before long, however, Abdul Razak reached an agreement with SUPP whereby that party, although it did not formally join the Alliance, nevertheless pledged itself not to oppose the government's policy, including the passage of a Bill to entrench Malay privileges in the Constitution, in the Federal Parliament. This sign of cooperation in a party that had previously been resolutely anti-Malaysia and anti-Alliance, went a long way towards influencing the later return to elected government.

Abdul Razak had been so pessimistic of the likely outcome of the Sarawak State elections, that he had made a point of being in Kuching at the time that the results were declared so as to be ready immediately to negotiate some form of temporary coalition with one of the two main opposition parties. In the event, however, the Alliance did surprisingly well, for Parti Bumiputra, the SCA and Party Pesaka between them took twenty four of the forty eight seats. Then, due to the agreement that Abdul Razak was able to achieve with SUPP, a coalition government with thirty six seats was formed. This left only Snap, which held the remaining twelve seats, in opposition.

SELANGOR AND PERAK

There were then really only two major obstacles left to be overcome before Parliamentary democracy could be resumed: these were to settle the question of the composition of the future State governments for Selangor and Perak and the amending of the Constitution so as to prohibit further challenges to Malay privilege. The first of these was settled fairly easily, for in Perak three opposition Assemblymen — two from the PPP and one from the DAP — defected to the Alliance, which meant that it could then muster twenty two seats against eighteen; while in Selangor, one Gerakan Raayat and one Independent Assemblyman crossed over to give the Alliance a comfortable sixteen seats to twelve majority. The second was neatly disposed of by a decree that provided cover until the necessary legislation could later be introduced into, and enacted by, Parliament.

THE SEDITION ACT AND THE RUKUNEGARA

In mid-August 1970 Abdul Razak's National Operations Council, with the full cooperation and assent of the National Consultative Council, arbitrarily decreed the strengthening of the Sedition Act. Under this Amendment to the existing law, it immediately became a punishable offence for anyone to attack in public, or to advocate the suspension, alteration or abolition of the powers and privileges of the Paramount Ruler or all or any of the Malay Sultans, the law appertaining to citizenship, the use of Malay as the sole national and official language, or the special rights enjoyed by the Malays and certain other indigenous peoples. The stage was nearly set for a cautious return to constitutional government.

At the very end of August came National Day; and to mark the thirteenth anniversary of the attainment of Malayan, and the seventh of Malaysian, independence, large-scale celebrations, which Abdul Razak had decreed should be devoted to the promotion of the idea of intercommunal goodwill and national solidarity, were held throughout the country. In furtherance of this campaign, the Paramount Ruler launched the adoption of a National Ideology, the *Rukunegara,* which stressed that people of all racial origins should advance together towards a just and progressive society through belief in God, loyalty to king and country, upholding the Constitution and the rule of law, and the promotion of moral discipline, tolerance and mutual respect. National Day also saw the end of most of the remaining curfews, the legal resumption of all political activities which did not infringe the Sedition Act, and the release of a number of political detainees, including Lim Kit Siang whose imprisonment had exacerbated the already existing ill-feeling between the Democratic Action Party and the National Operations Council.

PRIME MINISTER

On that same momentous day, August 31st 1970, an era in Malayan and Malaysian political life ended, when Tunku Abdul Rahman announced his intention of giving up the Premiership which he had held since Independence and of devoting the evening of his life to the service of his religion as Secretary-General of the Islamic Secretariat that, some six months earlier, had been set up at Jeddah in Saudi Arabia. With the full approval of Abdul Razak, he also announced, as a sort of parting gesture, that the suspension of Parliament and of the various State Legislative Assemblies would end in February 1971.

On September 21st a new Paramount Ruler, Sultan Abdul Halim of Kedah, took the oath of office; and on the following day first accepted the resignation of Tunku Abdul Rahman and then appointed Abdul Razak as Prime Minister of Malaysia in his place. One day later, on September 23rd, Abdul Razak made public the composition of his new Cabinet, and the appointment of Tun Dr Ismail as his Deputy Prime Minister. With the advent of this new regime, the leaders of the Malayan Chinese Association formally abandoned their self-imposed exile from the Cabinet, with the result that Tun Tan Siew Sin once again became Minister of Finance, thus relieving Abdul Razak of the burden of that additional portfolio. There were also several newcomers in the line-up, the most notable among them being Hussein Onn, the son of Dato Onn, who had left private law practice at Abdul Razak's request and was now appointed to the post of Minister of Education.

THE RETURN OF PARLIAMENT

Five months later, on February 23rd 1971, the Paramount Ruler officiated at the State Opening of the new Parliament; and later in the day Abdul Razak, addressing the House of Representatives for the first time as Prime Minister in his own right, said:

> Mr Speaker, we meet today some twenty months late. I regret this as much as any Member of this House, but we all know why this had to be. The disturbances of May 1969 mark the darkest period in our national history. By dint of prudent and imaginative policies we have, however, carefully moved ourselves away from the abyss which then confronted us. Today life has generally returned to normal. But we shall be extremely foolish and irresponsible if we forget the lesson of 13th May. It would be easy for us to do nothing now and to hope that somehow things will turn out all right. But a country cannot be governed with hope. If we do not act, or if we do not take precautions now, we shall stand condemned before our people as failing in our duty.[8]

In Abdul Razak's opinion, the only way that an eventual catastrophic return to the conditions of May 13th could be avoided was by restructuring the whole economy of the country so as to correct racial imbalances in education, income, employment opportunities, and the ownership of industry and basic national resources. He recognised that in order to achieve this his government would have to be prepared to play a direct role in promoting many new commercial ventures, deciding their location and, in most cases, enforcing by legislation proportional representation by race among their work forces. This latter was a revolutionary new concept, fraught with grave political dangers, but it had to be faced if Malays were ever to participate with equality in the economic progress and prosperity of the nation.

Chapter Nineteen
Re-Alignment in Foreign Policy

Although Abdul Razak, in his capacity as Director of Operations, had been the *de facto* Head of Government from May 1969, he made no attempt to change the country's foreign policy for as long as Tunku Abdul Rahman held the title of Prime Minister; this despite his personal conviction that its conservatism and over-dependence upon alignment with the Western Democracies no longer adequately served Malaysia's needs. Soon after the Premiership had passed to him, however, Abdul Razak, faced with the continuing gradual rundown of British military power in Southeast Asia that inevitably would sooner or later lead to a total withdrawal, coupled with the determination of the United States progressively to disengage its armed forces from the various territories of Indo-China, began the implementation of his own plans, which he had formulated in the hope and expectation of securing the future safety and well-being of Malaysia.

These had as their main long-term objectives no less ambitious projects than the complete neutralization of the whole of Southeast Asia — something which he hoped to achieve with the full cooperation and concurrence of all of the leading world powers still concerned with the area — together with Malaysia's gradual re-alignment with the 'Third World' of Afro-Asia, especially the Pan-Islamic part of it, while still maintaining good relations with the West. He recognized, too, the urgent need to come to terms with the fast emerging Chinese nuclear 'super-power'; and the necessity of taking into consideration in all of his future policies the increasing strength and influence throughout Asia of Japan, particularly in the fields of commerce, industry and finance.

For the time being, however, Malaysia, with its small conventional army and embryo air-defence systems, still needed Western allies; and so in April 1970 Abdul Razak, in his capacity as Minister of Defence, was a prime mover in organizing the Five-Power Defence Pact, subscribed to by Australia, Britain, Malaysia, New Zealand and Singapore, that was signed in London. This, Abdul Razak assured his critics in Parliament, was intended as nothing more than a stop-gap measure, able to provide some sort of military cover until such times as a similar alliance with ASEAN* countries could replace it and further progress

---
*The Association of South East Asian Nations, comprising Malaysia, Indonesia, Thailand, the Philippines and Singapore.

be made in building the 'Zone of Peace and Neutrality' that all of them desired. When these latter projects became realities rather than dreams, he continued, the Five-Power defence arrangements would gradually be phased out, so that by the time neutralization was complete, there would be no foreign military forces left anywhere in the area to complicate matters.

As it turned out this withdrawal, at least as far as Malaysia was concerned, far exceeded the speed of neutralization, so that by mid-1975 the only foreign force of any consequence still based in the Malay Peninsula consisted of two squadrons of Royal Australian Air Force fighter planes. Following the communist victory and take-over in Indo-China, Britain decided to discontinue its small remaining naval presence in Singapore and this, together with the growing reluctance of the United States government and people to become further involved militarily in Southeast Asia, necessitated a rapid re-appraisal of Malaysia's defence needs and political attitudes. It was time to begin phasing out alliances of doubtful military value and instead to pin the country's hopes of survival on the speeding up of neutralization, or at least the acceptance by the super-powers of Southeast Asia as a non-aligned buffer zone.

INDENTIFYING WITH THE THIRD WORLD

Malaysia had joined the non-aligned group of nations in September 1969; and in April the following year had sent a full team of representatives, headed by Ghazali Shafie who was at that time Permanent Secretary to the Ministry of Foreign Affairs, to Dar-es-Salaam, the capital of Tanzania, where its first meeting was being held. Later that same year Abdul Razak, then Director of Operations as well as Deputy Prime Minister, had personally led the delegation to the Third Summit Conference held in Lusaka, Zambia.

So great an importance did he attribute to these meetings, in fact, that he again put in a personal appearance at the very high level Fourth Conference that was held in North Africa early in September 1973; although to do so meant that he, the Prime Minister, had to leave Malaysia in the middle of the celebrations that had been arranged in conjunction with National Day. On arrival in Algiers, at a time when the preliminaries to the Conference had already been completed by subordinates, Abdul Razak took over leadership of the Malaysian team from Ghazali Shafie, by then a Minister in his Cabinet, who had been representing him at the meetings of Foreign Ministers. These had successfully prepared the ground for the true Summit.

When, on September 6th, his turn came to address the representatives of the seventy-six countries participating in the Conference, Abdul Razak urged member States to combine their strength in order to fight as a powerful united force for a more equitable share of world economic opportunities for their peoples.

> The developed nations are using the emerging era of detente to increase the tempo of their economic activity and to enjoy a higher proportion of the growing prosperity of the world, [he said]. The developing nations, on the other hand, are struggling against a host of barriers to provide their peoples with a modicum of material satisfaction. The gap between the two groups of nations, as is only too well known, continues to grow; and .... the developed world has hitherto taken only half-hearted measures to assist in rectifying the imbalance in economic and trade opportunities. Instead, developed countries have been more preoccupied with pandering to the selfish demands of economic nationalism.
>
> .... The developed countries must be made to realise that economic tension and friction can only be ameliorated through the provision of more fair and favourable access to their markets for the products of developing countries and at stable, equitable and remunerative prices. We should therefore act in concert to present a common approach and to secure an increasing share of the growth in international trade, commensurate with our needs for economic development and on the basis of non-reciprocity, non-discrimination and preferential treatment ....
>
> .... For more than two decades now we in the Third World have pleaded our case for a fairer share of the world's growing prosperity and for a more rapid transfer to us of the developed world's technology and know-how. During this period we have pressed for a more meaningful and mature international division of labour which maximises the welfare of all. Let us acknowledge that our success so far has been minimal. Indeed, the developed world appears to have moved strongly toward forming its own 'clubs', quite blind and unheeding of our problems plans and persuasions.
>
> It is in this context that I feel that we .... should seek to intensify our own efforts which lead us to self-reliance and independence of action, as the underpinning for our non-alignment and the framework for shaping our own identity and independence. We should .... seek to achieve the fullest development of our own resources — whether land or oil — and our economic potential for the welfare of all our peoples. This is the basic thrust and goal of Malaysia's own development strategy — the creation of wide-based opportunities for all our people to participate in ....

These latter sentiments later began to show through in Malaysia's internal policies, when Abdul Razak's government increasingly demanded that the country's natural resources, commerce and industry should be controlled locally and not be subject to excessive exploitation by foreign interests.

SUPPORT FOR PAN-ISLAM

Despite its stand on non-alignment and neutralization, Abdul Razak's government — because the official religion of the country and the actual religion of the Malay race, and so of the majority of the leading politicians, was Islam — was strongly partisan in the various Arab-Israeli conflicts. When, for example, in October 1973 the Egyptians and Syrians launched coordinated surprise attacks on Israeli military positions in the Suez Canal and Golan Heights areas, a move that led to a renewal of active warfare, the Malaysian government permitted monetary contributions to be solicited from the general public and even the enlistment of volunteers — though response to the latter was negligible — to aid the Palestinian cause.

Such well publicised support ensured, however, that when King Faisal of Saudi Arabia led the Arab nations in an oil embargo on the United States and Holland and restricted supplies of that vital commodity to other countries whose attitude to the war they equated with covert support for Israel, Malaysia was placed on the list of privileged recipients. Despite such an assurance of continuing and adequate supplies of essential fuels for its expanding economy, Malaysia could not escape the serious financial consequences of the unprecedented increase in prices; which inevitably led to cut-backs in, and the pruning of, certain sections of the current Five-Year Development Plan. Unwelcome and disruptive as such unavoidable brakes upon progress proved to be, this lesson in economic warfare, and the knowledge that it was likely to be repeated whenever the producing nations felt that they could get away with it, did have the beneficial effect of encouraging Abdul Razak's government to speed up the exploitation of the country's own recently discovered deposits of both oil and natural gas; and of ensuring that these were kept firmly within Malaysia's own control.

RAPPROCHMENT WITH CHINA

In May 1971, in furtherance of one of his most important objectives on the road to peace — neutralization of Southeast Asia — Abdul Razak began making conciliatory overtures towards Communist China, a complete reversal of the country's former policy. The opening move in this revised strategy involved the despatch of a 19-delegate trade mission to Peking. There, its carefully selected leader, Tengku Razaleigh — an emerging contender for high position in the UMNO executive — not only succeeded in promoting the first direct commercial exchanges between the two countries, but also, acting upon Abdul Razak's instructions, held unofficial political talks with various Chinese administrators, including Prime Minister Chou En-lai, which were aimed at exploring the feasibility of eventually establishing full diplomatic relations.

This was a bold move for Abdul Razak to initiate, for communist terrorist guerillas were still active and extremely dangerous in both the Malay Peninsula and the Borneo states; and the possibility that a

Chinese embassy in Kuala Lumpur might encourage and sustain them could not be discounted. It was, however, a calculated risk that paid off at least temporarily, for at a later stage, when Abdul Razak was himself handling negotiations, China officially withdrew its active support and recognition from the local communist insurgents and declared that in future it would provide them with neither money nor armaments.

When speaking on the subject of his government's new foreign policy in the House of Representatives on July 26th, 1971, Abdul Razak began carefully to prepare Members of Parliament to accept his intended fundamental change of political direction. He pointed out to them that it was time for radical re-thinking on relations with China with the realisation and acceptance of the very obvious fact that that country was now a great power with an important and expanding role to play in international affairs. Fear of her undoubted military capacity for aggression and territorial expansion should be tempered by the knowledge of her leaders' growing willingness to establish normal relations with non-communist countries. This, he suggested, was a policy likely to be accelerated by the recent visit to Peking of Dr Kissinger of the United States, especially as that event was soon to be followed by an even more momentous attempt at de-escalating tension through the projected travels of President Nixon. Smaller countries, observing the intentions of the super-powers, must trim their political sails accordingly in order to stay afloat when the winds of change were blowing strongly.

He then went on to clarify Malaysia's new stand, which recent developments had necessitated, on the China-Taiwan controversy. This, he stated, was simply that there could only be one government of mainland China and that that was without any doubt located in Peking. Malaysia would in future act on that assumption, but at the same time would support the inalienable right of the people of Taiwan to decide their own future for themselves. In recognising the Peking regime as the sole and legal government of China, Malaysia also felt it logical to support its claim for a seat in the United Nations; with the reservation that this was not to be at the expense of unseating the Taiwan delegation.

It was to be his government's policy, Abdul Razak continued, in time to establish diplomatic relations with all countries — no matter what their political persuasions — that were prepared to respect Malaysia's sovereignty and independence; for their internal policies and ideologies were solely the concern of their own people. In formulating the country's new foreign policy, he told M.P.'s bluntly, 'we can only proceed by accepting the world as it is not as we should like it to be .....'. This notwithstanding, the hoped-for detente with international communism would not in any way affect his government's stated policy of continuing to fight and defeat communist terrorists, or for that matter insurgents of any other political opinion, operating within Malaysia; for these were two entirely separate issues. Any communist regime establishing relations with Malaysia would have to accept this precept; just as Malaysia had already publicly accepted the right of other countries to pursue, without outside interference, their own aims and ideologies within their own sovereign territories. That such a stand was generally acceptable, was shown when diplomatic relations were successfully established with both North Korea and North Vietnam.

The protracted and at times difficult negotiations with Peking were brought to successful conclusion in May 1974: and on the 28th of that month Abdul Razak, taking the initiative among Southeast Asian heads of government, began six-day official visit to China. During the course of his talks with Chairman Mao Tze-tung and Prime Minister Chou En-lai, he settled at first hand all remaining points of controversy and reached agreement for an exchange of ambassadors. He also obtained from the Chinese leaders a promise that no further attempts would be made by them to alienate the local Chinese communities from their loyalty towards Malaysia; and a formal statement that the insurrection still being maintained by the Malayan Communist Party was purely an internal matter, the outcome of which was no concern of the People's Republic. With these matters settled, a Malaysian ambassador arrived in Peking in the middle of December 1974 and a Chinese ambassador in Kuala Lumpur two months later.

A further outcome of this heads of government meeting, was China's tentative support for the neutralization proposals for Southeast Asia; a project which by then had become of some interest to the Chinese as one way to combat what they felt to be the growing encirclement of their country by the Soviet Union. This matter became of even greater importance to them when, on April 30th 1975, Saigon — and with it the whole of South Vietnam — fell to the Viet Cong; for North Vietnam, militarily by far the most powerful country in Southeast Asia, was classified by them as a Russian satellite, or at best as a client state. The unpalatable fact of North Vietnam's power, coupled with American reluctance any longer to become involved in the area's battles, was also not lost upon member states of ASEAN, whose leaders quickly scrambled to emulate Abdul Razak's example in encouraging detente with the new communist regimes in both Saigon and Cambodia; and with the longer established one in China.

THE NEUTRALIZATION OF SOUTHEAST ASIA

One of the most ambitious projects in Abdul Razak's plan for re-aligning his country's foreign policy — and one of the most difficult to achieve because of its total dependence for success upon the co-operation and goodwill of other, more powerful, nations — was undoubtedly the move away from reliance upon foreign military support, provided in the past mainly by Britain and the United States, towards the neutralization of the whole of Southeast Asia and its integration into a single 'Zone of Peace'. The main difficulty arose because it was one thing for the countries concerned, even if they could agree among themselves, which was by no means certain, to declare their territories neutralized, but quite another, when lacking any form of effective military deterrent, to force outside acceptance of neutralization, whenever it happened to clash with the interests or expansionist ambitions of more powerful countries, especially the super-powers. It could be achieved only by obtaining their prior agreement and maintained tenuously mainly by playing one off against the other in the hope of their finding it to their advantage to recognise Southeast Asia as a demilitarized and non-partisan buffer zone.

On October 1st, 1971, Abdul Razak, indefatigable in seeking world support for his thesis, carried his plans for neutralization to the United Nations General Assembly in New York, where he invited the delegates to accept it. The response was encouraging. During this same session of the international body, he took the opportunity to meet with the Foreign Ministers of the four other ASEAN countries and to arrange for them to confer together in Kuala Lumpur in order to coordinate their thinking on this matter. This conference eventually took place in the Malaysian capital in late November. When it ended, a joint communique was issued, which included a declaration of all five countries' intention to work together to attain 'the recognition of, and respect for, Southeast Asia as a Zone of Peace, Freedom and Neutrality, free from any form or manner of interference by outside powers'; and a pledge to concentrate their efforts on broadening the areas in which they currently co-operated and to work for even closer mutually beneficial relationships.

In this closing address to this meeting, Abdul Razak said:

> .... The acceptance of this Declaration by the Foreign Ministers of the countries who are here today representing as we do nearly 200 million people, signifies an important and vital step in our efforts to ensure a new era of peace and stability in Southeast Asia. Above all, this Declaration shows our determination to shape our destiny ourselves, to safeguard our independence and national integrity.
>
> Whether we will succeed in the further steps ahead depends on our ability to work together. We cannot expect others to respect us as independent and sovereign countries unless we are ourselves prepared to work to maintain our independence .... and unless we show our determination to ... be free from any form of external interference.
>
> It is my hope that other countries in Southeast Asia will share our aspirations and objectives .... and that in due course they will join us to work together. With the active support and collaboration of these other countries for our Declaration, we hope that other powers outside this

region and in particular China, the Soviet Union and the United States, will recognise and respect .... Southeast Asia as a Zone of Peace .... At the same time, it should be emphasized that these objectives can only be attained if all countries show that they will scrupulously respect our independence and integrity and that they will not interfere in any manner in our internal affairs, either overtly or covertly. This is the only basis on which we can proceed. We cannot be neutral — no one has a right to expect us to be neutral — if there is any form of interference in our internal affairs.

Having said all this, it should be clear that we have no illusions about the long and difficult road ahead of us. I have always felt that in all endeavours we should have our feet planted firmly on the ground — but at the same time be guided by a clear vision of the future. The task on which we are now embarking is important — indeed it vitally affects our very existence as independent states and peoples. We are all fully aware that any mistake entails grave risks....

Even within the framework of ASEAN, however, there were many unresolved tensions that at times seemed ready to threaten its very existence. Foremost among these was the continuing claim of the Philippines to sovereignty over Sabah, a point of contention which, despite Malaysian pleas that it be dropped in the interests of regional co-operation, Manila continued to press. To this discord was soon added an accusation by the Philippines Executive that the State government of Sabah was infringing the Kuala Lumpur Declaration by interfering in its internal affairs; specifically by providing a refuge and a training ground for members of the dissident Moro National Liberation Front[1], and by smuggling arms and explosives to their compatriots in the Sulu Islands and Mindanao.

Meanwhile, Abdul Razak continued his personal efforts to obtain support for the neutralization plan in those countries of Southeast Asia that were not members of ASEAN. During his 1974 official visit to Burma, for example, he tried to gain the interest of President U Ne Win; but soon found that the Burmese, while prepared to support the proposals in principle, remained unconvinced that the ASEAN countries really intended to break away completely from dependence on the West. They proved to be even more sceptical of communist promises of non-intervention. Burma had for many years been fighting a fratricidal war against its own left-wing insurgents; and as the situation in Vietnam became progressively more favourable to the communists, that of Burma became correspondingly more desperate.

As soon as it became obvious that the whole of Indo-China was eventually to be ruled by the communists, the fate of the neutralization plan seemed to hinge more and more upon the attitude towards it of the government of the Democratic Republic of Vietnam; for if even part of the vast stores of arms and ammunition captured in the south of that country were distributed to dissident elements throughout Southeast Asia, all hope of peace would fast disappear. The Thais panicked and started to drive out the Americans; but Abdul Razak, despite being offered many opinions to the contrary, remained convinced that the Vietnamese would, in the foreseeable future, stay within their own borders. This, he admitted, was mainly because after three decades of almost continuous internal strife, their country needed a long period of peace while its shattered economy was rebuilt. Additionally, with China on its flank, Vietnam needed all the friendly neighbours it could find.

RESURGENCE OF TERRORISM

A disquieting factor in this reckoning was soon provided, however, by a resurgence of communist activity in the Malay Peninsula. Policemen, particularly Chinese detectives engaged on security projects, were assaulted or murdered; the deputy superintendent of a detention camp assassinated; and the country's chief of the national police force gunned down in daylight in the centre of Kuala Lumpur. Ambushes in the northern States claimed the lives not only of members of the security forces, but also those of civilians working for them; and all too soon limited nightly curfews were back in force, and the re-introduction of national service announced.

At about 5 am on August 26th, 1975, members of a militant communist splinter organisation blew up part of the National Monument that was located in the centre of Kuala Lumpur, not far from the Parliament Building. The main explosion was apparently premature, for booby traps discovered soon afterward indicated that several bombs were scheduled to be detonated by timing devices during the flag-raising ceremony carried out there daily by members of the armed forces. This daring and provocative action was followed, early in September, by a grenade attack on the Kuala Lumpur headquarters of the Police Field Force, a para-military *gendarmerie* unit, that left two men dead and another fifty-one injured.

The outcry that resulted from these two major demonstrations of terrorist ability to strike right in the heart of the Federal Capital, led Abdul Razak to introduce the Emergency Essential (Community Self Reliance) Regulations, by means of which a vigilante force, in which all male citizens between the ages of 18 and 55 were liable to serve, was to be formed. The members of this organisation were made responsible for patrolling, and maintaining the security of, their own community areas. In addition, a workers' volunteer force, armed with shotguns, was enrolled to patrol strategic coastal areas, in order to prevent communist gun-runners from supplying the terrorists with even more sophisticated weapons.

It soon became evident that despite the establishment of diplomatic relations with China, and the cordial commercial and cultural exchanges that had taken place between the two countries, Malaysia would have to learn to live with the Peoples Republic's continued support, at least in the field of propaganda, of the local insurgents. Despite complaints from Kuala Lumpur, no attempt had been made by the Peking regime to silence the Malayan Communist Party's China-based radio station, which daily churned out vituperative personal attacks on members of the 'right-wing' Malaysian government[2]; and Abdul Razak had been forced to order an official protest lodged with the Chinese ambassador after the Peking government had sent a congratulatory message to the proscribed Malayan Communist Party on the occasion of its 45th anniversary.

Chapter Twenty
Restructuring the Economy

The May 1969 riots, terrible and traumatic as they had been, had at least served the purpose of bringing out into the open what so many people had been trying for so long to pretend did not exist — outright distrust and widespread antipathy among the members of the main racial divisions of the country's population. This, Abdul Razak recognized, was a most dangerous sickness in the body of the nation; and one that only major surgery could hope to remove. It would inevitably involve, he felt sure, nothing less than a complete restructuring of the country's economy, the alteration of many of its traditional ways of life and, above all, a more equitable distribution both of its wealth and its opportunities for advancement. There were, as Lee Kuan Yew had been at pains to point out some years before, poor people in all racial groups; but for a number of basic reasons the Malays and other indigenous peoples were, taken *en masse,* 'less equal' than the others.

THE 1970 CENSUS REPORT

An analysis of the 1970 Census Report showed, for example, that the mean monthly income of Malay households was 179 Malaysian dollars; a figure that compared unfavourably with that of the Chinese at 387 and the Indians at 310 dollars [1]. This was because nearly 70 per cent. of those Malays officially classified as being gainfully employed, earned their living in the rural areas from some form of agriculture. Such enterprises were often carried on in uneconomic sized holdings, using traditional and largely inefficient methods, either through ignorance of modern procedures, lack of technical training, or for want of adequate capital. These were the smallholders, tenant farmers and share-croppers, whose dependence upon outside financing and marketing, usually by non-Malay moneylenders and their business associates, made peasant poverty self-perpetuating.

Although the central and various state governments' development schemes had gone some way towards alleviating the worst of rural poverty, the rapid growth of the peasant population had led to overcrowding, with consequent economic hardship, in many country areas. It was an unpalatable fact that Abdul Razak's government had to face, that 90 per cent. of all households where the total income was below 100 Malaysian dollars a month, and over 76 per cent. where it was between

100 and 200 dollars, were in the rural areas where Malays accounted for over 65 per cent. of the total population. This situation had been exacerbated in recent years by a progressive decline in agricultural commodity prices, especially for rubber, that was coincidental with substantial increases in the cost of machinery, transportation and fertilizers, and in the general expenses of ordinary living.

THE NEW ECONOMIC POLICY

It had become obvious, therefore, that if a lasting peace between the main communities was to be preserved, the standard of living of the Malays would have to be raised to a level where they no longer found themselves in a position inferior to that of the Chinese and Indians, either socially or financially. This, Abdul Razak saw, could only be achieved by ensuring that they became 'full partners in all aspects of the economic life of the nation[2]', rather than just the tillers and armed defenders of its soil. He therefore ordered the Economic Planning Unit attached to the Prime Minister's Department to formulate a completely new economic policy with this proviso in mind; and during the course of 1970, this objective became the basis of the Second Malaysia Five-Year Development Plan that was due to be put into operation from the beginning of January 1971.

This radical new economic policy was designed to operate in two parts; but with each main division in many ways complementary to the other. The first of these lines of attack was aimed at reducing poverty levels generally by raising the incomes of, and increasing the employment opportunities for, all Malaysians irrespective of their racial origins. The second, and rather more controversial part, was aimed at restructuring Malaysian society so as to correct, in the words of the officials who formulated it, 'those imbalances which tended to perpetuate the identification of race with economic function'; that is with Malay dependence on agriculture and Chinese domination of commerce and industry.

Obviously not all Malays could, or would wish to, disassociate themselves from agriculture, nor would it be good for the country that they should do so; and so Abdul Razak decided that one of the new Plan's first priorities should be to improve life in the rural areas, by affording the people there similar amenities to those enjoyed in modern and progressive urban communities. Much more revolutionary in concept than this, however, was Abdul Razak's declared intention to create a completely new Malay commercial and industrial community that would be capable of directing, managing and working enterprises, at all levels of complexity, on a par with similar, established communities of other races. This meant, of course, that it would be necessary to provide suitable technical education and managerial and commercial training, both theoretical and practical, on an unprecedented scale. It also meant that there would have to be an almost total re-organisation of the traditional structure of the nation's work force; with the probability of having to enact unpopular legislation in order to bring about equality of opportunity, or even the introduction of privileged concessions, so as to provide employment places for the many tens of thousands of Malays eagerly awaiting a chance to participate in the hitherto unattainable rewards of commerce and industry.

RESTRUCTURING THE WORK FORCE

It therefore became an important part of Abdul Razak's new employment policy to try to persuade, and if this failed to put government pressure upon, employers gradually to re-structure their work forces until at all levels, including that of top management, they reflected the racial percentages of the Malaysian population. This was, of necessity, to be a long-term project, for had any attempt been made to displace large numbers of Chinese and Indian workers in order to fill their jobs with Malays, such action would inevitably have led to further serious outbreaks of inter-communal violence. It therefore became essential to create additional employment opportunities through expansion and diversification.

Meanwhile, Abdul Razak's government gave precedence, whenever new ventures were being started, to those that were labour intensive rather than to prestige projects dependent upon automation or which favoured large-scale mechanisation. These new industries were then encouraged by various financial and other incentives, such as tax holidays for periods up to ten years and by large-scale government and State expenditure on public utilities, roads and other infrastructure, to locate themselves in selected smaller towns. These development areas were situated in places where rural youths, most of them Malays, were in the process of undergoing free basic technical training that would enable them to quit the already overcrowded agricultural industry and take up the newly created jobs in the factories.

Although there had, even before independence, been a desultory movement of Malays away from agriculture into industry, such youths, because of their lack of technical training, were usually to be found in the lower grades of such employment, working as unskilled labourers, messengers, drivers, or security guards. Few had secured promotion to technical or senior clerical posts, and even fewer had achieved managerial or even supervisory positions. As a relevant step toward altering this, Abdul Razak's government decreed that any firms wishing to take advantage of the tax and other concessions, that were among the most valuable benefits accruing from the acquisition of pioneer industry status, would in future be expected to ensure that the racial composition of the new company's work force was in accordance with the employment conditions laid down in the national economic policy. He also let it be understood that failure to do so would result in loss of those privileges, even if they had already been granted.

In 1975, in extension of this pressure policy, the government put into law the Industrial Co-ordination Act, which provided that every enterprise engaged in manufacturing of any kind, no matter how long it had been in operation, must be licensed by the relevant Ministry supervising that particular activity; and that the Minister involved could attach any conditions to the new licence that he considered in the national interest. If these conditions were not carried out in full, the licence could be revoked and the company prevented from continuing in business. This punitive measure was aimed primarily at those already established foreign and non-Malay Malaysian firms — particularly those owned and run by Chinese — which had persistently failed to give Malays an increased share both in total employment and in the better paid jobs [3].

EMPLOYMENT PROBLEMS

One of the greatest difficulties that Abdul Razak's government experienced in implementing its employment policy was that with a rapidly expanding population — which in the five years covered by the Second Malaysia Plan was expected to increase from just short of 11 million to over 12½ million — most of the newly created opportunities would, instead of reducing the level of unemployment, which in 1970 stood at around 275,000. be needed for the 650,000 estimated additions to the job-seekers. This situation held out little prospect for improvement in the lot of those unfortunates in the rural areas who, while officially classified as employed, were in economic reality badly underemployed.

The Second Malaysia Plan was designed to create some 600,000 new jobs which, even if the target was fully achieved, would still mean a small numerical increase in unemployment. This could only be countered by increasing job opportunities in already established businesses and in government service. Three practical measures were instituted by Abdul Razak's government to aid this: statutory control was introduced to limit the amount of overtime that any one employee could work; the payroll tax was abolished; and the retiring age was compulsorily set at 55.

Unemployment was found to be very largely a problem of youth, as over 60 per cent. of those without work of any kind were aged between 15 and 25. This, in view of the terrorist and subversive elements already active in the country, was a potentially dangerous security situation; as many of these youths, driven to desperation by poverty and frustration, might well be enticed into the extremist camp. The unemployment problem was exacerbated because the bulk of school-leavers, being in many cases far better educated than their parents, were no longer satisfied to follow then into work, even if it was available, that was laborious, tedious, dirty and financially and socially unrewarding[4].

WORKER-CAPITALISTS

In Abdul Razak's view, one of the major economic imbalances that had to be corrected in favour of the Malays had to do with the restructuring of the ownership of wealth other than land. In 1970 a review of the total share capital of all limited companies registered in Malaysia, showed for example, that 61 per cent. of the equity was in the hands of foreigners, 22.5 per cent. was held by the Chinese, and only about 2 per cent. was owned by Malays[5]. He therefore set a target, scheduled to be achieved by 1990, that was in twenty years from inception of this scheme, whereby Malays would own 30 per cent. of the total share capital of all Malaysian private enterprises.

This was to be achieved in stages, by methods that would not hold back or frustrate the development and industrialisation of the country with outside help and participation. One such measure was to force all newly approved manufacturing projects to reserve a proportion of their issued shares — this had risen to 30 per cent. by 1973 — for purchase only by Malays. At the same time, efforts were made to reduce foreign holdings in the non-manufacturing sectors of the economy — 45 per cent. of all foreign investment in the country in 1970 was in rubber and other estates and in mining — in favour of the Malays, so that by 1990 the proportion of the country's total share capital held by non-Malaysians would have fallen to roughly 30 per cent. of the whole. This, of course, was working only in percentages; for continued industrial development of the Federation, with a consequent increase in the number of limited companies, would allow plenty of scope for new foreign investment within the limits of the 30 per cent. of the total arbitrarily imposed. Should these targets be achieved, that would leave 40 per cent. of the total as the permissible share for all non-indigenous Malaysians.

All of this was fairly simple to plan, but less easy to put into practice. This was mainly due to the difficulty of getting the ordinary wage-earning Malays, as against the privileged wealthy few, to invest in shares, or even to retain those that they had already bought. Malays generally like to have their main holding of wealth in land and property; and usually only buy shares when they are offered at privileged prices, that is in the reserved issue, and then only in order to sell them at a profit as soon as possible. By mid-1973 they had taken up only about one-fifth of the total shares that had been allocated to them in pioneer status new enterprises[6]. To help overcome this sales resistance, which was based to some extent on fear of innovation and of loss of hard-earned capital, Abdul Razak's government encouraged the setting up of a number of unit trusts, operated by national corporations, in order to mobilize Malay household savings in a way that, due to the spread of investment, offered the purchasers the greatest security.

PUBLIC AND JOINT ENTERPRISES

Although Malaysia was strongly wedded to the private enterprise type of economy, as against that favoured in socialist countries, Abdul Razak soon found that in order to achieve the desired restructuring process, an increased measure of government participation in at least some sectors of commerce and industry was both necessary and desirable. This was carried through in part by extending the activities of national corporations like MARA (*Majlis Amanah Raayat*) and PERNAS (*Perbadanan Nasional*), which provided technical and financial assistance for existing Malay enterprises and help in setting up completely new ones, particularly in selected development areas where private enterprise was unwilling to venture. In addition, these corporations set up a number of specialised businesses which they initially owned and ran; but which it was intended should in time be transferred to private Malay ownership.

One of the most significant advantages that was expected to accrue from such enterprises, was the opportunity they would provide for the practical training of many of those Malays who were to form the new commercial and industrial community. Only the government, using the tax-payers' money, could afford first to train the personnel and then set up industry in that area to absorb it into full employment. Lack of capital, the bane of such enterprises when run privately, would be solved by continuing government support, either through direct low interest loans, or through financial participation. In some instances marketing facilities would be provided by state corporations.

In order to increase Malay participation in the construction industry, for example, Abdul Razak's government set up a special corporation, that was financed and managed by Pernas. Its chief aim was to train Malay contractors so that eventually they could compete on equal terms with their counterparts from other communities. When this objective had been achieved, Abdul Razak declared, it would then be government policy to give such contractors priority in many State and national development projects. In the meantime, all government contracts for repair and maintainance the cost of which was below ten thousand Malaysian dollars were normally to be reserved for Malays. This was because most of them operated on a very small scale and could not tender competitively if larger Chinese concerns were able to oppose them.

Insurance was another field of commerce in which, in Abdul Razak's considered opinion, it was necessary for the government to intervene. This was because, of the ninety one insurance companies operating in the country in 1970 only fourteen were incorporated in Malaysia and in only ten of those was the majority stock-holding held by Malaysians [7]. In order therefore to develop a stronger locally-controlled industry in which Malays would have the chance to participate, the government, in 1970, set up the Malaysian National Insurance Company as a subsidiary of Pernas; and in June 1973, formed the Malaysian National Reinsurance Berhad as a joint venture in which Pernas was the majority shareholder, and the ten locally-owned insurance companies participants. In this same year, 1973, legislation was passed that required all new insurance companies incorporated in Malaysia to allocate a minimum of 30 per cent. of their issued share capital to Malays or other indigenous people.

ECONOMIC NATIONALISM

A further basic target of Abdul Razak's new economic plan was to introduce measures that would eventually free important parts of the country's economy from foreign domination and at the same time ensure that Malaysians, particularly the Malays, took an increasing share in controlling their own primary produce such as rubber, palm oil and tin. This was to be achieved not through outright nationalisation, but mainly through the purchase of a substantial, or even majority, interest in key companies by buying up their shares on the stockmarket, or through direct offers to their foreign stock-holders. In the first instance, such blocks of shares would be acquired by various Pernas subsidiaries; but later sold to Malaysians, with first preference going to Malays. It was hoped, in this manner, to obtain such a wide spread of these securities, that the country would become in fact, as well as in theory, a property-owning democracy; while Malays would be helped to reach the target of owning 30 per cent. of Malaysia's private wealth more quickly than the previously specified year of 1990.

When oil and natural gas were discovered in territorial waters, Abdul Razak moved quickly to ensure that control of all aspects of these new natural resources should remain firmly in Malaysian hands. A monopoly state-owned corporation, PETRONAS (*Petroliam Nasional Berhad*), was set up in 1974 with sole rights — except when direct permission for the licencing of foreign firms was given by the Prime Minister[8] — to the refining, processing and manufacture of all petroleum and petro-chemical products.

In April 1975 this control was extended when all companies engaged in the marketing of petroleum and petro-chemicals were required to create a new class of management shares, representing one per cent.

of the firm's paid-up capital, which were to be taken up only by Petronas. Each of these management shares was to carry the equivalent voting rights of 500 ordinary shares[9]. It was a move, said Abdul Razak when answering criticism of backdoor nationalisation by obtaining enforced control of directoral boards at a minimum outlay of capital, which aimed mainly at exerting pressure on existing oil firms to give Malays a greater share in the profitable retailing of petrol from stations throughout the country.

NECESSITY FOR A NATIONAL FRONT

By the time that the Second Malaysia Development Plan had been in operation for about a year, it became obvious to Abdul Razak that much of the effort that should have gone into the implementation of the new economic policy was being dissipated in inter-party bickering. In the case of the Party Islam (PMIP), this took the form of deliberate obstruction and non-cooperation; a policy that adversely affected the progress of a large section of the very poorest among the Malays, those living in the four northern States of the Peninsula. With the predominantly non-Malay parties that remained outside of the Alliance the problem was different, for with them opposition was mainly concentrated upon frustrating his plans for increasing the Malay share in the economy and in the more remunerative sectors of employment; a move which they seemed to equate with an automatic reduction in the living standards of their own supporters. In this negative action they were being partly successful; and Abdul Razak realised that unless he could eliminate this opposition, or at least a substantial part of it, by absorbing it, his efforts were likely to fall far short of their target. Despite considerable dissention from within the existing Alliance, he therefore decided to try to form a National Front Coalition Government; and to incorporate into it as wide a cross-section of political opinion and communal interests as he possibly could.

Abdul Razak's first success occurred in Penang where, in February 1972, he was able personally to arrange with the leaders of the majority political party, the ruling Gerakan Raayat, for the local Alliance to join them in a coalition in the State Assembly. This successful recovery of at least a share in the government of a State that had been lost to the Alliance in the debacle of the 1969 elections, was followed a little less than three months later by a similar agreement with the Peoples Progressive Party in Perak. There the Alliance already governed the State, but the inclusion of the PPP gave it, at least in theory, a wider popular base, especially among the Chinese. The Perak coalition, which unlike that in Penang did not extend to the Federal Parliament, was criticised as unnecessary by powerful interests in both the MCA and UMNO; and was made to work satisfactorily only through the strength of Abdul Razak's determination that it should do so.

At the beginning of May 1972, Abdul Razak opened negotiations aimed at bringing about yet another, and infinitely more important, political association, this time between the Alliance and the principal Malay opposition party that formerly had been known as the Pan-Malayan Islamic Party (PMIP) but had since changed its name to the Party Islam (PAS). In these negotiations many concessions had had to be made — far too many in the opinion of some of his colleagues — but all concerned agreed that Abdul Razak had displayed great skill, ingenuity and perseverance in these political manoeuvrings, particularly in the way he applied pressure through control of the distribution of Federal Government development funds for use in the PAS-controlled State of Kelantan.

On September 5th a coalition, that would operate at both Parliamentary and State Assembly levels, was finally agreed upon; and nearly four months later, after a further bout of tough bargaining, Abdul Razak announced that not only would this collaboration become fully operative on January 1st, 1973, but that on that date Datuk Mohammed Asri, the leader of Party Islam, would join the Federal Cabinet as Minister for Land Development and a Minister with Special Functions. For the Alliance such a coalition guaranteed an easy passage in fighting the next Federal elections; and an immediate share in running the State Government of Kelantan, where the PAS held nineteen seats to the eleven that had been won by UMNO. This latest achievement by Abdul Razak meant that every State government in Malaysia was then run either by the Alliance alone, or by a coalition in which it was able to wield considerable influence. In the Federal Parliament too, the government now found itself without any effective form of opposition to worry about.

THE 1974 ELECTIONS: PRE-ELECTION DIFFICULTIES

On Nomination Day, October 6th 1971, the ruling Alliance coalition in Sabah had won, unopposed, all thirty two seats in the elections for the State Assembly: twenty eight of them going to the United Sabah National Organisation (USNO) and four to the Sabah Chinese Association. This success had not been attained without some minor embarrassment for Abdul Razak and his colleagues of the Grand Alliance, however, for the disqualification of all ten of the opposing Independent candidates, on the grounds that every one of them had failed properly to complete his nomination papers, was criticized by some sections of the foreign press as smacking of sharp electoral practice.

Within UMNO, the senior partner in both the Alliance and the National Front, the danger of the party splitting into two diverging camps seemed to have been avoided when, on March 7th 1972, Dr Mahathir bin Mohammed, who had been expelled in September 1969 after trying, unsuccessfully, to force the resignation of the then Prime Minister, Tunku Abdul Rahman, was re-admitted to full membership. He was later to be brought into the Cabinet as a senior Minister; another example of Abdul Razak's skill in co-opting former opponents into his regime.

During 1972 the Alliance did quite well in by-elections for the Federal Parliament, for it won all three of them; but in January 1973 it as a political whole and UMNO in particular, suffered a minor shock at the result in the contest for the predominantly Malay constituency of Kuala Kedah. Although the latest of Abdul Razak's coalition agreements had led to the withdrawal from the by-election of Party Islam, which formerly had provided the main opposition in that constituency, the UMNO candidate on this occasion — former Federal Minister Senu Abdul Rahman, who had been narrowly defeated in Kedah in the 1969 elections — obtained a much smaller majority than had been expected in a straight fight with an Independent; even though the latter was the daughter of a Malay who had received much publicity for consistently opposing what he and his followers considered to be the Alliance government's ultra-conservative land policy.

A few days later, five of the political organisations still remaining in opposition, the Democratic Action Party (DAP), the Social Justice Party (Pekemas), Parti Marhaen — a pro-Indonesian Malay organisation, the Sarawak National Party (Snap) and the United Sabah Action Party, decided to form a united front in order to oppose Abdul Razak's National Front, both immediately and in the forthcoming elections. In that same month, these parties elected Lim Kit Siang of the DAP to be Leader of the Opposition in the Federal Parliament, a position that had been vacated by Datuk Mohammed Asri when his party had joined the National Front.

A further embarrassment to Abdul Razak as leader of the National Front, and to the Alliance in general, was caused by the power struggles that in 1973 were waged with considerable bitterness and vilification for the leadership of both the Malayan Chinese Association and the Malayan Indian Congress. On May 30th of that year, for example, Dr Lim Keng Yaik, a Minister with Special Functions in the Federal Government, was forced to resign after he had failed in an attempt to replace Tan Siew Sin as President of the MCA; while on June 28th a hard and protracted struggle for the Presidency of the MIC ended when V.T. Sambanthan, who had led that party for the past eighteen years, unwillingly resigned, under pressure from his Cabinet colleagues, in favour of his deputy, V. Manickevasagam, who, it was claimed, represented a younger and more dynamic section of the Congress.

These ferments and divisions within the main non-Malay progovernment political parties were particularly unwelcome to Abdul Razak, because they took place at a time of renewed inter-racial tension and clamorous dissatisfaction with the Alliance education policy. This was due to the National Language issue, a constant point of intercommunal controversy. The specific cause of friction, was the results of examinations for the certificate in secondary education, which showed that large numbers of Chinese and Indian students had failed solely because of their inability to pass a compulsory paper in the Malay language.

There were fears in all three main communal parties in the Alliance that this issue might, in the future, drive many non-Malays to vote for the opposition. All these matters, educational and hierarchical, were resolved in time for the 1974 elections, however, and despite the defection of a few ultra-nationalistic UMNO stalwarts who joined dissident members of the PAS in founding a new Malay opposition party that they called KITA (*Kaum Insaf Tanah Ayer*), the Alliance, as the mainstay of the National Front, went to the polls with all the outward signs of unanimity of interest and of purpose.

ELECTION RESULTS

At the time that Parliament was dissolved, the National Front held 119 seats out of a total of 144; leaving the combined opposition with only 25 seats, far short of the one third or more they needed in order to block further amendments to the country's Constitution, one of their primary concerns. On July 8th, 1973, this Constitution — in one of the few amendments that had not worried or outraged the opposition — had been altered by Parliament so as to make Kuala Lumpur, formerly the capital of the State of Selangor, into Federal Territory; and to provide it with five Parliamentary constituencies, but to exclude it from participation in any future State election. Later, due to the restructuring of certain electoral boundaries, a further five Parliamentary constituencies were added throughout the country, bringing the total number of seats to be contested in the 1974 elections to 154.

Polling Day for Peninsular Malaysia was August 24th; while in Sabah and Sarawak polling, as usual, was due to commence on the same day but, because of difficulties of communication and transportation, was scheduled to continue over an extended period. Although there was some fear, especially in Kuala Lumpur and in some northern rural areas, that communist terrorists, or other leftwing partisans, might try to disrupt polling, the entire election passed off without incident. This was probably due mainly to the unprecedented scale of the security precautions mounted by the police and army; and partly to the memory of the horrors of May 13th, 1969, still present in the minds of most candidates, which caused them to speak of controversial matters with considerable circumspection.

The results of this appeal to the judgement of the voters proved to be a great personal triumph for Abdul Razak — fighting a general election for the first time as Prime Minister — and a vindication of his determined efforts, often in the face of high-powered opposition from within his own party as well as from some sections of the MCA and MIC, to bring into being the multi-racial and politically wide-based National Front. He himself was returned unopposed in his usual Pahang constituency of Pekan, for the Party Islam which had, on the last three occasions that he had contested a Parliamentary seat, provided his opponent, was no longer in opposition. When all the results had been declared, the National Front was found to have secured 135 Parliamentary seats, a majority of 116 over its opponents of all parties, who together had managed to win in only 19 constituencies.

Among the few successful opposition candidates, those from the Democratic Action Party had secured nine seats, the Sarawak National Party nine and the Social Justice Party (Pekemas) just one; the latter seat having been won by the narrow margin of 666 votes, largely on personal popularity, by the moderate socialist Dr Tan Chee Khoon. There had been one major reverse for the National Front, however, in Perak, where the Peoples Progressive Party, because of Chinese dissatisfaction over its association with, and presumed domination by, the Alliance, had lost all its former Parliamentary seats. Abdul Razak recognised and rewarded this sacrifice, by keeping the PPP in the National Front despite its lack of popular support; and by enabling its leader, S.P. Seenivasagam, to remain in active politics, until his early death, by nominating him a Member of the Senate.

The Malay opposition to the National Front, was represented by the radical Socialist Peoples Party and KITA, which — even though three of its candidates had been independent MP's in the previous Parliament — failed to obtain even a single seat. This meant that such opposition as had emerged was predominantly Chinese in electoral support. Significantly, however, the victories of the largely Chinese, left-wing, Democratic Action Party had been gained not so much at the expense of the conservative MCA, but from the newly pro-Alliance Peoples Progressive Party and the trade union orientated socialist opposition party, the Gerakan Raayat. The MCA had, in fact, improved its position in the Alliance by winning 19 of the 23 seats it had contested, four more than it had held before the dissolution of Parliament.[10]

In the State elections, the National Front had successfully retained its control over all eleven of the Legislative Assemblies of Peninsular

Malaysia. It won every seat in the States of Pahang, Kelantan and Perlis; and had better than a two-thirds majority in each of the other eight. It won 24 out of 26 seats in Kedah, 23 out of 27 in Penang, 31 out of 42 in Perak (its worst showing), 21 out of 24 in Negri Sembilan, 27 out of 28 in Trengganu, 30 out of 33 in Selangor — where the opposition's loss was the exclusion of Kuala Lumpur, 16 out of 20 in Malacca and 31 out of 32 in Johore [11]. These impressive results were due very largely to the electoral coalition between the Alliance and Party Islam (PMIP), which negated the usual split in the Malay vote. One new and, to Abdul Razak and the other UMNO leaders at least, disturbing development, was the election in Perak for the first time on the DAP ticket of two Malay Assemblymen. This seemed to indicate that sometime, though perhaps not in the immediate future, the main electoral contests in Malaysia, as in most other countries, would be fought by parties based less upon racial origin or religious and cultural differences, than upon economic and social ideology.

In Borneo, results of the elections in Sarawak gave the National Front an easy victory with 30 seats against the 18 secured by the Sarawak National Party (SNAP) which, with its old rival SUPP included in the government coalition, was on its own in opposition. There had been no contest on a State level in Sabah, where the Legislative Assembly, in which at that time the Alliance held all of the seats, was not due to be dissolved until sometime in 1976. Political alliances in this latter State were already strained close to breaking point, however, and events were soon to produce an opposition to the autocratic and seemingly indestructible regime of Tun Mustapha, the peripatetic Chief Minister.

AN OPPOSITION IN SABAH

The authoritarian form of government practiced in Sabah under the Chief Ministership of Mustapha bin Datu Harun, was often at variance with the policies advocated by Kuala Lumpur; and so the solution which presented itself to Abdul Razak was to bring the controversial State leader into his post-election Federal Cabinet where, it was hoped, collective responsibility would make him more amenable to discipline. Abdul Razak therefore officially declared Mustapha the new Minister of Defence — an appointment ranking a prestigious number three in the Federal government's hierarchy — and hoped that the period of tension between them would soon be resolved. This was not to be, however, for the State leader, although he did not directly reject the offer, made no attempt either to take up his appointment or to resign as Chief Minister of Sabah.

In January 1975 Mustapha, finding himself in serious disagreement with Abdul Razak and the central government over the use of Federal funds allocated for development in Sabah, took the local Alliance organisation that he headed out of the National Front; a coalition of which he had been a constant critic since the time of its formation. There was the usual crop of rumours circulating about Sabah seceding from Malaysia and of either 'going it alone', or joining with the Muslim parts of the Philippines to form a single independent country. Such threats to the security of the Federation, impractical as they may have been in reality, eventually led to the appearance of a new opposition party called Berjaya which, Mustapha immediately claimed, was inspired by certain elements in Kuala Lumpur, including he suggested the Secretary-General of the National Front, in the hope that it would effectively replace him and his power-base, the United Sabah National Organisation (USNO), as the government of the north Bornean territory.

Berjaya was founded on July 12th, 1975, when a number of USNO State Assemblymen, several of them State Ministers, defected during one of Mustapha's frequent visits to Europe. This new party, it was soon revealed, was led by Sabah's Head of State, and Mustapha's long-time political rival Haji Mohammed Fuad Stevens, who as quickly as practicable resigned his constitutional position in order to become Berjaya's President and take an active part in its attempts to rally voters for what it hoped would be an early election. There was little doubt that Abdul Razak and others in the National Front were optimistic that a free election in Sabah would result in the establishment of a strong opposition to Mustapha's independent and often embarrassing policies.*

---

*In fact in the Sabah State elections in April 1976, Berjaya won 28 seats to USNO's 20 and Mustapha's party went out of office.

Epilogue

The sudden death of the Malaysian Prime Minister in London in January 1976 took the majority of his fellow countrymen by complete surprise. It had been known for some time that he had been unwell and recent photographs had shown that Abdul Razak had lost a great deal of weight; but few realised the serious condition of his health and the nature of the disease. Abdul Razak had gone first on holiday to France and then on 22nd December 1975 went to London for treatment for leukaemia, a disease which had been diagnosed six years earlier. However he had kept the knowledge of his ailment to himself and to only one or two others throughout these years. Abdul Razak had in 1970 been given much less than six years to live but he had seemingly held his own against the encroachments of the disease. At first in London he seemed to respond to treatment but then a relapse occurred and his death came quickly on 14th January at the London Clinic, before he could return to Malaysia.

Abdul Razak died at the age of 53, in his sixth year as Prime Minister, but he had been at the centre of his country's affairs for more than twenty years. His achievements were formidable for he had been the driving force in government since the time of the negotiations leading to Malaya's independence in 1957. As his country's first Minister of Education he had completely recast the educational system, both in its structure and also its content. The Razak Report on Education was a landmark in the history of Malaya for it not only introduced common syllabuses for schools in the various media but also introduced the policy of having Malay as the eventual medium of instruction in all schools. The Razak Report began the unification of the younger generation through education.

At that time in the late 1950's education was closely bound up with internal security for the Emergency was still in being and some Chinese Middle Schools were still centres of discontent. It was a natural transition therefore when Abdul Razak moved into the Ministry of Home Affairs as his next appointment, at the same time becoming Deputy Prime Minister to his friend and colleague, Tunku Abdul Rahman. In this Ministry he was closely involved in the final ending of the Emergency with the elimination of the Malayan Communist Party as formidable fighting force when the remnants of its army were either killed or forced to surrender. By 1960 the whole of Peninsular Malaya had become a 'White area' and the Emergency Regulations which had been in force since 1948 were able to be repealed.

Having dealt with the overt Communist menace Abdul Razak then turned his attention to removing the causes on which communism could breed — especially rural poverty. He took on the post of Minister of National and Rural Development and set about raising the living standards of those in the rural areas through the same organised means as he had used to defeat the terrorists. He began a systematic, planned campaign, for there was nothing haphazard in his methods. Although he became famous for the military style operations rooms which he set up in each district, his was not a chair-bound campaign for he himself was out in the field, inspecting land schemes and other development projects. He drove himself hard travelling hundreds of miles through the length and breadth of the country.

Abdul Razak took an important part in the negotiations leading up to the formation of Malaysia though he had never been an uncritical supporter of the project. He had not up to this time taken a great deal of interest in foreign policy matters leaving external affairs to his Prime Minister, the Tunku. And even in the negotiations for Malaysia, Abdul Razak was mainly involved in the nuts and bolts of the details of the internal arrangements between Malaya and her new partners. His own misgivings seemed to be partly justified by the adverse reaction from Indonesia and the latter's policy of confrontation which followed. He himself however was faced with new burdens being responsible as Minister of Defence for protecting, with the assistance of his allies, the new country of Malaysia from Indonesian invasion.

Successively therefore as Minister of Education, Minister of Home Affairs, Minister of National and Rural Development, and as Minister of Defence, Abdul Razak had been involved in his country's major problems since independence. The climax came in 1969, when in the grave racial crisis that threatened in the aftermath of the General Election, Abdul Razak took supreme control of the country's legislative and administrative machinery, suppressed the riots and then found himself a dictator responsible for the whole government. A reluctant dictator, it should be said, for as soon as was practical he returned his emergency powers to Parliament and became a democratically selected Prime Minister.

Much however still had to be done for the riots of May 13th had emphasised the fact that the rather leisurely *laissez-faire* progress of the previous administration would not produce the equal society necessary if the main races were to live prosperously side by side. It was at this point in time that he learned of his terminal condition but this made him even more determined to push on with his reformist policies as rapidly as possible. In effect he did much more than speed up processes of economic and social change which had already been set in motion, — he altered the whole style of government, introducing changes which were gradual but definite.

At first public attention was focussed on the more obvious changes; economic, with the restructuring of society; international, the new non-aligned foreign policy leading to the establishment of diplomatic relations (a calculated risk) with the Peoples Republic of China in 1974; and political, the attempt to obtain a 'consensus', and the elimination of friction among the parties and races in Malaysia, by the formation of a coalition, the National Front. However while the policies changed so did the method of government.

Abdul Razak had never been a radical and had never had a liking for confrontation in politics. He therefore made his personnel changes gradually and, considering the time there was available, possibly too slowly; but at the same time attempting to ruffle as few feathers as possible. Gradually the old style politicians, the old guard who had been in UMNO since the 1950's and had accompanied the Tunku throughout, were pensioned off. They were replaced by younger men, more often than not university educated and left of centre in their political outlook. The result was a definite rise in the intellectual calibre of the majority of the Cabinet. These changes did not always please the old guard, as for example, when Abdul Razak brought back individuals like Dr. Mathathir who had previously fallen foul of the Tunku; but he was able to carry them through with the support of his Deputy Prime Ministers, first Dr. Ismail, and after the latter's early death, Datuk Hussein Onn. It is probable that the main effect of these changes had not been properly seen before Abdul Razak's own death for, as had been said, he was one who made haste slowly. Nevertheless a new pattern had been introduced.

Abdul Razak had not been able to achieve all his aims before he died for he was still trying to solve two problems. He had realised that due to the great opportunities that had become available in the rapid development of the Malaysian economy the canker of corruption had taken a definite hold. He had in fact turned his attention to this problem by giving greater powers to the National Bureau of Investigation and by making use of the results of its investigations. It was mainly at the State Government level that the main evidence of corruption existed and usually there was enough evidence to convince the person concerned that early 'retirement' was the easiest solution. A beginning had been made in the attack on corruption though there had obviously been much heart searching before decisions to proceed legally were taken.

Epilogue

The other problem unsolved at Abdul Razak's death was that of Sabah, already referred to in the last chapter. His attempt to remove Mustapha, the over-mighty subject, had not so far proved successful and it seemed that he might in fact have misjudged the situation by encouraging the formation of a rival political party. However, although the coconut did not fall at the first shy, Abdul Razak by enforcing Kuala Lumpur's control of law and order in Sabah, did set the ground rules for the election success of Berjaya and the electoral defeat of Mustapha, which took place after his own death.

It is, of course, too soon after Abdul Razak's death to attempt any final assessment of the man and his contribution to the history of Malaysia. Assessments of all historically important figures change as the emphasis of time changes, but there can be little doubt that whenever the story of the first twenty years of independant Malaya and Malaysia is written about, the role of Abdul Razak will have an important place. Only future historians writing with the benefit of hindsight will be able to say whether it was his contribution to education or rural development or national security which had the most permanent effect. And again only they will be able to judge the crucial part which Abdul Razak played in returning the country to Parliamentary government in 1970. But whatever the final verdict there can be no doubt that when Abdul Razak died Malaysia mourned the passing of a man who had unselfishly contributed the whole of his working life for the benefit of his fellow countrymen. "By any standards Tun Razak was a great man with many achievements to his credit."*

**Financial Times 5th April 1976.

References

CHAPTER 1

1. *Mid-Term Review of the Second Malaysia Plan 1971-1975*, pp. 23-24, quoting the Census of Population for 1970: in Peninsular Malaysia (to which the inter-racial troubles were confined) Malays accounted for 52.7 per cent. of the total population, Chinese for 35.8 per cent., Indians for 10.7 per cent., and various others for the remaining 0.8 per cent.
2. *The Straits Times*, July 15th, 1972. From a speech by Dato Seenivasagam, M.P., Leader of the Peoples Progressive Party, at a dinner given in honour of Tun Abdul Razak on July 14th.
3. *The Malays in Malaya* by One Of Them, pp. 103-104.
4. 'A History of Pahang' by Dr W. Linehan, in the *Journal of the Malayan Branch of the Royal Asiatic Society*, volume 14, part 2, 1936, p. 43; and 'A History of Johore' by Sir Richard Winstedt, in the *Journal of the Malayan Branch of the Royal Asiatic Society*, volume 10, part 3, 1932, p. 50.
5. 'A History of Pahang' by Dr W. Linehan, p. 195.
6. Ibid., p. 195.
7. Ibid., p. 104.
8. Ibid., p. 147.
9. *Malaysia* by J.M. Gullick, p. 56.

CHAPTER 2

1. The Malayan, or Straits, dollar was at that time tied to Sterling with a fixed rate of two shillings and four pence, or roughly US$0.50.
2. Annual Report of the Federated Malay States for 1920, quoted in *The Modern Malay* by L.R. Wheeler, p. 155.
3. *A Brief History of Islam* by M.A. Rauf, pp. 97-98.
4. *A Survey of Muslim Institutions and Culture* by M.A. Hanifi, p. 87.
5. The description of the Purification Ceremony, Installation and Investiture are taken from eye-witness accounts, supplemented by reports that appeared in the *Straits Times* from 23rd to 29th June, 1932.
6. Personal interview with Encik Ishak Haji Muhammad on 28/10/71.
7. The root of the shrub *Derris elliptica*.
8. This debate took place on August 10th, 1939 .... Padi-planting means rice-growing.

CHAPTER 3

1. Personal interview with Encik Ishak Haji Muhammad.

2. *Malay Nationalism 1900-1945* by Radin Soenarno, pp. 11-12.
3. *Political Attitudes of the Malays* by Abdul Latiff bin Sahan p.2, Fn. 4-5, University of Malaya, Singapore, unpublished BA exercise.
4. *Nationalism in Malaya* by T.H. Silcock and Ungku Abdul Aziz, p. 280.
5. Ibid., p. 276.
6. Ibid., p. 277.
7. *British Military Administration in the Far East 1943-46* by F.S.V. Donnison, p. 379.
8. *Indian Society and Politics in Malaya 1900-1941*, by G. Palanivel, p. 107.
9. *The War Against Japan* by Major-General S. Woodburn Kirby (ed.), vol. I, p. 6.
10. Ibid., vol. I, p. 85.
11. Advertisement in *The Straits Times* of December 1st, 1941.
12. *The War Against Japan* by Major-General S. Woodburn Kirby (ed.), vol. I, p. 183.
13. Ibid., vol. I, p. 183.
14. Ibid., vol. I, p. 183.
15. *The Straits Times*, December 8th, 1941.
16. Quoted in *The Civil Defence of Malaya* by Sir George Maxwell (ed.), p. 73.
17. Ibid., pp. 106-108.
18. Ibid., p. 75.
19. Ibid., p. 74.

CHAPTER 4

1. *Singapore under The Japanese 1942-1945* by Lee Ah Chai, pp. 30-32.
2. *Perak Times* of December 9th, 1943.
3. *Singapore under The Japanese 1942-1945* by Lee Ah Chai, p. 9.
4. Ibid., pp. 9-10.
5. Personal interview with Dato Yeop Mahidin bin Sharif.
6. Personal interview with Dato Yeop Mahidin bin Sharif.

CHAPTER 5

1. *Post Surrender Tasks* by Admiral Lord Louis Mountbatten, pp. 183-184.
2. Report to the Combined Chiefs of Staff 1943-45 by Admiral Lord Louis Mountbatten, p. 282.
3. *The Chinese in Malaya* by V. Purcell, p. 263 and *British Military Administration in the Far East 1943-46* by F.S.V. Donnison, pp. 384-385.

4. Report on the British Military Administration of Malaya, September 1945 to March 1946, p. 40.
5. *Three Decades of Malayan Trials* by Dato R. Rajasooria, p. 80.
6. Report on the British Military Administration of Malaya, September 1945 to March 1946, p. 41; *Three Decades of Malayan Trials* by Dato R. Rajasooria, p. 80, gives a death toll of more than 80.
7. *Three Decades of Malayan Trials* by Dato R. Rajasooria, p. 81.
8. *British Military Administration in the Far East 1943-46* by F.S.V. Donnison, p. 137.
9. Comd. 6724 of 1944.
10. *British Military Administration in the Far East 1943-46* by F.S.V. Donnison, p. 381.
11. Ibid., p. 138.
12. Quoted in *British Malaya,* August 1946, p. 52.
13. *Utusan Melayu* 16/10/1945 and *Warta Negara* 10/11/1945, quoted in 'Dato Onn and Malay Nationalism' by Ishak bin Tadin in *Journal of Southeast Asian History,* University of Malaya, Singapore, vol. I, No. 1, March 1960, pp. 64-65.
14. *Utusan Melayu* 22/12/1945, quoted in 'Dato Onn and Malay Nationalism', p. 67.
15. *The Malayan Union* by James de V. Allen, p. 21.
16. Report on the British Military Administration of Malaya, September 1945 to March 1946, p. 62.
17. *Prince and Premier* by Harry Miller, pp. 77-78.
18. Communication from Lord Ogmore.
19. Communication from Lord Ogmore.
20. Reported in *British Malaya,* August 1946, pp. 52-53.
21. Ibid., p. 53.
22. Quoted in 'Hidop Melayu', The Department of Malay Union Affairs, Malay League of Perak, Ipoh, 1946, p. 7.
23. Report on the British Military Administration of Malaya, September 1945 to March 1946, p. 39.
24. *British Malaya, August 1946*

CHAPTER 6

1. *British Malaya,* October 1948, p. 83.
2. *The Art of the Possible: The Memoirs of Lord Butler,* p. 40.
3. *Churchill Revised: A Critical Assessment,* p. 112.
4. *As it Happened* by the Rt. Hon. Clement R. Attlee, pp. 109-110.
5. Communication from Lord Ogmore.
6. *Background to Indonesia's Policy Towards Malaysia,* Fed. Dept. of Information Kuala Lumpur, 1964, pp. 6 and 20-21.

CHAPTER 7
1. *The Holy Quran,* chapter 4, verse 3.
2. *The Straits Times,* September 27th, 1952.
3. *Politics in a Plural Society* by R.K. Vasil, pp. 68-69.
4. *Malaysian Politics* by Gordon P. Means, p. 135.
5. *Prince and Premier* by Harry Miller, p. 158.

CHAPTER 8
1. Report on the First Election of Members to the Legislative Council of the Federation of Malaya, p. 11.
2. Ibid., p. 10.
3. *The Straits Times,* June 4th, 1955.
4. Election Report, p. 30.
5. Legislative Council Debates, Official Report of the Second Legislative Council (first session), p. 23.
6. *British Malaya,* September 1955, p. 26.
7. Ibid., October 1955, p. 19.
8. Ibid., June 1956, p. 19.
9. Ibid., p. 19.
10. Legislative Council Debates, 16th May 1956, p. 1144-1158.
11. *Malayan Politics* by Gordon P. Means, p. 203.
12. Ibid., p. 203.
13. *Riot and Revolution in Singapore and Malaya 1945-1963* by Richard Clutterbuck, p. 98.
14. Legislative Council Debates, 16th May 1956, p. 1158.

CHAPTER 9
1. Communication from Lord Ogmore.
2. *Prince and Premier* by Harry Miller, p. 203.
3. *Malaysian Politics* by Gordon P. Means, p. 173.
4. *Malaya,* July 1958, pp. 18-19.
5. *Riot and Revolution in Singapore and Malaya 1945-1963,* by Richard Clutterbuck, p. 206.
6. *Malaya,* August 1958, pp. 16-17.
7. Ibid., p. 17.
8. *Malaya,* September 1958, pp. 15-17 and 24.
9. Ibid., pp. 16-17.
10. *The Communist Threat to the Federation of Malaya,* a reproduction of Legislative Council Paper No. 23 of 1959, Government Press, Kuala Lumpur, p. 20.
11. *Malaya,* September 1958, pp. 17 and 24.
12. *Malaya,* November 1958, pp. 37-38; and *The Straits Times* of October 4th, 1958.

CHAPTER 10
1. *Malaya,* May 1959, p. 18.
2. *Malaysian Politics* by Gordon P. Means, p. 206.
3. *The May 13th Tragedy:* A Report by the National Operations Council, p. 17.
4. Ibid., p. 18.
5. *The Straits Times* of May 10th, 1959.
6. *Malaysian Politics* by Gordon P. Means, p. 212.
7. Ibid., p. 213.
8. Ibid., p. 214.
9. *UMNO and the 1959 Election* by D. Moore. A doctoral thesis (unpublished), University of California, 1960, p. 83.
10. Ibid., p. 59.
11. *Politics in a Plural Society* by R.K. Vasil, p. 172.

CHAPTER 11
1. *The Straits Times,* January 1st, 1960.
2. *Studies in the Rural Economy of Southeast Asia* by E.K. Fisk, p. 90.
3. Ibid., pp. 94-95.
4. Ibid., footnote 7 to page 93.
5. *Development Implementation in Malaysia* by Tun Abdul Razak.
6. In 'Suggested Brief for State Development Officers' Conference on 12th July, 1960, at the National Development Operations Room'.
7. *Studies in the Rural Economy of Southeast Asia* by E.K. Fisk, p. 102; and Interim Review of Development in Malaya under the Second Five-Year Plan, p. 7.
8. Speech to the National Press Club of Australia, in Canberra, 14th April, 1967.

CHAPTER 12
1. Al-Batanuni, quoted in *A Pilgrim in Arabia* by R. St. J. Philby, p. 26.
2. Ibid., p. 41.
3. *The Life and Times of Mahommed* by Paul Hamlyn, p. 40.
4. The University of Malaya Gazette, vol. 2, No. 3, 1961, p. 3.
5. Ibid., pp. 5-9.
6. *The Annual Register for 1961,* pp. 94-95.

CHAPTER 13
1. *Malaysia: Selected Historical Readings.* Compiled by John Bastin and R.W. Winks p. 398.
2. Ibid., p. 414, quoting a government statement issued jointly by the Prime Ministers of Malaya and the United Kingdom in August —

taken from *Sari Berita,* Weekly Digest of the Malayan Press, 2nd August, 1962, pp. 1-2.
3. *Malaysian Politics* by Gordon P. Means, p. 305.
4. Ibid., footnote 48 to p. 312.
5. *The Dimensions of Conflict in Southeast Asia* by Bernard K. Gordon, p. 69.
6. *The Annual Register 1963,* p. 95.
7. *The Dimensions of Conflict in Southeast Asia* by Bernard K. Gordon, p. 71.
8. *The Annual Register 1963,* p. 96.
9. *The Separation of Singapore from Malaysia* by Nancy McHenry Fletcher, p. 12, quotes from *The Guardian* newspaper of July 5th, 1963.
10. *The Annual Register 1963,* pp. 96-97.
11. Ibid., p. 97.

CHAPTER 14

1. *The Malayan Parliamentary Election of 1964* by K.J. Ratnam and R.S. Milne, p. 339; quoting from Mr Lee Kuan Yew's Eve of Poll broadcast.
2. *The Straits Times* of April 16th, 1964.
3. *The Malayan Parliamentary Election of 1964* by K.R. Ratnam and R.S. Milne, p. 16.
4. Ibid., p. 112; quoting a White Paper — Cmd. 12 of 1965 — and *The Straits Times* of April 23rd, 1964.
5. Ibid., p. 112; quoting the *Straits Times* of March 17th, 1964.
6. *The Dimensions of Conflict in Southeast Asia* by Bernard K. Gordon, p. 110; quoting from 'Records of the First Foreign Ministerial meeting held at the Official Residence of the Japanese Foreign Minister on June 18th, 1964'.
7. Ibid., p. 111.
8. Ibid., p. 114; quoting 'Record of the meeting of Heads of Government held on June 20th, 1964'.

CHAPTER 15

1. *Malaysian Politics* by Gordon P. Means, p. 343.
2. Ibid., p. 343.
3. *Malaysia — Age of Revolution.* Ministry of Culture. Singapore. 1965. Speeches made by Prime Minister Lee Kuan Yew in New Zealand and Australia, March-April 1965.
4. *The Annual Register 1965.*
5. *Malaysian Politics* by Gordon P. Means, p. 341.
6. Speech by Tun Abdul Razak in Dewan Raayat (Lower House of Parliament) June 3rd, 1965. In *Speeches by the Deputy Prime*

Minister, Tun Abdul Razak bin Dato Hussein, Al Haj, 1965. pp., 34-46.

CHAPTER 16

1. *The May 13 Tragedy: A Report* by the National Operations Council, Preface, p. 111.
2. *Malaysian Politics* by Gordon P. Means, p. 365.
3. *The Separation of Singapore from Malaysia* by Nancy McHenry Fletcher, p. 20: based on report in the Straits Budget of July 21st, 1965.
4. Ibid., p. 18.
5. Ibid., p. 19.
6. *Malaysia: New States in a New Nation* by R.S. Milne & K.J. Ratnam, p. 233.
7. Ibid., p. 221.
8. Ibid., p. 222.
9. Speech by Deputy Prime Minister Tun Abdul Razak in the Dewan Raayat on June 3rd, 1965, in reply to an Amendment to the Royal Address.
10. *Malaysia: New States in a New Nation* by R.S. Milne & K.J. Ratnam, p. 224.
11. Statement to Parliament on the situation in Sarawak by the Deputy Prime Minister Tun Abdul Razak, on Monday September 19th, 1966.
12. Speech by the Deputy Prime Minister Tun Abdul Razak in moving a Bill entitled "An Act to Amend the Federal Constitution" in Parliament on Monday, September 19th, 1966.
13. *The Annual Register 1967,* p. 93.
14. Statement to Parliament on the situation in Sarawak by the Deputy Prime Minister Tun Abdul Razak on Monday 19th September 1966.
15. *The May 13 Tragedy: A Report* by the National Operations Council, p. 12.
16. *May 13: Before and After* by Tunku Abdul Rahman, pp, 10-11.
17. Ibid., p. 30.
18. Ibid., p. 32.
19. Ibid., p. 30.
20. Ibid., p. 46.
21. *The May 13 Tragedy: A Report* by the National Operations Council, p. 12.
22. Ibid., p. 27 and *May 13: Before and After* by Tunku Abdul Rahman, p. 48.
23. *May 13: Before and After* by Tunku Abdul Rahman, p. 48.
24. Ibid., p. 52.

25. Ibid., p. 56 and *The May 13 Tragedy: A Report* by the National Operations Council, pp. 27-28.

CHAPTER 17
1. Report on the Parliamentary and State Legislative Assembly General Elections 1969 of the States of Malaya, Sabah and Sarawak.
2. *Malaysia: New States in a New Nation* by R.S. Milne & K.J. Ratnam, p. 181.
3. *The May Thirteenth Incident* by Goh Cheng Teik, pp. 12-15.
4. Ibid., p. 21 and footnote 6.

CHAPTER 18
1. *The Annual Register 1969.*
2. *May 13: Before and After* by Tunku Abdul Rahman, pp. 113-114.
3. Ibid., p. 118.
4. *Far East Economic Review Year Book, 1971,* pp. 221-222.
5. *Malaysia Official Year Book 1970,* p. 1.
6. *Far East Economic Review,* May 21st, 1970, p. 8.
7. Report on the Parliamentary and State Legislative Assembly General Elections 1969 of the States of Malaya, Sabah and Sarawak, p. 44.
8. Dewan Ra'ayat, Official Report, 23rd February 1971, pp. 53-54.

CHAPTER 19
1. *Far East Economic Review,* August 28th, 1975, p. 28.
2. *Newsweek,* June 16th, 1975.
3. *The New Straits Times,* 28/9/75, 29/9/75 and 3/10/75.

CHAPTER 20
1. *Mid-Term Review of the Second Malaysia Plan 1971-1975,* p. 9.
2. *Second Malaysia Plan 1971-1975,* p. 1.
3. *Far East Economic Review,* May 16th, 1975, p. 66.
4. *Second Malaysia Plan 1971-1975,* pp. 99-100.
5. *Mid-Term Review of the Second Malaysia Plan 1971-1975,* pp. 10-11.
6. Ibid., p. 145.
7. Ibid., p. 155.
8. *Far East Economic Review,* May 16th, 1975, p. 63.
9. Ibid., p. 63.
10. *Asia Research Bulletin,* September 30th, 1974.
11. Ibid.,

Bibliography

GOVERNMENT PUBLICATIONS

Report on the First Election of Members to the Legislative Council of the Federation of Malaya, Government Printer, Kuala Lumpur, 1955.

Report on the Parliamentary and State Elections 1959, Government Printer, Kuala Lumpur, 1960.

Report on the Parliamentary and State Legislative Assembly General Elections 1964 of the States of Malaya, Government Printer, Kuala Lumpur, 1965.

'Legislative Council Debates', *Official Report of the Second Legislative Council*, Government Printer, Kuala Lumpur.

Federated Malay States, *Annual Reports*.

Federation of Malaya, *Annual Reports*.

Report of the British Military Administration of Malaya, September 1945 to March 1946, Kuala Lumpur, 1946.

Comd. 6724 of 1944.

Background to Indonesia's policy towards Malaysia, Federal Department of Information, Kuala Lumpur, 1964.

Report on the Barnes Report on Malay Education and the Fenn-Wu Report on Chinese Education, Kuala Lumpur, 1951.

Report of the Education Committee 1956 (The Razak Report), Kuala Lumpur, 1956.

Malaya and its Civil Administration Prior to the Japanese Occupation, War Office, London, 1944.

'Post-Surrender Tasks': Section E of the *Report to the Combined Chiefs of Staff by the Supreme Allied Commander South-Asia 1943-1945, Vice-Admiral The Earl Mountbatten of Burma*, H.M.S.O., London.

University of Malaya Gazette, vol. 2, No. 3, 1961.

Foreign Affairs Malaysia 1966-1971.

Speeches by the Deputy Prime Minister Tun Abdul Razak bin Dato Hussein, Al-Haj, 1965-1967, 3 volumes, Johore Bahru, State Printer Johore, 1969.

Report on the Parliamentary and State Legislative Assembly General Election 1969 of the States of Malaya, Sabah and Sarawak, Kuala Lumpur, Government Printer, 1972.

The May 13 Tragedy: A Report by the National Operations Council, Kuala Lumpur, 1969.

Second Malaysia Plan 1971-1975 Kuala Lumpur, Government Printer, 1971.

Mid-Term Review of the Second Malaysia Plan 1971-1975. Kuala Lumpur, Government Printer, 1973.

The Communist Threat to the Federation of Malaya, a reproduction of Legislative Council Paper No. 23 of 1959, Kuala Lumpur, Government Press.

Malaysia — Age of Revolution. Speeches made by Prime Minister Lee Kuan Yew in New Zealand and Australia, March-April 1965, Singapore, Ministry of Culture, 1965.

PUBLISHED WORKS: BOOKS AND ARTICLES

Abdul Rahman, Tunku *May 13: Before and After* Utusan Melayu Press, Kuala Lumpur, 1969.
Allen, James de V. *The Malayan Union* Monograph No. 10, S.E.Asian Studies, Yale University, U.S.A., 1946.
Anon *The Malays in Malaya* Malayan Publishing House, Singapore, 1928.
Attlee, Rt. Hon. C.R. *As it Happened* Heinemann, London, 1954.
Bastin, J. & R.W. Winks *Malaysia: Selected Historical Readings* Oxford University Press, Kuala Lumpur, 1966.
Butler, Lord R. *The Art of the Possible: The Memoirs of Lord Butler K.G. C.H.* Hamish Hamilton, London, 1971.
Clutterbuck, Richard *Riot and Revolution in Singapore and Malaya 1945-1963* Faber & Faber, London, 1973.
Donnison, F.S.V. *British Military Administration in the Far East 1943-46* H.M.S.O., London, 1956.
Emerson, R. *Malaysia* The MacMillan Co., London, 1937. (reissued 1964 by University of Malaya Press, Kuala Lumpur).
Fish, E.K. *Studies in the Rural Economy of Southeast Asia* Eastern Universities Press, for University of London Press, Singapore, 1964.
Fletcher, Nancy McHenry *The Separation of Singapore From Malaysia* Department of Asian Studies, Cornell University, Ithaca, N.Y., 1969.
Goh Cheng Teik *The May Thirteenth Incident and Democracy in Malaysia* Oxford University Press, Kuala Lumpur, 1971.
Gordon, Bernard K. *The Dimensions of Conflict in Southeast Asia* Prentice-Hall, New Jersey, 1966.
Gullick, J.M. *Malaysia* Ernest Benn, London, 1969.
Hamlyn, Paul *The Life and Times of Mahommed* Paul Hamlyn, London, 1968.
Hanifi, M.A. *A Survey of Muslim Institutions and Culture* S.H. Mahommed Ashraf, Lahore, 1962.
Ishak bin Tadin 'Dato Onn and Malay Nationalism' *Journal of Southeast Asian History Vol. 1* University of Malaya, Singapore, 1960.
Kirby, Maj. Gen. S.W. (ed) *The War Against Japan Vol. 1* H.M.S.O., London, 1957.
Linehan, Dr. W 'A History of Pahang' *Journal of Malayan Branch Royal Asiatic Society Vol. 14 Part 2* 1936.
Maxwell, Sir George (ed) *The Civil Defence of Malaya* Hutchinson, London.
Means, Gordon P. *Malaysian Politics* University of London Press, London, 1970.

Miller, Harry *Prince and Premier* G. Harrap, London, 1959. Donald Moore, Singapore, 1959.
Milne, R.S. & K.J. Ratnam *Malaysia: New States in a New Nation* Frank Cass, London, 1974.
Palanivel, G. 'Aspects of Indian Society and Politics in Malaya 1900 — 1941' *Jernal Sejarah Universiti Malaya Vol.* X 1971/72, pp. 98 — III. 1972.
Philby, H. St. J. *A Pilgrimage in Arabia* Robert Hale., London, 1946.
Purcell, V. *The Chinese in Malaya* Oxford University Press, London, 1948.
Rajasooria, Dato R. *Three Decades of Malayan Trials* Kuala Lumpur, 1960.
Ratnam, K.J. & R.S. Milne *The Malayan Parliamentary Election of 1964* University of Malaya Press, Kuala Lumpur, 1967.
Rauf, Dr. M.A. *A Brief History of Islam: with special reference to Malaya* Oxford University Press, Kuala Lumpur, 1964.
Silcock, T.H. & Ungku Abdul Aziz *Nationalism in Malaya* in *Asian Nationalism and the West* The MacMillan Company, New York, 1953.
Soenarno, Radin 'Malay Nationalism' *Journal of Southeast Asian History I (1)* 1960.
Taylor, A.J. (ed) *Churchill Revised: A Critical Assessment* The Dial Press Inc., New York, 1969.
Vasil, R.K. *Politics in a Plural Society* Oxford University Press, Kuala Lumpur, 1971.
Vasil, R.K. *The Malaysian General Election of 1969* Oxford University Press, Kuala Lumpur, 1972.
Wheeler, L.R. *The Modern Malay* Allen & Unwin, London, 1928.
Winstedt, Sir Richard 'A History of Johore' *Journal of Malayan Branch Royal Asiatic Society Vol.* 10 Part 3 1932.
The Annual Registers for 1961, 1963, 1965, 1967, 1969 Longman, London.

UNPUBLISHED THESES

Abdul Latiff bin Sahan 'Political Attitudes of the Malays', BA exercise. University of Malaya, Singapore, 1959.
Lee Ah Chai 'Singapore Under the Japanese 1942-45', BA exercise. University of Malaya, Singapore, 1956.
Moore, D. 'UMNO and the 1959 Election', Doctoral Thesis. University of California, 1960.

NEWSPAPERS AND PERIODICALS

The Perak Times
The Straits Times
The New Straits Times Malaysia
Sunday Times
Sunday Mail

Bibliography

The Daily Telegraph, London
Utusan Melayu
Warta Negara
Far East Economic Review, Hong Kong.
Far East Economic Review Yearbooks
British Malaya — The Journal of the British Association of Malaya.
Hidop Melayu — The Department of Malay Union Affairs, Malay League of Perak, Ipoh, 1946.
Asia Research Bulletin
Newsweek

Index

Abdul Aziz Ishak, 165-6
Abdul Ghaffar Baba, 208, 245
Abdul Rahman, Tunku, 1, 2, 66, 70, 72, 74, 84, 85, 86, 93, 94, 98, 106, 107, 108, 110, 111, 112, 117, 118, 120, 121, 126, 128, 148, 149, 150, 151, 154, 157, 158, 165, 167, 171, 172, 177, 178, 179, 180, 182, 185, 196, 197, 207, 212, 215, 219-20, 222, 241
Abubakar Tafawa Belewa, Sir, 181, 182, 183
Adam Malik, 184, 185, 186
Algiers, 223-4
Ali, Sultan of Pahang, 9
Alliance, the, 91, 93, 94, 95, 97, 98, 103, 104, 105, 106, 108, 110, 114, 115, 116, 117, 118, 120, 121, 122, 123, 124, 126, 127, 128, 130, 146, 147, 148, 152, 164, 165, 166, 167, 168, 169, 170, 172, 173, 175, 176, 177, 191, 193, 194, 196, 197, 198, 202, 203, 204, 206, 207, 213, 216, 217, 218, 219, 233, 239, 240, 241, 242, 243, 244, 245
Ambler, D.J., 51
America, United States of, 149, 154, 158, 170, 222, 225, 227, 228, 229,
Arulanandom, Justice, 71
Association of South East Asian Nations (ASEAN), 196, 222, 223, 226, 227, 228, 229
Atlee, Clement, 73
Australia, 180, 222, 223
Azahari, M.A., 152, 155, 156, 159

Baling Talks, 112
Barisan Socialis, 151, 163
Bentong, 44, 45, 46, 49, 52, 87, 123
Berjaya, 245

Birth ceremony, 12-3
Borneo, 3, 5, 149, 151, 152, 154, 159, 160, 161, 170, 171, 180, 190, 191, 204, 217, 225, 239, 244
British, 3, 4, 5, 6, 7, 10, 12, 15, 19, 20, 24, 26, 29, 30, 31, 32, 33, 34, 35, 37, 41, 42, 43, 44, 46, 47, 49, 50, 51, 52, 55, 56, 60, 61, 63, 65, 68, 69, 74, 76, 91, 93, 105, 106, 107, 109, 110, 111, 112, 120, 125, 148, 149, 150, 151, 152, 153, 154, 155, 156, 157, 158, 159, 161, 162, 170, 180, 181, 182, 183, 211, 222, 223, 228
Brunei, 3, 148, 152, 153, 154, 155, 156, 157, 158, 160, 161, 163, 168, 194, 195
Bugis, 8, 9, 14
Burma, 229

Census Report 1970, 232-3
China, Peoples Republic, 222, 225-7, 229, 230, 231
Chinese schools, 32, 99, 173
Chinese secret societies, 195, 201, 206, 208, 210-1, 213, 214
Chou En-lai, 225, 227
Churchill, Sir Winston, 36, 73
Cobbold, Lord, 153
Colour bar, 35
Commonwealth, 158, 179, 181, 182, 183
Communist, 29, 32, 33, 45, 49, 52, 54, 56, 57, 58, 72, 78, 83, 90, 96, 97, 98, 103, 107, 111, 112, 113, 114, 127, 129, 149, 150, 161, 163, 168, 173, 177, 181, 184, 185, 190, 194, 198, 199, 200, 210, 211, 213, 214, 217, 223, 225, 226, 227, 229, 230, 231, 243
Confrontation, 155, 156-9, 160, 164, 165, 168, 170-2, 180, 181, 184, 185, 196

Defence and Internal Security, Minister of 111, 113, 126, 129, 154, 170, 194
Democratic Action Party (DAP), 180, 197, 198, 204, 206, 207, 216, 219, 241, 243, 244
Des Alwi, 75, 77, 78, 79, 184, 185
Director of Operations, 212, 216, 222, 223

Economic Planning Unit, 233
Economic policy, 233-9
Education, Minister of, 27, 95, 98, 145
Education problems, 92, 99, 100, 101, 102, 103, 118, 242
Egypt, 138, 225
Elections (1952), 91
    (1955), 93, 95, 96, 97, 98, 112, 117
    (1959), 110, 117, 119-126, 128
    (1964), 164-170
    (1969), 196-9, 202, 203-6, 217-8
    (1974), 241-5
Emergency Regulations, 1, 100, 114, 115, 177, 216, 230
Emergency, State of, 36, 72, 83, 208, 211

Fatimah (mother of Tun Razak), 11, 12, 16
Federal Land Development Authority, 137
Federal Legislative Council 31, 71, 86, 87, 88, 91, 92, 93, 94, 98, 100, 112, 121
Force 136, 50, 51, 53, 54, 55, 56

Gammons, L.D., 62, 64
Ghazali Shafie, Tan Sri, 28, 46, 47, 50, 51, 58, 181, 185, 209, 212, 223
Gerakan Rakyat Malaysia, 195, 197, 198, 204, 206, 207, 219, 239,
Goh Keng Swee, Dr, 71, 179, 180
Gurney, Sir Henry, 72, 112

Haj, the, 138-144
Harun b. Haji Idris, Datuk, 166, 206, 207, 208, 209
Hatta, Ahmad, 75, 76
Home Affairs, Minister of, 1, 202, 205, 212
Hung League (Triads), 6, 32, 211
Hussein, Dato (father of Tun Razak), 10, 11, 13, 14, 16, 18, 31, 43, 44, 46, 49, 62, 71, 72, 80, 86, 87, 88
Hussein Onn, Datuk, 84, 220

Ibrahim, Sultan, 105
Immigration, 6, 7, 31-32, 33-34
Independence (*Merdeka*), 96, 98, 103, 105-107, 110, 113, 134, 144
Independence of Malaya Party, '91 92, 96
Indian National Army, 47, 48, 50, 57
Indonesia, 29, 48, 75, 76, 78, 100, 110, 117, 125, 148, 149, 152, 155, 156, 157, 158, 159, 160, 163, 164, 165, 168, 170, 171, 174, 177, 180, 184, 185, 190, 194, 196
Installation, (of Sultan of Pahang), 16-18
Ismail bin Abdul Rahman, Tun Dr., 106, 108, 190, 212, 220

Jaffar, Tunku, 77, 78, 79
Jambu Langgar, 13, 14, 44
Japanese, 28, 32, 33, 35, 36, 37, 38, 39, 41, 42, 43, 44, 45, 46, 47, 49, 50, 51, 52, 53, 54, 55, 56, 57, 58, 61, 64, 69, 75, 76, 111, 125, 148, 155, 161, 162, 222
Java, 4, 76
Johore, 5, 6, 7, 8, 9, 17, 37, 42, 51, 88, 89, 105, 106, 112, 113, 169, 172, 196, 213, 244

Kedah, 6, 42, 48, 114, 169, 185, 195, 198, 213, 214, 241, 244
Kelantan, 6, 39, 41, 42, 48, 62, 106, 120, 122, 123, 160, 168, 169, 198, 240, 244

Keris, 17, 83
Kesatuan Melayu Muda (KMM), 28, 30, 31
Kuala Lipis, 46, 51, 52, 53, 54, 58, 83, 84, 87, 90
Kuala Lumpur, 1, 19, 31, 37, 41, 55, 61, 63, 80, 84, 86, 87, 91, 110, 112, 113, 138, 152, 153, 154, 158, 163, 171, 174, 184, 185, 195, 200, 201, 205, 206, 207, 208, 213, 214, 226, 229, 230, 231, 242, 243, 244
Kuantan, 43, 90
Kuomintang, 32, 53, 57

Labour Party, 194, 195, 196
Language policy, 92, 96, 98, 101, 103, 109, 145, 146, 163, 173, 193, 199, 219, 242
Lansdowne, Lord, 154
Lee, Tun Sir H.S., 91, 106, 108
Lee Kuan Yew, 68, 71, 130, 149, 150, 151, 154, 158, 159, 163, 164, 173, 175, 176, 177, 178, 179, 232
Lim Chong Eu, Dr., 118, 121, 166, 195, 206
Lincolns Inn, 88, 145
London, 63, 67, 68, 69, 71, 73, 79, 83, 93, 104, 105, 106, 107, 145, 153, 154, 158, 178, 179, 222
London, University of, 69, 145

Macapagal, President, 154, 157
Macassar, 9
MacMichael, Sir Harold, 61, 62, 64
Magsaysay award, 137
Mahathir bin Mohammed, Dr., 215-6, 241
Mahmud, Sultan of Johore, 7
Maphilindo, 157, 158
Malacca, 4, 5, 7, 60, 107, 147, 160, 178, 204, 208, 213, 244
Malay Administrative Service, 25, 26, 28, 58
Malay College, 10, 19-21, 22, 23, 24, 25, 26, 27, 34, 153
Malay nationalists, 3, 27, 29, 56, 148, 167, 198
Malay Peninsula, 3, 4-6, 7, 14, 25, 28, 29, 32, 34, 35, 37, 39, 45, 47, 48, 50, 52, 55, 56, 57, 60, 64, 74, 100, 101, 124, 148, 159, 164, 167, 172, 190, 191, 202, 211, 223, 225, 230. 242
Malay Society of Great Britain, 66, 70, 71
Malay States, Federated, 6, 9, 15, 16, 18, 34, 36, 41, 56, 61, 65, 211
Malaya, Federation of, 3, 65, 67, 71, 83, 89, 99, 107, 110, 114, 123, 134, 146, 148, 149, 150, 151, 152, 156, 159, 163, 173
Malaya, University of, 26, 144, 145, 146
Malayan Chinese Association (MCA), 91, 92, 93, 95, 96, 103, 109, 117, 118, 120, 121, 124, 146, 147, 148, 161, 164, 166, 167, 175, 177, 178, 197, 198, 205, 212, 213, 220, 240, 241, 242, 243
Malayan Civil Service, 57, 83
Malayan Communist Party, 30, 33, 49, 50, 65, 67, 87, 98, 99, 111, 112, 114, 115, 227, 231
Malayan Forum, 71
Malayan Indian Congress (MIC), 91, 95, 96, 109, 120, 121, 164, 197, 212, 241, 243
Malayan Peoples' Anti-Japanese Army, 49, 50, 51, 52, 56, 57, 59, 61,
Malayan Union, 60, 61, 62, 63, 65, 66, 67, 71
Malaysia, 4, 136, 137, 147, 148, 149, 150, 151, 153, 154, 155, 156, 157, 158, 159, 160, 161, 162, 163, 165, 166, 167, 170, 171, 172, 173, 175, 176, 177, 178, 179, 180, 181, 182, 184, 185, 189, 190, 193, 194, 195, 197, 200, 218, 220, 222, 223, 224, 225, 226, 227, 229, 234, 235, 236, 238, 245
Mao Tse-tung, 227
May 13th, 1, 2, 186, 189, 202, 206-11, 213, 220, 232, 243
Mecca, 138, 139, 140, 141, 143, 144, 145

Index

Medina, 143-4
Mountbatten, Lord Louis, 54, 55, 56, 61
Muslim Society, of Singapore, 27, 28
Mustapha bin Datuk Harun, Tun, 162, 163, 192, 244
Muhammad Khir Johari, 138, 196

National Front, 239-40, 241, 242, 243, 244, 245
National Consultative Council, 216, 219
National Operations Council, 1, 211, 212, 219
National and Rural Development, Minister of, 1, 97, 127, 128, 129
National Service, 113
Negri Sembilan, 5, 169, 204, 244
New Zealand, 180, 222
Nigeria, 181, 182, 183
Ningkan, Dato Stephen K, 192, 193, 203

Onn bin Jaafar, Dato, 57, 63, 84, 85, 87, 91, 95, 96, 122, 123, 126
Operations rooms, 131, 132, 133

Pahang, 5, 6, 9, 12, 15, 16, 17, 18, 19, 21, 28, 41, 43, 44, 45, 46, 47, 48, 49, 50, 51, 52, 57, 62, 79, 80, 83, 86, 87, 89, 90, 94, 96, 122, 123, 169, 203, 205, 243, 244
Pan-Islam, 222, 224-5
Pan Malayan Islamic Party (PMIP later PAS), 96, 97, 120, 122, 123, 125, 126, 160, 166, 167, 168, 169, 170, 175, 180, 197, 198, 203, 204, 205, 207, 215, 239, 240, 242, 243, 244
Paris, 78, 79
Parliament, 1, 110, 121, 152, 153, 160, 162, 164, 168, 169, 173, 177, 180, 193, 194, 195, 197, 199, 202, 203, 204, 211, 216, 217, 220, 222, 226, 230, 240, 241, 242, 243, 244
Parti Bumiputra, 161, 203, 218

Party Negara, 95, 96, 120, 122, 126
Party Pesaka, 161, 192, 193, 203, 218
Pekan, 9, 11, 13, 14, 16, 21, 42, 43, 44, 52, 54, 90, 122, 123, 169, 203, 243
Peking, 225, 226, 227, 231
Penang, 5, 40, 42, 55, 56, 60, 65, 99, 100, 166, 176, 178, 193-4, 197, 199, 200, 204, 205, 213, 239, 244
Peoples Action Party (PAP), 150, 151, 152, 159, 163, 164, 167, 169, 170, 172, 174, 175, 176, 177, 178, 179, 180
Peoples Progressive Party (PPP), 116, 120, 122, 124, 125, 126, 147, 167, 169, 170, 176, 197, 198, 204, 219, 240, 243
Perak, 5, 6, 17, 18, 19, 30, 63, 64, 70, 86, 106, 114, 118, 119, 124, 167, 195, 196, 199, 204, 205, 206, 207, 217, 218-9, 240, 243, 244
Perlis, 6, 42, 48, 244
Pernas, 237, 238
Philippines, the, 149, 154, 155, 156, 157, 158, 159, 163, 170, 171, 185, 196, 197, 229, 245

Quran, 16, 89, 139, 140, 141, 143
Quranic Schools, 15-6

Racial problems, 3, 6, 7, 31-2, 46, 56, 57, 72, 84, 95, 98, 108, 130, 232, 233, 234
Raffles College, 25, 26, 27, 28, 36, 37, 38, 39, 40, 58, 68
Rahah bte Haji Noah, Toh Puan, 87, 88, 89, 122
Raub, 12, 58, 62, 63, 123
Razak Report, 100-3, 104, 145
Razaleigh, Tengku, 225
Rees-Williams, D (Lord Ogmore), 64, 74, 93, 106
Reid Commission, 108-9
Rhodesia, 181-3

Riots, 65, 175, 189, 197, 213, 217, 232
  riots in Kuala Lumpur, 208-11
  riots in Pangkor, 118-9
  riots in Penang, 194-5
  riots in Singapore, 173-4
Rural development, 96, 11, 127-137, 232-4

Sabah (British North Borneo), 3, 5, 136, 137, 147, 148, 151, 152, 153, 155, 156, 157, 158, 159, 160, 161, 162-3, 169, 170, 176, 178, 180, 185, 186, 191, 193, 194, 197, 202, 204, 217, 218, 229, 240, 242, 243, 244, 245
Sambanthan, Tun V.T., 112, 242
Sarawak, 3, 64, 136, 137, 147, 148, 151, 152, 153, 155, 156, 157, 158, 159, 160-2, 169, 170, 176, 177, 178, 180, 186, 190, 191, 192, 194, 202, 203, 204, 217-8, 239, 242, 244
Sarawak National Party (SNAP), 161, 162, 192, 193, 203, 218, 241, 244
Sarawak United Peoples Party (SUPP), 160, 161, 162, 176, 192, 203, 218, 239, 244
Sardon Haji Jubir, Tan Sri, 28, 59
Saudi Arabia, 138, 220, 225
Second World War, 3, 23-4, 25, 35-41, 55, 75, 124, 155, 161
Seenivasagam, D.R., 147
Seenivasagam, S.P., 2, 243
Selangor, 5, 6, 86, 91, 92, 98, 106, 110, 199, 204, 205, 206, 207, 213, 218, 242, 244
Semantan, 94, 97
Shahbandar, Dato, 9, 10, 16, 19, 43, 83, 122
Shahrir, Sutan, 75, 76, 77, 184
Singapore, 3, 5, 6, 25, 31, 33, 34, 35, 36, 37, 39, 40, 43, 45, 49, 51, 55, 56, 57, 60, 64, 65, 68, 71, 83, 99, 107, 112, 118, 136, 147, 148, 149, 150, 151, 152, 154, 156, 158, 159, 163, 164, 169, 171, 172, 173, 174, 175, 176, 177, 178, 179, 180, 182, 184, 185, 190, 194, 195, 213, 222, 223
Socialist Front, 120, 122, 123, 124, 125, 126, 160, 163, 164, 166, 167, 168, 169, 170, 175
Soviet Union (Russia), 50, 52, 227, 229
Stevens, Donald (later Tun Fuad), 162, 163, 192, 245
Straits Settlements, 5, 16, 31, 33, 41
Subandrio, Dr., 75, 77, 157, 170, 171, 184
Suharto, General, 184, 186
Sukarno, President, 75, 76, 125, 155, 157, 158, 159, 163, 165, 167, 168, 170, 171, 172, 180, 181, 183, 184, 185
Sultan Idris Training College, 28, 30
Sumatra, 4, 8, 76
Syed Jaafar Albar, 167, 173, 174

Taib Andak, Tan Sri, 70, 72, 79, 80, 83, 87, 88, 89,
Taib Mahmud, Datuk, 192, 193
Tan Siew Sin, Tun, 154, 164, 191, 220, 242
Temenggong Jugah, Tan Sri, 192, 193
Temerloh, 13, 44, 45, 46, 97, 123
Tan Chee Khoon, Dr., 194, 195, 243
Templer, Sir Gerald, 89, 90, 94, 111, 112, 113, 127
Terauchi, F.M., Count, 47, 55, 76
Thailand (Siam), 4, 5, 6, 40, 48, 112-3, 114, 123, 148, 190, 213, 230
Toh Chin Chye, 71
Trengganu, 6, 48, 120, 122, 123, 244

UMNO, 2, 63, 64, 65, 66, 77, 83, 84, 85, 86, 87, 88, 91, 92, 93, 95, 103, 105, 107, 116, 117, 118, 120, 121, 123, 125, 128, 148, 149, 152,

164, 165, 166, 167, 173, 174, 175, 176, 177, 178, 192, 193, 195, 197, 198, 199, 200, 204, 205, 206, 207, 208, 215, 217, 225, 240, 241, 242, 243
UMNO Youth, 84, 206
United Nations, 159, 181, 226, 228
United Pasokmomogun Kadazan Organisation (UPKO), 162, 192, 202, 203
United Sabah National Organisation (USNO), 162, 163, 192, 202, 204, 218, 240, 245

Vietnam (Indo-China), 222, 227, 229, 230

Wataniah, 48, 49, 50, 51, 53, 54, 56, 57, 58, 63, 68, 87
Wedding, 88-9
Wilson, Harold, 181, 182, 183

Yeop Mahidin, Dato, 48-9, 87

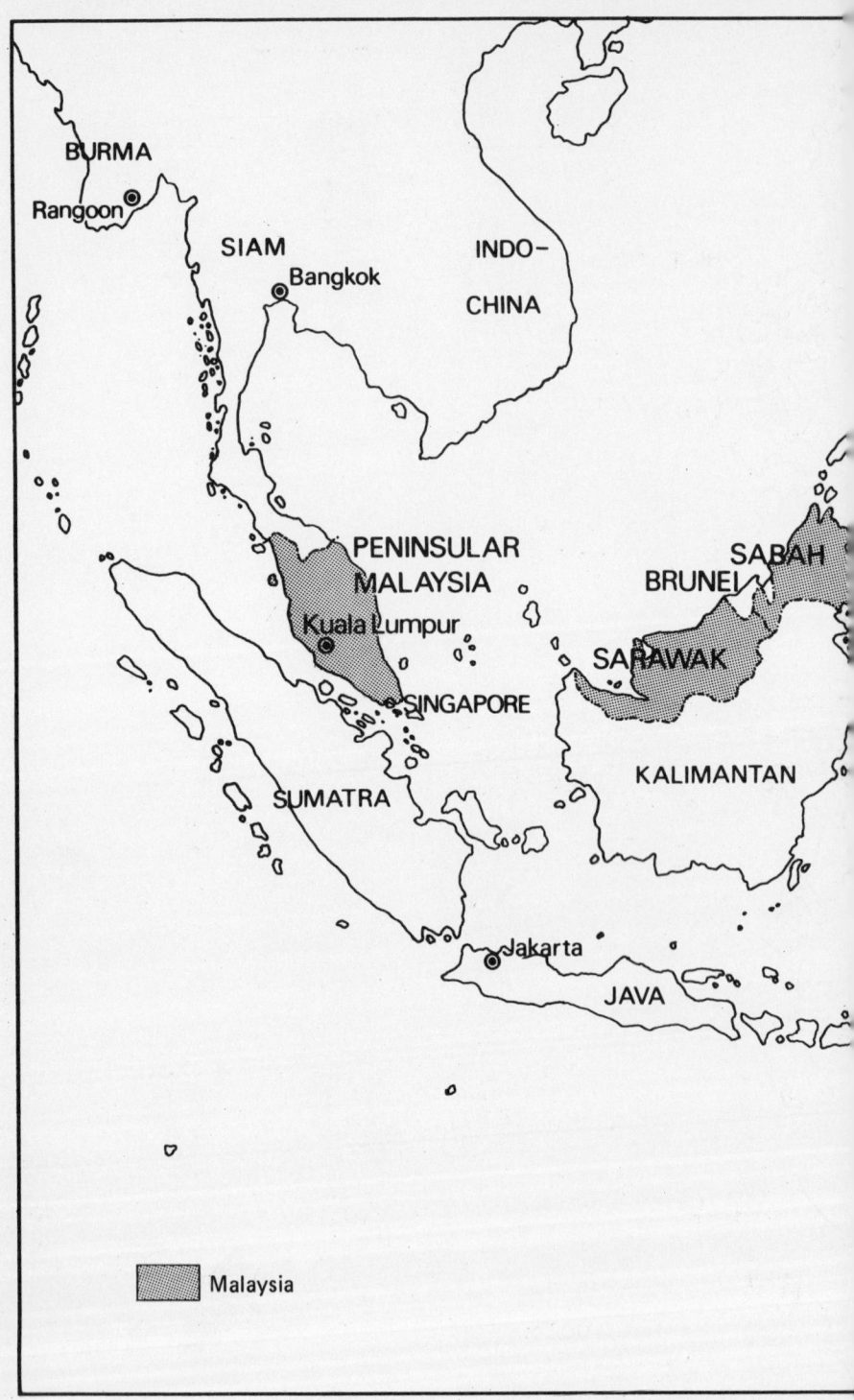